INDIA'S BATTLEFIELDS

From Kurukshetra to Balakot

Updated Edition

INCLUDES 'OP SINDOOR'

INDIA'S BATTLEFIELDS
From Kurukshetra to Balakot

Updated Edition

INCLUDES 'OP SINDOOR'

Ajay Singh

Edited by

Monisha Naik-Singh

PENTAGON PRESS LLP

First published in 2020
Updated in 2025 by
PENTAGON PRESS LLP
206, Peacock Lane, Shahpur Jat
New Delhi-110049, India
Contact: 011-26490600

Typeset in AGaramond, 11.5 Point
Printed at Aegean Offset Printers, Greater Noida

ISBN 978-81-988370-9-7

www.pentagonpress.in

To

Ragini

Who, in any case, is all our words.

CONTENTS

Preface *xi*

1 THE SACRED GROUNDS
Battle of Kurukshetra 1

2 THE JHELUM RIVER CROSSING
Battle of Jhelum River 7

3 VICTORY AND DEFEAT AT TARAIN
The Battles of Tarain 13

4 AN EMPIRE FORGED THROUGH CANNON SMOKE
The First Battle of Panipat 19

5 CONSOLIDATING AN EMPIRE
Battle of Khanua 25

6 GHAGHRA
The Battle of Ghaghra 30

7 A CHESSBOARD OF AN EMPIRE
Battle of Chausa 33

8 THE OUTSKIRTS OF AN EMPIRE
Battle of Tuglaqabad 37

9 THE CUSP OF VICTORY
Second Battle of Panipat 41

10 THE 'CITY OF VICTORY'
Battle of Talikota 45

11 THE PASS OF BLOOD
The Battle of Haldi Ghati 51

12 THE THRONE OF BLOOD
The Battle of Samugarh 57

13 "GAD AALA PAN SINH GELA"
The Capture of Sinhgarh Fort 62

14 THE BATTLE OF MANEUVER
The Battle of Palkhed 68

15 A TRAITOR'S BATTLE
The Battle of Palashi 74

16 'THE BLACKEST DAY IN INDIA'S HISTORY'
Third Battle of Panipat 79

17 ESTABLISHING IMPERIAL RULE
Battle of Buxar 86

18 THE TIGER OF SRIRANGAPATNAM
The Anglo-Mysore Wars 90

19 THE VICTORY PILLAR
Battle of Bhima Koregaon 96

20 BLOOD IN THE SUTLUJ
Anglo-Sikh Wars 101

21 THE FIRST FIRES OF INDEPENDENCE
India's First War of Independence 108

22 THE LAST STAND AT SARAGARHI
Battle of Saragarhi 114

23 THE RACE TO SRINAGAR
Battle for Kashmir 118

24 SAVING KASHMIR
The Indo-Pak War of Kashmir 124

25 TANKS AT 11,500 FEET
Battle of Zojila 129

26 GOA'S LIBERATION – AFTER 451 YEARS
Battle for Goa 134

27 DEBACLE IN THE HIGH HIMALAYAS
1962 Indo-China War 140

28 THE LAST STAND OF 'C' COMPANY: 13 KUMAON
Battle of Rezang La 144

29 CAPTURED ON GROUND, LOST ON THE TABLE
Capture of Haji Pir Pass 148

30 BLOODY SEPTEMBER
Indo-Pak War 1965 152

31 GIVING THE CHINESE A BLOODY NOSE AT NATHU LA
Battles of Nathu La and Cho La 161

32 THE OPENING SALVOES
Land and Air Battle at Garibpur 166

33 CREATING A NATION IN 13 DAYS
1971 Indo-Pak War 170

34 RAID ON KARACHI
The Attack on Karachi 186

35 "BREAKFAST AT LONGEWALA"
Battle of Longewala 191

36 GALLANTRY ON BOTH SIDES OF THE BASANTAR
Battle of Basantar/Nawapind 196

37 THE COLDEST WAR
Siachen 202

38 FROM 'QUAID' TO 'BANA'
The Capture of Bana Post 209

39 INDIA'S FORAY INTO SRI LANKA
Operation Pawan 214

40 INTO OPERATIONS WITH A TOURIST MAP
OPERATION CACTUS in the Maldives 218

41 THE HEIGHTS OF VICTORY
Kargil 224

42 KASHMIR
Pulwama, Balakot and Beyond 231

43 'OP SINDOOR'
India's Retaliation against Terror 237

Index 249

PREFACE

The story of Indian warfare is not really a happy one. Most battles fought by Indian armies against outsiders have seen them coming out as second best. The outcome of India's battles can be gauged by the fact that, in the pre-Independence era, the last Indian ruler to sit on the throne of Delhi was Prithviraj Chauhan in 1192. (Not considering the 21 day regime of Hemu in November 1556) and the last major victory by an Indian army over an outside force was when the Rajputs defeated Mohammed Ghori in the First Battle of Tarain way back in 1191.

India – or rather the Indian sub-continent – has been fortunate that it has natural protection through the Indian Ocean in the South, East and West; by the Himalayas to its North and Northeast; and the Hindu Kush mountains to its Northwest. India's neglect of its maritime legacy opened its shores to stronger naval powers, mainly the Arabs in the Seventh Century and the European powers from the Seventeenth Century onwards. The mighty Himalayas protected India till they were breached by the Chinese in 1962. But the real threat came from the Northwest. From here, armies marched in through the six major passes of the Hindu Kush Mountains – the Bolan, Gomal, Khyber, Kunjerab, Parpik and Mintaka passes. These passes were breached around the Ninth Century and since then India had been subjected to a stream of foreign invaders, who came, defeated local armies, looted and established their own Empires in the sub-continent.

A deep analysis of Indian warfare brings out one fact. Indian warriors were invariably skilful and individually very brave and courageous. But, military leaders neglected the organisational structure of their armies. They did not adapt to new concepts of warfare and often remained rooted in the past. Nor did they embrace technology. This enabled smaller, compact, but better equipped armies to repeatedly defeat larger Indian armies – most of whom were a conglomeration of clans and individual soldiers who had never trained or fought together, and often relied on equipment which was a generation or so behind their adversaries. The leaders were brave – like their soldiers – but often lacked generalship. Rather than coordinate actions, fine-tune the deployment of forces, move of reserves, or the launching of counter-attacks, they chose to lead reckless charges which provided local tactical victories but were often at the expense of the overall outcome of the battle.

The results were visible in some of the most crucial battles of Indian history. The Afghans, Turks, Uzbeks and other invaders from Central Asia used nimble, fast moving cavalry to outmanoeuvre large Indian armies who remained rooted in the traditional concepts of static, muscular battle. The First Battle of Panipat saw another outsider, Babur, use cannons and muskets to mow down the advancing ranks of Ibrahim Lodhi's army and then use heavy cavalry to attack from the flanks and rear to deliver the *coup de grace*. Similar tactics enabled him to defeat the Rajputs, who were not even aware of the impact of guns and cannons and charged blindly into them in the Battle of Khanua. The neglect of gunpowder, technology and modern concepts of war has cost us dearly.

The British, with well-drilled, organised and well-equipped forces (composed largely of 'native' troops) repeatedly defeated Indian armies using modern concepts of war; aided with the simple stratagem of dividing them from within. A telling feature is how often defeat has come about through treachery from within. Turning an Indian against an Indian was a doctrine the British used to perfection in their depredation of the country.

The Post-Independence period though, has much to show. The performance of Indian Armed forces in all actions, save 1962, has been commendable. In a way, the crushing defeat in the Sino-Indian War of 1962 was a blessing. It shook us out of our misplaced concepts of pacifism and set us off on a course to build up the armed forces and develop military doctrines. The results were there for all to see in the subsequent 1965 and 1971 Indo-Pak wars and all operations thereafter. There has been a gradual shift in our strategic thinking over the years – for the better. Pro-active action, utilising all elements of national power and aggressive pursuit of national interests are concepts that are slowly taking sway.

The book intends to bring out the Story of Indian Warfare and reveal what happened on our battlefields – warts and all. The versions of most battles have usually come down to us from foreign sources. Names and places have been changed to suit the victor. For example, the King of Pauravas who battled Alexandra by the Jhelum River is remembered as Porus. That was not his real name. It was the name given to him by the Greeks. Similarly the Battles of Plassey and Seringapatnam are anglicised versions of the locations where they took place. But then, there is no place called Plassey or Seringapatnam. The correct names of these places were Palashi and Srirangapatnam. And that is how they have been referred to in the book.

A total of 42 battles have been covered, beginning from the seminal Battle of Kurukshetra, which has shaped the psyche of Indian war-fighting, right down to the present day actions in Uri, Pulwama and Balakot. The aim is to present a spectrum of Indian warfare in a realistic and objective manner. Perhaps, the knowledge of the past would enable us to deal better with the conflicts of the present day and of those that may arise in the future.

New Delhi
November 2019

Ajay Singh

1

Around October/November 3102 BC
THE SACRED GROUNDS

Battle of Kurukshetra

The Epic War

Like all stories, we must start from where it all started. The story of Indian warfare began over 5000 years ago on the sacred ground of Kurukshetra – a triangular swath of flat, open ground that lays around 140 kilometres northwest of Delhi and forms an ideal battleground. Kurukshetra – literally, the abode of the Kurus – was also considered sacred ground and called Dharmakshetra –

the abode of righteousness. In that epic battle, those who fell on its soil automatically attained salvation. Around it lie Panipat, Thaneshwar and Karnal, equally illustrious battlefields that have shaped India's history for over 2000 years. Yet, none of those battles can match the effect of the Battle of Kurukshetra – the 18-day war between Good and Evil, Right and Wrong – which left an indelible impact on the Indian psyche.

No one is really sure when the battle took place, or indeed if it did take place at all. Yes, a major battle did take place as was described in the Mahabharata, but was it really the gigantic war that sucked in all the kingdoms of India or was it just a skirmish amplified beyond proportion? Historians give it varying dates, ranging from 5000 BC to 500 BC. Yet, various clues, such as the position of the stars and the depiction of events in the Mahabharata, place the battle at around 3100 BC or so. A general timeframe of around mid-October to mid-November in the year 3102 BC is the commonly accepted date based on the mention of three solar eclipses that took place in the months preceding the battle that were seen as an indication of great death and destruction. But even this celestial event, which has been calculated by astronomers to have taken place that year, is largely conjecture.

But yes, an 18-day war of great death and destruction did take place on the Kurukshetra plains. As per the Mahabharata, it involved 4 million participants and caused over 3 million casualties, but an objective assessment of the timeframe and the destructive power of weaponry available seem to indicate a figure which is less than a tenth of this. The scale of the battle seems to have been magnified to titanic proportions, and then the whole event took on a story of its own through the pages of the Mahabharata – India's greatest epic.

Yet, whatever be the scale of the actual war, no battle has impacted the Indian psyche so strongly. It led to the concept of 'Dharma' and of fighting only 'righteous wars'. Perhaps that is the reason that no Indian ruler embarked on expansionism policies beyond the sub-continent, or failed to act pro-actively against perceived threats. This battle also spawned a range of warrior-heroes: Arjuna, Karna, Bhima, Duryodhana, Bhishma, Dronacharya, and many others whose exploits fill the pages of the Mahabharata. This emphasis on personal valour and hero-worship has permeated itself into the Indian concept of war-fighting. Indian armies have traditionally produced great and skilled individuals, but have grossly neglected organisational structures, processes and doctrines (on which even the Mahabharata largely glosses over). This fatal flaw has remained with Indian war-fighting doctrines for centuries thereafter.

The Major Kingdoms of the Time

The Carnage at Kurukshetra

This battle between the Kauravas and their cousins, the Pandavas was little more than a war of succession. The Pandavas returned after 13 years of exile to reclaim the territory which they had lost to their cousins in a rigged game of dice. The proud, arrogant Duryodhana – the eldest scion of the Kauravas – refused to part with even five needle points of territory and the situation was set for war.

The Kauravas and their allies had mustered a force of 11 Akshauhinis – or divisions – with each Akshauhini having 21,870 chariots, 21,870 elephants, 65,610 horses and 109,350 infantry, in a battle formation of 218,700 fighters in the ratio of 1 chariot: 1 elephant: 3 cavalry: 5 infantry soldiers. The 11 Akshauhinis (2,405,700 warriors) of the Kauravas were countered by a force of 7 Akshauhinis (1,530,900 warriors) of the Pandavas. Over 4 million soldiers thus participated in the war as per the Mahabharata. But an objective look shows that the very space for deployment does not exist in that area. The figures thus can be realistically reduced to a tenth.

The two armies arrayed on either side of the vast plains of Kurukshetra with the Kauravas on the East and the Pandavas on the West. The Kauravas placed 10 Akshauhinis in a phalanx formation with elephants forming the body, the chariots comprising the head and cavalry on the wings. One Akshauhini was with the Commander-in-Chief, Bhishma, for his personal protection. The Pandavas were similarly arrayed with their 7 divisions. As the two gigantic armies of friends and cousins faced off, Arjuna, the great warrior, weakened and put down his bow. The treatise of the Bhagwat Gita that Krishna then gave to rouse him to fight the righteous war is perhaps the most profound philosophical work of all time.

On the first day of the war, the Pandava formation was cut down by Bhishma with enormous casualties. The day belonged to the Kauravas, but on the second day, Bhishma's charioteer was killed by an arrow making the horses bolt away from the battlefield. The leaderless Kaurava army suffered equally grave losses and the scores were even.

The Pandavas realised that the only way they could hope to win would be by killing Bhishma. They formed a crescent formation with Bhima and Arjuna on the right and left horns, which closed in to cut off Bhishma and kill that wily, venerable warrior. Bhishma eluded them and for 10 days, the slaughter of the Pandava forces continued. Finally, Krishna suggested the strategy of using Shikhandi, a eunuch. Bhishma had vowed never to fight a woman and refused to shoot at Shikhandi, with Arjuna positioned behind him showering arrows on Bhishm. With arrows on each part of his body, the great warrior finally fell from his chariot and lay with his body resting on a bed of arrows. Arjuna fired three arrows beneath his head to support it and released an underground spring of cool water towards the mouth of the wounded warrior. Bhishma, who had a boon of *Iccha Mrityu* (self-willed death), eventually embraced death only when the war ended, after giving instructions to Yudhisthira on the art of governance.

On the eleventh day, Dronacharya, the teacher of both the Pandavas and the Kauravas took over as Commander in Chief of the Kaurava Army. He changed his strategy to capturing Yudhisthira alive so as to force the Pandavas to sue for peace. With Arjuna by his side, this would not be possible. Over the next three days, Arjuna was engaged in a remote corner of the battlefield, while the rest of the Pandavas were lured towards a complex formation of intertwining layers of defences called *Chakravyuh.* Only Abhimanyu, Arjuna's son, knew how to break into the *Chakravyuh,* but he did not know how to get out. He broke through the formation and created an opening, but before the rest of the Pandavas could follow, the *Chakravyuh* was closed again and Abhimanyu was trapped and killed within.

The *Chakravyuh*

After 15 days of mutual slaughter, the war changed course again. Dronacharya was tricked into believing that his son Ashwatthama had been killed – a lie borne out by none other than Yudhisthira, the truthful. The broken-hearted old warrior laid down his arms and was killed. Karna now took over as the Commander in Chief of the Kaurava forces.

The character of Karna is perhaps the most complex in the pantheon of heroes of the Mahabharata. Born illegitimately through a union of queen Kunti with the Sun God, he was befriended by Duryodhan and in return gave him unflinching loyalty. He rebuffed persuasion by Krishna to switch sides to the Pandavas and take over as king, being the eldest son. He even promised not to kill any of the Pandavas, save Arjun, assuring his mother Kunti that she would still have five sons at the end of the war. He fought as the Commander in Chief for two days, in which he duelled and defeated all the Pandavas, only to let them go. Yet in his final, fatal encounter with Arjuna, his chariot wheel got stuck in the mud of the churned-up battlefield. As he tried to take out the stuck wheel, Arjuna, goaded by Krishna, fired his arrows, killing that noble warrior. That ignoble act was against all norms of warfare prevalent at the time.

It is strange that the war which was hailed as a war of 'right' versus 'wrong' saw rules being flouted and trickery resorted to by almost every participant (except maybe Karna). In fact the concept of 'right' was twisted to suit the end of almost every participant, most notably by Krishna himself.

With Kaurava leaders dead and most of the Kaurava brothers killed, the battle continued for one more day. On the eighteenth and final day, Duryodhan was finally killed in a mace fight with Bhima where once again the rules were flouted. Duryodhan was struck below the waist and mortally wounded. But the death toll was still not over. Even as the funeral pyres were burning for hundreds of miles across the plains accompanied by the wailing of women and children, the Pandava camp was attacked at night by the surviving Kaurava leaders who burnt it to the ground. The Pandavas survived, but the flames took away all their remaining children.

One question that is often asked is how so much death and destruction were wrought over in just 18 days. Given the primitive technology of the time, it seems implausible. Yet the Mahabharata gives clues as to the kinds of weaponry utilised – most of them arrow based. There were Agni Astras, which could cause fires, and were perhaps arrows tipped with Naptha. There were Naga Astras, which converted into venomous snakes on impact, but could have been merely fanciful interpretations of arrows coated with snake venom. There were also remotely guided weapons such as Krishna's Sudarshan Chakra that returned to his hands after unerringly decapitating the enemy. There were quivers which provided an unending supply of arrows (which could just have been judicious use of space in Arjuna's chariot which ensured that he never ran out of arrows in the day's battle). And there are references to nuclear weapons, such as the Brahmastra and the Bramashirshashtra (which was ten times more powerful), which participants on both sides were known to possess but did not use because of the destruction and lingering effects they would have on the environment. Some of the weaponry described may have been just flights of fancy and imagination, but it indicates that the technology and knowledge base of Ancient India was far superior to the rest of the contemporary world.

Just 12 major figures on both sides survived the war. Yudhisthira, the righteous, took over the throne and ruled wisely and well for 36 years. But it would have been a desolate kingdom of widowed women, orphaned children and old men. Perhaps the cost was too high, and the means used to attain the victory were not commensurate to the end. But the story does not dwell on that. It just tells that at the end of it all, it sufficed that the right cause had won.

2

Mid-May 326 BC
THE JHELUM RIVER CROSSING

Battle of Jhelum River

This battle goes so back in time, that no one knows the exact date. The Battle of Hydaspes, between Alexander the Great and King Porus took place sometime in Mid-May 326 BC according to Greek historians. Indian sources, who call it the Battle of Jhelum River, put it somewhere in the monsoon of 326 BC (which can be anytime from June to October). While the exact date of the battle is lost in antiquity, its impact is not.

The story began when Alexander, the greatest conquering hero in history, marched across Europe and Asia in his attempt to conquer the very end of the earth. He crossed the Hindu Kush Mountains in late 327 BC and entered the Indian sub-continent. India then was a string of independent kingdoms perpetually fighting with each other. Most of the border states in present-day Afghanistan and Pakistan were easily subjugated. Others capitulated without a fight. The Raja of Taxila also gave him his beautiful daughter as a wife, with 30 elephants as dowry.

Alexander

Yet Porus, the six and a half foot tall monarch of the Paurava kingdom between the Jhelum and Beas Rivers, refused to accede to Alexander and chose to fight. He made his stand on the banks of the Jhelum River, what is now known as the first recorded battle between an Indian ruler and a foreign invader.

It is strange that the name of this Indian hero has been lost in time. It was the king of Pauravas who fought Alexander – and not a man named Porus. Porus was the name given to him by the Greeks. And that unfortunately is also the name history remembers him by.

Porus's army of around 20,000-25,000 infantry, 2500 cavalry, 600 chariots and 150 elephants was camped and waiting for Alexander across the Jhelum River, which marked the borders of Porus's kingdom. The Greeks army was centered around a force of around 15,000 excellent Cavalry and around 1,20,000 archers and infantry. This was a battle-hardened army which had conquered half the known world and had perfected the concepts of fire and maneuver. The Greeks definitely held a clear edge in both numbers and quality.

The two armies faced off across the Jhelum for over a month. The Jhelum was in flood and Porus occupied its only crossing place. Unable to cross, Alexander send his scouting parties along the river and one of them discovered a site 20 kilometers upstream. Here a small island in the middle of the swollen river, named Adnana, would enable them to get across. It would be a dangerous crossing, but it was a gamble that Alexander was willing to take.

On the night of a violent thunderstorm, Alexander moved out with 13,000 of his Macedonian cavalry and Scythian archers towards Adnana, taking a wide circuit to avoid detection. The rest of his army remained in camp, with the campfires burning and the hustle of activity still depicted. Alexander's force reached Adnana and around midnight began the crossing, some on improvised rafts and boats, most swimming across on their horses. Over 200 were swept away in the fast-flowing waters, but by morning the force was across and had established a Phalanx on the other side.

The Greek Phalanx consisted of a tight formation of Infantry with large overlapping shields to provide tortoise like protection. Each man was armed with a *sarissa*, a 24-foot-long spear to impale acharging horse or man. On the sides were archers and to the rear were the Cavalry. It was a time-tested formation, which would hold the enemy ahead of the Phalanx while the cavalry swooped down from the flanks to launch the *coup de grace*.

The Greek Phalanx

Porus scouts relayed the news of Alexander's crossing and he sent a covering force under his eldest son to counter it. The chariot borne encountered the Greeks in the area of the Karri Plain, a flat open ground, in which their chariots got stuck in the wet, swampy soil and were then decimated by Greek archers and cavalry.

With his Advance Force easily defeated, Porus now moved his entire army to counter the threat on his flanks. His ponderous army moved slowly, reaching the Karri Plain where Alexander's army was deployed. The first clash took place between the cavalry of the two forces, where the Greeks simply out-maneuvered them from their flanks. With his cavalry defeated, Porus now decided to attack the Greek lines frontally, using his elephants as a battering ram in the concepts of the time.

The Greek Phalanx had never been broken in any of their earlier battles, but then neither had they faced elephants before. Yet Alexander had studied elephants and their habits carefully (thanks to the dowry of elephants he had received from the king of Taxila) and changed tactics to counter them. Instead of making his Phalanx in a solid wall, he now deployed them in files with gaps of 8-10 feet in between. The charging elephants would thus be funneled into the gaps from where they could be attacked on to their vulnerable sides and rear.

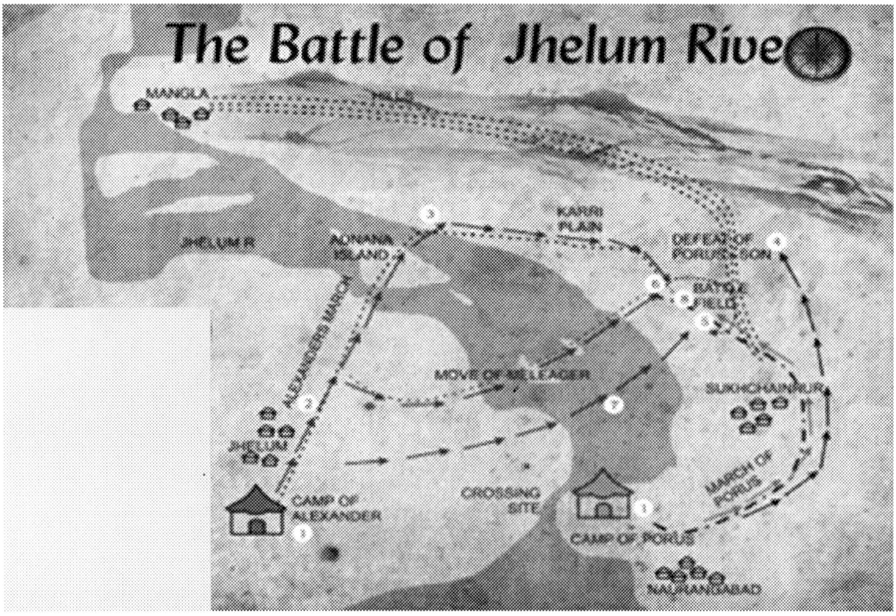

The Battle

From Greek accounts, the Indian attack was one of the most violent and determined assaults they had faced. Yet unknown to Porus, another element of the Greek army – a 10,000 strong force under General Meleager – had also crossed the river during the battle and were now behind them and attacked Porus' forces from the rear. Hemmed in by the phalanx in front and Greek cavalry behind them, Porus decided to make one last charge on the Greek ranks.

Porus led this attack himself and the force of the assault broke the Greek Phalanx – the first time it had ever been broken. For the next two hours or so, fierce hand-to-hand fighting raged with immense casualties to both sides. Finally, Alexander sent an emissary to Porus, proposing a truce. Porus who had been wounded and had his elephant beneath him killed was fighting a fierce dismounted action and responded to the emissary's offer with a hurled javelin. Finally Alexander himself approached him and after offering his condolences for the loss of both his sons in the battle proposed a truce to halt further bloodshed. Porus finally accepted and when asked how he would like to be treated gave the classical reply, "As a king would treat another king."

The truce was called around four or five in the evening, but the drama was not over. As the armies were regrouping, collecting their dead and attending to the wounded, Alexander's force in the camp on the other side of the river, crossed over, and not aware of the truce, attacked the Indians from the rear, causing over 2000 casualties till order was restored. Both armies withdrew and licked their wounds and Alexander made his plans for further inroads into India to reach the end of the world, which he was convinced lay across it.

The Truce

This was not to be. His armies, tired and dispirited in the battle with "the most formidable foe we have faced" (as per the Greek historian Plutarch) and fearful of even more formidable foes ahead, refused to move further. At the banks of the Beas River, they mutinied, forcing Alexander to begin his long journey across his conquered territories back to Greece.

In the first recorded battle with a foreign invader, the Indian armies had acquitted themselves well as valiant individual fighters, but not as a cohesive collective force. That trend would continue throughout the centuries as a stream of invaders attacked India. Indian armies would fight valiantly, but eventually individual skill and valour would prove no match for new concepts and technologies that the invaders brought in their wake. And the outcomes of each battle would be distressingly the same.

3

End of May 1192
VICTORY AND DEFEAT AT TARAIN

The Battles of Tarain

The bards of Rajasthan still sing stories of Prithviraj Chauhan, the last Hindu ruler to sit on the throne of Delhi (that is, if you discount Hemu's fifteen-day reign in 1526, before the Second battle of Panipat. For more details, see 'The Cusp of Victory'). A courageous warrior, he expanded the Rajput Empire across all of North India. As a dashing prince, he stole the heart of Princess Sanyogita, and abducted her from her own *swayamwara.* Captured by Mohammed Ghori, he was imprisoned and blinded, but attained revenge by slaying his captor, using just the sound of a gong to direct his arrow. Tales of him are the stuff of legends, but like all stories, the truth lies somewhere in between.

Prithviraj Chauhan

The story of Prithviraj Chauhan and his fateful encounter with Shihabuddin Muizzuddin Mohammed Bin Sam of Ghor, or Mohammed Ghori as history remembers him, goes back to the mid-12th century. The Chahamana Empire of the Chauhans extended from Punjab to Bihar and upto Gujarat in the South. As it inched westwards, it also touched the borders of the Timurid Empire of Mohammed Ghori, based in present-day Afghanistan. It was but inevitable that the two dominant empires of the time would clash.

Mohammed Ghori had launched a series of raids into India from 1175 onwards, even moving as far south as Gujarat. His forays were not always successful. In 1178, he was soundly defeated by the Chalukyas in the Battle of Gadahatta (near modern-day Mount Abu) and barely managed to escape back to Afghanistan. Yet within a decade, he had rebuilt his army and by 1190 had expanded his kingdom towards the Punjab, touching on the edges of Prithviraj Chauhan's kingdom. Border clashes between the Rajputs and the Timurid forces intensified and slowly the stage was being set for a confrontation.

The decisive moment came in the winter of 1190 when Mohammed Ghori captured the fortress of Tabarhindah (modern-day Bhatinda) – a vital fortress on the outskirts of the Chauhan Empire. This was a provocation Prithviraj Chauhan could not ignore and in early 1191, he set out to confront Ghori with an army of around 200,000 Cavalry and 3000 elephants. The two large armies, virtually evenly matched, met at Tarain – near modern-day Karnal – and here the first major clash of arms took place.

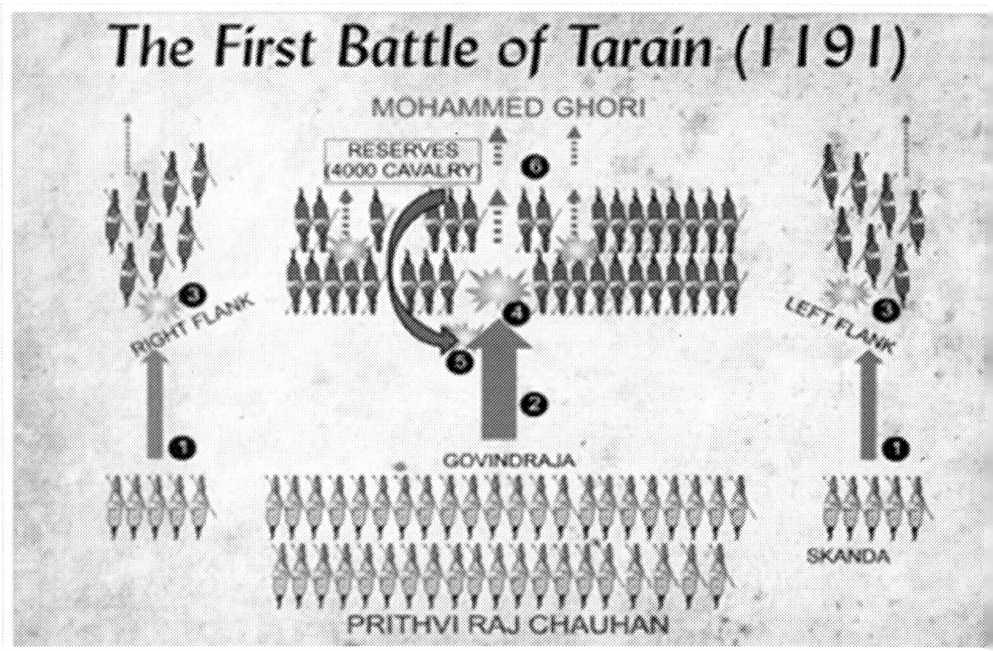

The First Battle

The First Battle of Tarain was a classical set-piece battle that the Indian excelled in. In a fierce day-long battle, the Rajputs got the better of their opponents. Their attacks simply smashed the Timurid lines and routed them. Mohammed Ghori himself was wounded and had to be carried away from the battlefield. His army broke and fled and were pursued by the Rajputs for around 40 kilometers. Yet, at a time when Ghori's entire army could have been eliminated once and for all, the Rajputs misplaced sense of chivalry and fair play did not permit them to attack a defeated enemy. Ghori and the remnants of his army were allowed to withdraw back to the safety of Afghanistan and there the threat coiled itself once again.

The First Battle of Tarain affected its principal actors differently. Prithviraj Chauhan became overconfident and careless, flush with victory. Ghori, however, became a man possessed. After his wounds healed, he set about forming a new army of Turks, Tajiks and Afghans. He changed his tactics and organization and developed small compact units of cavalry and infantry, each assigned specific roles. A year later, he was ready and marched into India at the head of over 120,000 well-armed and well-trained troops.

Prithviraj Chauhan had spent a year of indolence. He had abducted and married Sanyogita, the beautiful daughter of his rival Raja Jayachand of Kannauj, and now spent most of his time with his new queen, neglecting the matters of state. Rather than focusing on the threat that Ghori still posed, he ignored the frontiers of his empire and concentrated on petty squabbles with his fellow Indian chiefs. No frontier outposts were placed, nor did he receive any information of Ghori's activities and preparations. In fact, he only awoke to the threat sometime in March 1192, when Mohammed Ghori entered his empire and again captured the fortress of Tabarhindah.

When Prithviraj Chauhan marched out to meet Ghori again, he was not as well prepared as was a year earlier. Two of his major Generals, Skanda and Udayaraja, who had been the architects of his earlier victory, were out campaigning elsewhere with their armies. An overconfident Prithviraj did not even recall them for this decisive battle. He had gathered a force of around 100,000–120,000 men, but it was not a cohesive force. Rather it was a conglomeration of small chiefs and their armies hastily assembled together. Once again, the two armies met at Tarain, just 10 kilometers southeast of their earlier battle for an even more decisive encounter.

The two armies encamped opposite each other for a fortnight and negotiations began. Chauhan sent Ghori a letter proposing that they demarcate the line between the two empires. He suggested that the line be along the areas already captured by Ghori and even allowed him to keep the prized fortress of Tabarhinda. Ghori replied in a meek, subservient manner saying that he could not act on his own but would await instructions from his brother in Ghazni. It was a well-crafted letter and its obsequious tone lulled the Rajputs into a misplaced sense of complacency. A temporary truce was established and the Rajputs let down their guard.

For a fortnight or so, this 'truce' remained. While the Rajputs indulged in feasting and merry making, Ghori was putting his plans in place. On night, at around three in the morning, he launched a furious attack on the Rajput camp that virtually reached upto Prithviraj's own tent. The only thing that saved the situation was that the Cavalry were kept in the center, which soon regrouped and drove out the raiding party. By then, however, much damage had been done.

The so-called truce was now over, and the next morning the two armies assembled for battle. The Rajputs lined up in their traditional formation with Prithviraj himself in the center and two strong formations of all arms on either flank. Ghori's army was already ready and waiting on the edge of the Tarain plain with a strong force of infantry in the Center, and two battlegroups of around 10,000 light cavalry each, on either flank. In the rear was a reserve of 12,000 heavy cavalry – each man strongly armed and heavily mailed. It was an unconventional deployment that Ghori had adapted after having learnt his lessons in the first battle. This time he would not engage the Rajputs in the conventional battle they excelled in. He would use his cavalry to break their ranks.

The Rajput army was already a little disoriented from the unexpected raid of the night and even as their pendulous army was forming up, it came under first attack. One of the light cavalry groups of around 10,000 horsemen rode up to a flank and fired showers of arrows onto the packed Rajput ranks. Each horseman was armed with a composite double-curved bow, a small bow which could be fired while on the move, and which provided a range 70 yards more than the traditional long bows of the Rajputs. The Rajput ranks turned to meet this threat, but the light cavalry did not attack. Instead, after firing volleys of arrows, they simply wheeled away.

And then the next attack came in from the opposite flank.

Again the arrows showered down and the casualties mounted. Again the Rajput ranks turned to redeploy to meet the threat and again the cavalry wheeled away without making actual contact.

Four times Ghori repeated this maneuver. His light cavalry rode in from the flanks, fired and raced away without offering combat. By noon, the Rajput ranks were ragged, the men exhausted, and the formation had lost cohesion by constant shifting. A gap appeared in the Rajput lines and here Ghori launched his fifth and most powerful attack. A force of 12,000 heavy cavalry and around 70,000 infantry tore through the Rajput lines.

The heavy cavalry scythed through the disorganized Rajput ranks. Their own cavalry was dispersed in small groups and unable to concentrate and offer a coordinated resistance. In this battle, the light cavalry attacked along the flanks and faced with these unconventional tactics, the Rajput lines collapsed. Hemmed in from all sides, they were unable to maneuver or fight. Around 50,000-70,000 Rajput warriors and most of their leaders fell that day. Prithviraj Chauhan was forced to leave the battlefield, but was pursued and captured near Sirsa and taken to Ghori's camp.

The defeat at Tarain marked the end of an era. The Chauhan Empire collapsed and Mohammed Ghori now established his sway up to the Yamuna. He paced his favorite General – Qutb-ud-din-Aibak – on the throne of Delhi and with it began the Delhi Sultanate and the beginning of Muslim rule in India.

And what of Prithviraj Chauhan? Legend has it that he was blinded with hot irons and imprisoned in Ghazni. Here his court poet, Chand Bardai persuaded Mohammed Ghori to let the blind king display his archery skills. As Prithviraj notched his arrow, Chand Bardai recited a couplet giving away the location of Ghori in the courtroom. Prithviraj fired in that direction, killing Ghori instantly. He himself was stabbed to death by Chand Bardai allowing him to die in a manner befitting a king.

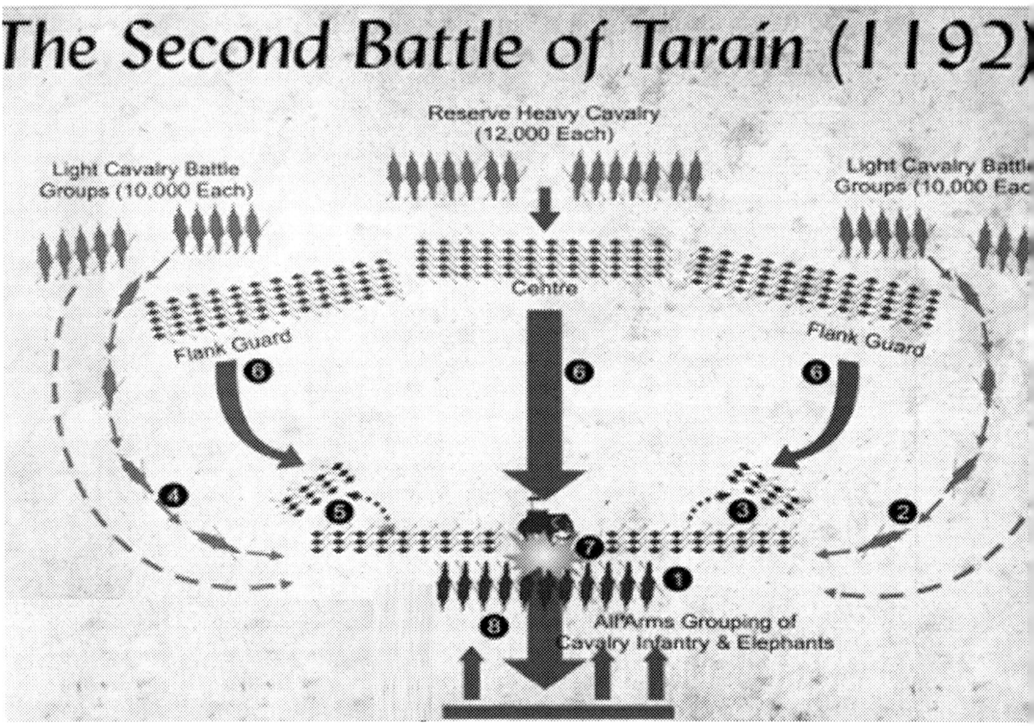

The Second Battle

But the truth is different. Prithviraj was blinded and tortured to death by Mohammed Ghori shortly after his capture and his body was buried at the entrance of Ghazni fort, where all who entered the fort could walk over it. Ghori himself died only in 1205, a full 14 years after the battle. But the legend remained and grew strong and like many stories became accepted as fact.

The truth was that Indian rulers could never really come together against a common foe. Their concepts of warfare and chivalry were antiquated and they relied on individual skill and courage, instead of modern tactics and doctrines. They were always too busy battling each other instead of an outsider. And that was the cause of their defeat and for the centuries of subjugation that followed.

4

21 April 1526
AN EMPIRE FORGED THROUGH CANNON SMOKE

The First Battle of Panipat

On 21 April 1526, an exceptionally hot Indian summer day, two armies faced off on the sun-baked fields of Panipat, just 70 kilometers North West of Delhi. The clash of arms that followed would last just six hours, but its impact would shape the nation for the next 300 years.

The story behind that epic clash began with Zahir-ud-Din Mohammed –

or Babur as history remembers him – who embarked on his quest for an empire. He was just 13 when his father, the ruler of Fergana, died, and he was hastily thrust on the throne. With that began his induction to the power play of Central Asian politics. Over the next decade and a half, he was pushed out of Fergana, then re-captured it, captured Samarkand, lost both, and then captured Kabul in 1504 that finally gave him a base. From there he cast his eyes covetously on India. Like his ancestors Timur Lane and Chengiz Khan, he launched repeated raids into the rich, undefended land, returning each time with treasures and experiences.

The flag of the Mughal Empire

Babur, founder of the Mughal Empire

Sultan Ibrahim Lodi (1517)

Babur and Ibrahim Lodi

His raids gave him a glimpse of the vast potential of India. His moment came when he was invited by Daulat Khan, the Governor of Punjab, to attack India and overthrow Ibrahim Lodi – the weak, ineffectual ruler who sat on the throne of Delhi. Ibrahim Lodi was a scion of the ruling Lodi dynasty, but had turned many of his own nobility and generals against him through his high-handedness. When Daulat Khan's invitation reached Babur, he found the temptation of Hindustan irresistible and made plans to come, not just to raid, but to rule.

He launched his first expedition in 1524. It was a disaster. His forces were defeated in the initial battles near Lahore itself. He fell out with Daulat Khan and in a pique he returned to Kabul. But that expedition taught him valuable lessons about his own weaknesses, his adversary and the conditions he would have to fight in. He returned again the next year and this time he was better prepared. He had built up an army of around 30,000 battle-hardened warriors, largely cavalry who were highly trained in the concepts of fire and move. Armed with double-curved, composite bows, they could fire on the move, and outranged their opponents by over 70 yards. Best of all, in his wagon train, he carried an artillery park of around two dozen *kazans,* or heavy mortars, around 40-50 *zarbzans* or light cannons, and around 1000 flintlocks. On the strength of his artillery, he would forge an empire.

Babur moved slowly from Kabul in November 1525. He crossed the Hindu Kush Mountains, the Chenab, Jhelum and Sutlej and reached Panipat in the end of March 1526. By then, the vast army of Ibrahim Lodi had already encamped in the vicinity of Panipat and were waiting for him. What is surprising is that Ibrahim Lodi allowed the invader to come so close. He should have engaged Babur at the Hindu Kush Mountains, or at any of the rivers he had to cross en route. The threat was virtually at the doorstep of Delhi when he decided to confront it.

Mughal Cavalry with double curved bow

Babur halted a little to the north of Panipat and established a defensive position using the town to cover one flank and some low hills to cover the other. In between he established a defensive line along a dried-up river bed which he converted into a ditch. Along the ditch he lined up his wagon carts, chained in pairs. Gaps of 60-70 yards were strategically placed through which his precious cannon could fire. On the flanks were larger gaps of around 150-200 yards through which his cavalry could sally. Behind that defensive line, he marshaled his forces and waited.

For three weeks both armies faced off, each waiting for the other to make the first move. None wanted to be the first to attack. Encounters were common as both sides clashed virtually on a daily basis, to gauge their opponent. Then on the night of 19 April, Babur launched a large raid with around 5000 men on the Afghan camp. The raid was a disaster. The raiding parties started late, moved in an uncoordinated manner and were detected by the Afghans, who attacked and forced the Mughals to flee leaving behind over 2000 dead. Babur, in his memoirs, claims it was a planned move, though in all probability it was just a botched-up raid. But it had its effect. Confident after their easy victory, the Afghans decided to attack the Mughal camp the next day – exactly what Babur hoped they would do.

That morning of 21 April 1526, the armies assembled to the sounds of drums, whistles and gongs. Babur deployed in a classical Turkish formation, with a light screening force ahead, a covering force behind them, and the main force assembled behind the defensive perimeter. Babur himself commanded the center (the *Kol*) with his son Humayun on the right flank (Baranghar) and his most trusted general, Mohammed Mirza on the left flank (Jaranghar). Light cavalry contingents called *Tulaqmas* operated on the flanks, and in the rear was the strong reserve – the *Iltimish* – of around 10,000 heavy cavalry. His artillery, the ace up his sleeve, were deployed behind the wagon line positioned to bring down fire between the gaps. Each gun was carefully concealed and camouflaged to amplify its surprise and shock effect.

The Afghan army lined up in rows of 200–300 extending over 200 files deep. Leading the charge were the time-tested elephants. Surprisingly, the Afghans had not even scouted the area and were not aware of the presence of the ditch or of Babur's defensive layout. Nor did they have any idea of the cannon they were about to encounter for the first time.

The leading elements of Ibrahim Lodi's army encountered the screen and the covering force which withdrew, drawing the army toward an open field which Babur had selected as his killing area. As they approached Babur's defensive layout, his guns opened up. The flash and thunder of guns scared the elephants who panicked and turned to flee, trampling over their own ranks. The gun fire took a heavy toll on the packed ranks, and to compound the effect, Babur sent his light cavalry on both flanks who fired their arrows at long ranges, wheeled away, returned and fired again, each time causing heavy casualties but not entering into decisive combat.

As the leading elements of Ibrahim Lodi's army were being mowed down, the rear was not aware of the carnage ahead and continued pushing forward compressing the ranks like a concertina. The leading elements could not advance because of the ditch ahead. The entire army was being pushed into a tight knot in which cannon, arrows and gunshot took a deadly toll. Adding to the chaos were the elephants running amok.

With Ibrahim Lodi's army trapped inside the killing area, Babur launched his *iltimish* – his reserve. His 10,000 heavily armed cavalry moved from a flank and tore through the rear of Ibrahim Lodi's forces slashing and cutting their way through the bewildered ranks. Hemmed in from all sides, the Afghan army could neither maneuver, nor fight. It was carnage. Ibrahim Lodi made a desperate attempt to break out with 5000 of his personal guard, but was killed himself. His body was discovered after the battle along with 25,000-30,000 Afghans who fell in the field of battle. His body was washed and ceremoniously buried. The rest were not so fortunate. Their bodies were decapitated and a small hillock was made of their severed heads as a grisly warning to any future contenders.

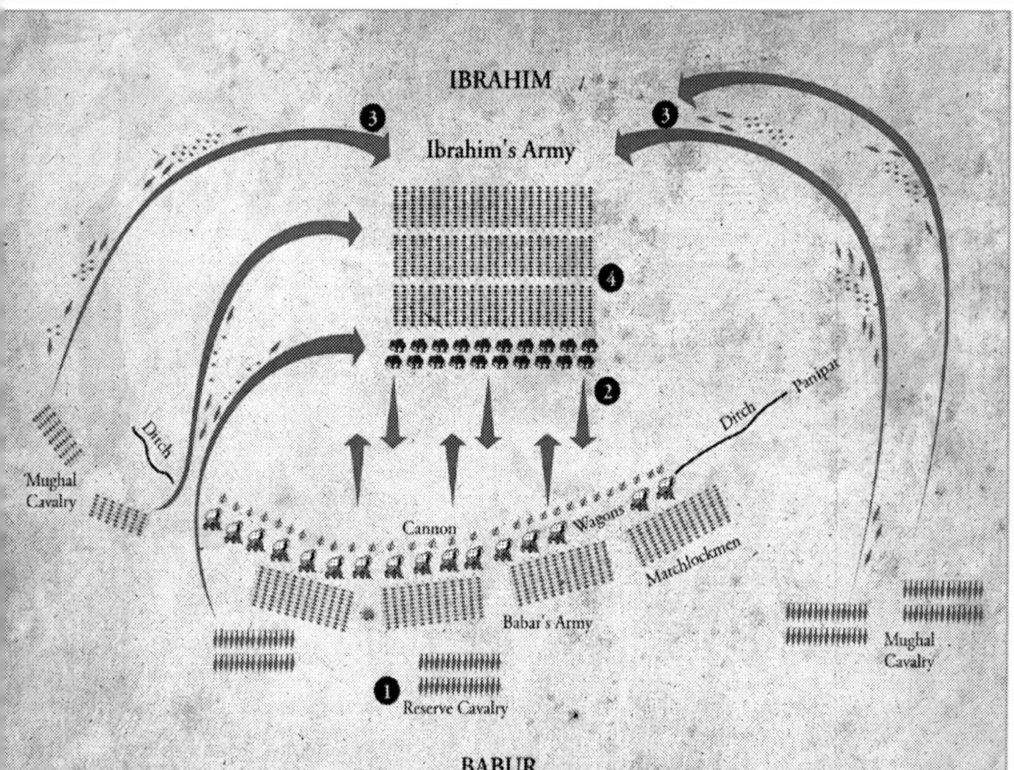

The Battle

By noon it was over. Babur himself describes it as, "*The battle commenced when the sun was spear high and lasted till midday when the enemy was completely broken. The mighty army, in the space of half a day, lay in the dust.*" In the space of just six hours, his army had defeated a force almost twice its size, and established the Mughal Empire in India. There would be other battles – Khanua (see 'Consolidating an Empire at Khanua'), Ghaghra (see 'The Battle of Ghaghra'), Chausa (see the Battle of Chausa), Bigram and many others – before the empire was finally consolidated. These battles too would be fought on the same principles of fire and maneuver and their outcome would be the same. When the cannon smoke cleared, it would be the green flag with a golden lion emblazoned within, the flag of the Mughal Empire, that would rise victoriously. This flag would hold sway over the entire country for the next 300 years.

5

17 March 1527
CONSOLIDATING AN EMPIRE

Battle of Khanua

Babur had wrested the throne of Delhi from Ibrahim Lodn the First Battle of Panipat (see An Empire Forged Through Cannon Smoke) on 21 April 1526. The easy victory over an enemy twice his force gave him a foothold into India. Yet to truly establish the Mughal Empire in India, he had to contend with the Rajputs under their charismatic chief Rana Sanga.

Rana Sanga, the one-eyed, one-limbed Rana of Mewar was the victor of over 80 battles and had assembled a confederacy of Rajput Chiefs against the Mughal invader. In fact, in 1525, Rana Sanga had sent a letter to Babur, asking him to attack Ibrahim Lodhi and even promised to attack Agra during the battle, but backed down. After Babur defeated Ibrahim Lodhi at Panipat, he imagined that he would loot and depart, leaving Delhi up for the taking. Babur's decision to stay in India led Rana Sanga to form a coalition of Rajput and Afghan Chiefs to evict the outsider.

Rana Sanga

In December 1526, he moved out of Mewar towards Agra, the seat of the Mughal Empire. The Rajput armies with over 7 major chiefs, 40 minor chieftains and 12,000 Afghans had a combined strength of 80,000 well-trained and courageous fighters. Yet, they depended on individual valor and skill and had no exposure to cannon and guns or the concepts of fire and maneuver which Babur had developed. Their rigid adherence to outdated concepts of war would cost them dear.

They crossed the River Gambhir and entered the Mughal Empire capturing the forts of Dholpur, Gwalior and Bayana. A large Mughal force that had been sent to relieve the siege of Bayana was comprehensively defeated. The Rajputs also got the better of their adversaries in most of the fights that occurred. At that time, the bulk of the Mughal army, under Humayun, was in the East, quelling an uprising of Afghan chiefs. They were hastily recalled and on 11 Feb 1527, Babur moved out to contest the advancing Rajput armies. As they advanced from Agra towards Khanua, the Advance Guard of over 2000 was intercepted by a force of Rajput cavalry and virtually decimated. News of Rajput valor and their skill at arms percolated down and a sense of defeatism crept into the Mughal camp.

Seeing the flagging morale, Babur assembled his army and in an emotional speech, smashed his bejeweled goblets and wine caskets, vowing to never drink again. He also declared a "*jihad against the infidels.*" The call had the desired effect. It galvanized his men out of their despair and rejuvenated them for the battle ahead.

Babur now set about making preparations. Additional reinforcements came in from Kabul which beefed up his strength. He set up camp in the area of Fatehpur Sikri, where he established a defensive perimeter with carts yoked together and linked with chains, with the gaps covered by the fire of his cannons. He also developed a new invention, a movable tripod. This was a triangular fortification on wheels which could allow his matchlock men and archers to fire behind its protection, and still move across the battlefield. In effect, he developed his camp to be a mobile defensive platform.

For over a month Babur remained in his camp. Surprisingly, the Rajputs did little to attack thus allowing Babur to consolidate. Negotiations also began between the two sides conducted by Taur Silhadi of Raisen who was an important chief of the Rajput Confederacy. He had recently converted to

Islam, and during the negotiations was convinced by Babur to change sides and defect during the battle. That monthlong period of inactivity also saw the differences between the perpetually warring Rajput chiefs come to the fore and signs of rift emerged in the alliance.

Finally on 17 March 1527, at the urgings of his Chiefs, Rana Sanga decided to attack Babur's camp. Babur had deployed his guns in the form of an all-round defense and had placed his infantry and archers in the center, with light cavalry in the flanks and a 10,000-strong force of heavy cavalry as the reserve. The initial Rajput charge was met with a storm of fire – something they had never encountered before. The faceless rain of shot and pellets took a huge toll that valor and individual skill could do little against. The Rajput Center, led by Rana Sanga himself, tried valiantly to close in with the enemy, but the elephants refused to attack, terrified by the cannon fire that they had encountered for the first time. Rana Sanga ordered the left and right flanks to attack and in spite of dreadful casualties, the Rajput ranks managed to close in. Taur Silhadi who had been entrusted with the important task of leading the left flank now abruptly left the battlefield with his entire contingent and deserted to the Mughal side – something that must have been agreed upon earlier. His departure left a gap in the Rajput formation, and seeing his moment, Babur launched his *tulugmas* – his cavalry reserves – that cut their way through the open flank and into the Rajput ranks.

Tapestry Depicting the Battle

With Mughal Cavalry on their flanks and fire pouring in from the front, the Rajputs fought desperately to break out of the encircling ring that surrounded them. Babur now moved his movable fortifications and guns forward hemming them into a tight knot in which they could neither maneuver nor fight effectively. Rana Sanga, leading the attack, had been repeatedly wounded and collapsed in the howdah of his elephant. The unconscious Rana was carried away to safety while the Rajputs tried to fight their way out of the closing Mughal ranks. But it was no longer a coordinated battle. By around 4 in the afternoon, the battle had been decided and it was all over.

Over 25,000 lay dead on the battlefield and the Mughals began the grisly practice of creating a mound of human heads on a hillock by the battlefield to commemorate their victory. Rana Sanga and the remnants of his army withdrew towards Mewar. He pledged never to enter Chittor, his capital, till he attained

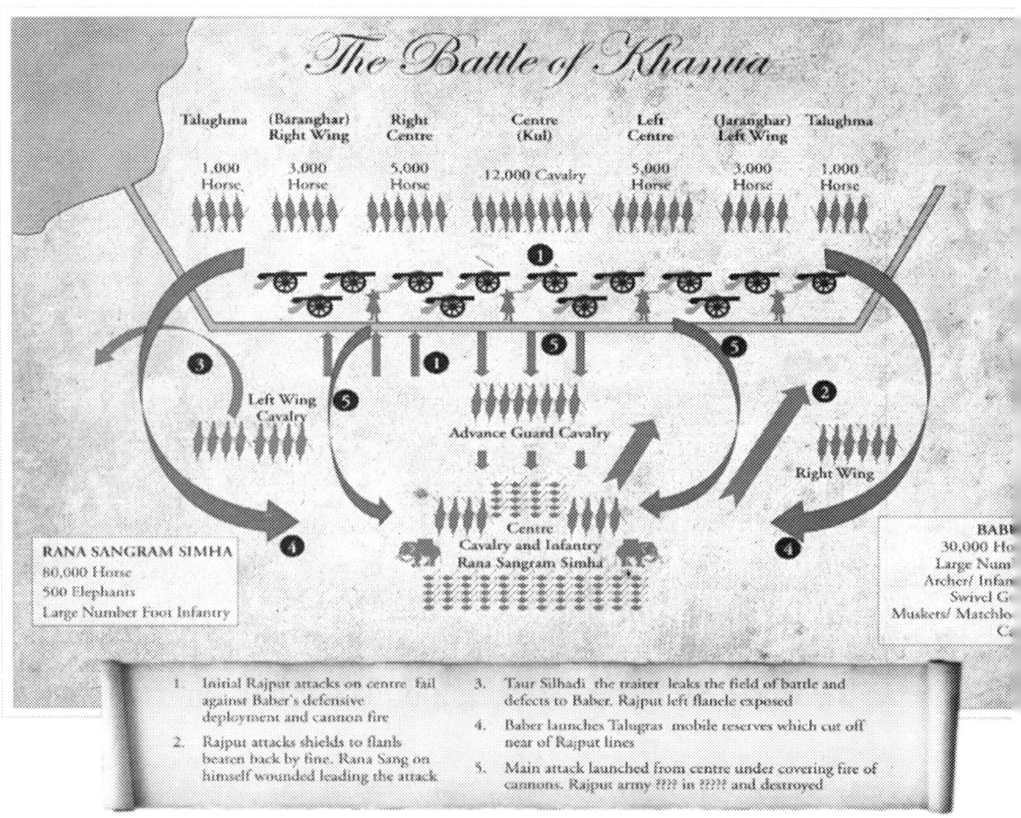

The Battle

victory. It was a promise he could not keep. Within a year he was dead, most probably poisoned by his own ministers in the incessant power play of politics, which has been the curse of Indian rulers. The Rajput chiefs who had been unified by his personality went back to their internal squabbling and infighting, and with him, the last major opposition to Mughal rule disappeared.

From then on, the Rajputs continued to hold on to their kingdoms but were never able to present a united front again. Babur consolidated his position with other victories and slowly expanded his empire laying the foundation for a three-century-long rule of the Mughal Empire over the Indian sub-continent. (Also see 'The Cusp of Victory – the Second Battle of Panipat'; 'The Pass of Blood – Haldi Ghati'; 'The Throne of Blood – Samugarh'.)

6

6 May 1529
GHAGHRA

The Battle of Ghaghra

Babur had attained the throne of Delhi after his victory over Ibrahim Lodhi in the battle of Panipat on 21 April 1526. He consolidated his hold over North India in the battle of Khanua the very next year with the defeat of the Rajputs under Rana Sanga. Yet, the Mughal Empire was still on shaky foundations. In the East, the Afghans were regrouping under Sultan Mahmud Lodi (the brother of Ibrahim Lodi) and Sultan Nusrat Lodi of Bengal. They had assembled an army of around 100,000, which was poised in Bengal to challenge Babur's claims to India. It was a threat he could not ignore.

Babur set out on his campaign to subjugate the Afghans in early 1529. He marched towards Bengal, defeating several minor Afghan chiefs along the way. Unlike his earlier campaigns on flat open grounds, here he encountered a series of vast, wide rivers. It was behind one of them – the Ghaghra River – that the Afghan Army was deployed.

As always, his army was outnumbered, and he depended on his excellent cannon and ever better tactics to save the day. The Afghan army was just north of the confluence of the Ganga and the Ghaghra Rivers, and he divided his army into two parts. The main contingent under General Askari moved with four divisions (around 40,000 men), while Babur himself moved with around two divisions towards the confluence of rivers. Nusrat Lodi had deployed his troops on the East bank of the Ghaghra River with defenses on a

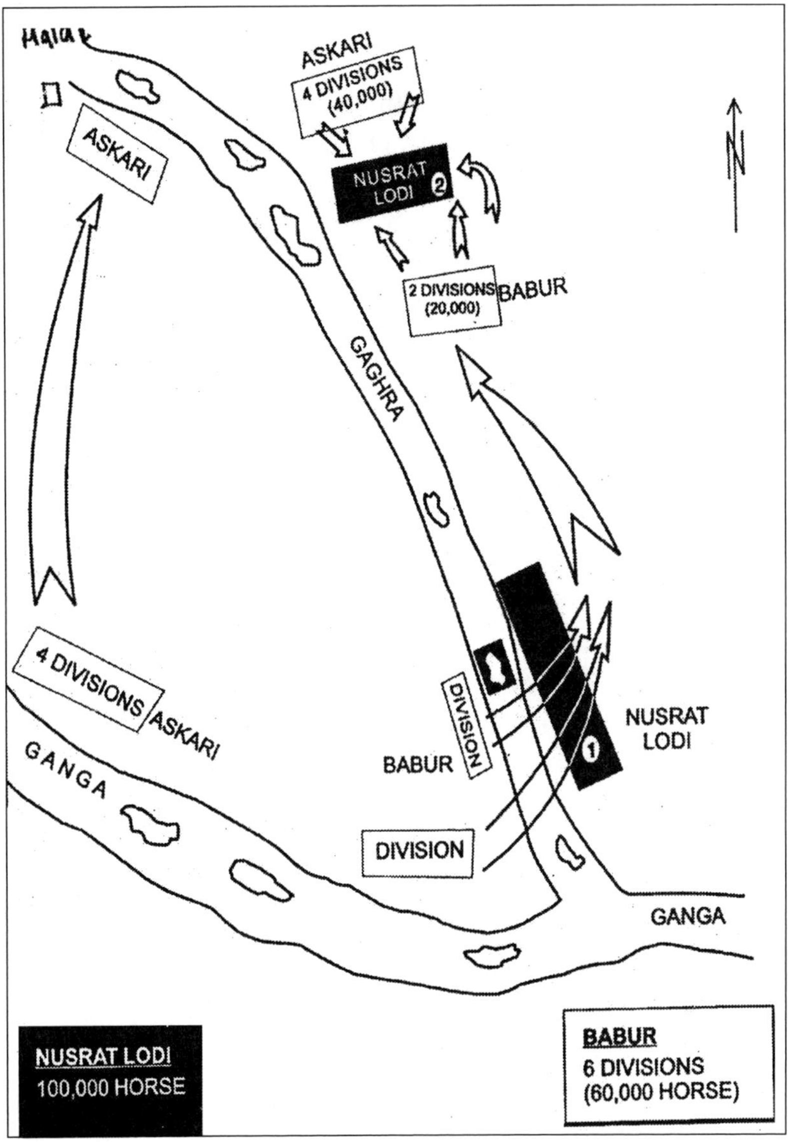

fortified island in the river. A flotilla of boats was also positioned near the banks to enable him to move his troops rapidly. The Ghaghra River was over half a mile wide and though not so deep at that time of the year, it was a formidable obstacle. Getting across with the Afghans holding the other side in strength would be a difficult proposition.

Babur resorted to the classical stratagem in the crossing of rivers. He moved Askari with his 40,000 men to attempt a crossing around 20 kilometers to the north. He himself was positioned with two divisions opposite Nusrat Lodi's force. His precious guns were raised on huge ramparts from where they could bring down fire on the Afghan positions on the other side. Their fire destroyed many of the boats anchored there and pinned down the Afghans, diverting attention from the main crossing that Askari was attempting elsewhere.

Around 20 kilometers to the North, Askari's four divisions crossed the Ghaghra River near the village of Haldi on the night of 05-06 May and were across by early morning on 06 May. Realizing the major threat, Nusrat Lodhi moved the bulk of his forces to counter them, thinning out his defences. Babur ordered his two divisions to cross, using reed rafts, small boats, and even swimming across on their horses. His cannon provided a steady barrage of fire and by mid-morning both his divisions were across and he had established a bridgehead on the other side.

Nusrat Lodi's army was in the process of engaging Askari's four divisions when it was violently attacked by Babur's two divisions from the rear. In spite of the exhaustion of executing a major river crossing just one night earlier, the Mughals still had the strength to launch their wheeling cavalry attacks that hemmed in the Afghans and comprehensively defeated them on the open plains by the banks of the Ghaghra.

Nusrat Lodi surrendered, and with this victory, Babur extended his empire from Kandahar to Bengal. In a period of three years, his army had won three major victories in spite of being heavily outnumbered in each case. Ghaghra would be his last major battle. He died the next year (1530), leaving the fledging Empire to his son Humayun hold, consolidate, and develop it into the mightiest Empire of the sub-continent.

7

26 June 1539
A CHESSBOARD OF AN EMPIRE

Battle of Chausa

Few historical figures have been as wrongly named as Humayun – which means lucky. This son of Babur inherited the Mughal Empire from his father Babur (see 'An Empire Carved from Cannon Smoke' – First Battle of Panipat and 'Consolidating an Empire – Battle of Khanua') and then spent the rest of his life trying to hold on to it. He spent his life almost as a figure on a chess board, moving from place to place, suffering defeat after defeat, till he finally re-established the Mughal Empire in India.

When Humayun ascended the throne in 1530 after the death of Babur, he had to contend with enemies all around. In Bengal and Bihar, the Afghans under Sher Shah Suri were on the rise. In Gujarat, Bahadur Shah was a major threat; the Rajputs were up in arms, and his own brothers eyed his throne covetously.

Humayun spent most of his early years quelling rebellion after rebellion. In 1537, he rushed to Gujarat to defeat Bahadur Shah, only to rush back to Agra when Sher Shah Suri marched towards the city. Humayun managed to save his capital and forced Sher Shah to withdraw, but now the battlelines between the Mughal Empire and the rising power of Suri were being drawn.

Humayun

Sher Shah Suri

Sher Shah Suri was a formidable opponent. He had risen from the ranks as a simple sepoy and got his name 'Sher' when he killed a tiger with his bare hands to save the Mughal Governor of Bihar. That act got him a position of prominence and he built upon it till he finally replaced the Governor and took control of all of Bihar. In 1537, he captured and looted Gaur – the capital of Mughal Bengal – and armed with its riches built up his own power in Bihar and Bengal.

Humayun could not let this rising threat go unchecked. In early 1539, he marched out with a huge army into Bihar to confront Suri. He captured Gaur and Charna, but in each battle he was being drawn deeper eastward and further from his own capital. In his long absence, his own brother now moved to usurp the throne.

With this new threat developing, Humayun rushed back towards Agra, only to find that Sher Shah had blocked his route back by positioning himself at Mungar on the Northern bank of the Ganges River. He was now forced to cross the Ganges and in doing so entered Sher Shah Suri's territory where Suri held the advantage. Suri attacked and harassed the Mughals repeatedly forcing them to re-cross the Ganges at Bihiya and get back to the Northern side.

As Humayun resumed his march towards Agra, Sher Shah awaited him in the vicinity of Chausa. The two armies camped opposite each other for over three months – from April to June 1539 – with neither willing to go on the offensive. Sher Shah deliberately delayed the battle, knowing that the Mughal army was being gradually weakened through illness and the constant campaigning of the past few months. His own army was getting reinforced by his Afghan and Rajput allies. Humayun however was isolated. His appeals for help to his brothers were unanswered and he was literally on his own.

In June, as the rains set in, a huge flash flood engulfed the Mughal camp that had been wrongly sited in the lowlands between the Ganges and the Karmanasa rivers. With the Mughal army in disarray, Sher Shah attacked. He divided his army in three divisions: one under his son Jalal Khan, one under his ablest general Khanwar Khan and the strongest division commanded personally by him. The three-pronged attack ripped through the Mughal camp and the army disintegrated under the shock attack. Over 8,000 Mughals were cut down, and twice as many drowned as they tried to cross the flooded Ganges. Humayun himself was carried across the river on an inflated water skin and he and the remnants of his army dragged their way back to Agra.

Flush with the victory, Sher Shah Suri took on the title of Sultan of Bihar and Bengal and began expanding his power westwards towards Agra. Humayun managed to cling on to power and reconstituted his army. Humayun was forced to confront his old nemesis, just a year later, as Suri's army came closer and closer towards Agra. He marched out to meet him and the two armies met on 17 May 1540 at Kannauj (250 kilometers east of Agra). Here Sher Shah, using superior tactics and field craft, inflicted another crushing defeat on the Mughals forcing Humayun to flee to Agra and then to Lahore and Kabul.

Sher Shah took over the throne and established the Suri Empire. His five years of rule (1540–1545) were eventful and he proved himself to be a good administrator. He extended the Grand Trunk Road from Chittagong to Peshawar, building rest houses and water tanks along the way. He developed the concept of 'Rupaya', a silver coin weighing exactly 178 grams, and copper coins called 'Paisa', currency names known even today. He introduced land reforms and fair taxation and ran a stable efficient government till his death in 1545.

Memorial to the Battle of Chausa

And what of Humayun? He wandered in exile for 15 years – a king on a chessboard moving from place to place. Then the Suri Empire was weakened by the death of Sher Shah Suri's son Islam Shah in 1554. Seizing his moment, Humayun marched back and defeated the Afghans in the Battle of Sirhind in 1555. Once again, the Mughal Empire re-established itself in India. This time it would be for keeps.

8

07 October 1556
THE OUTSKIRTS OF AN EMPIRE

Battle of Tuglaqabad

Tuglaqabad: Where the Battle was Fought

It was the year 1556. Medieval India was in its usual state of political chaos. The lion's flag of the Mughal Empire had been well-established in Delhi after Babur's victory over Ibrahim Lodi in the First Battle of Panipat in 1526 (see 'An Empire Forged through Cannon Smoke') and over the Rajputs at Khanua (see 'Consolidating an Empire'). But within 4 years, Babur was dead. His son Humayan struggled to hold the fledgling kingdom together, but battered on all sides, he was defeated by the Afghan chief Sher Shah Suri in the Battle of Chausa in 1539 (see 'A Chessboard of an Empire – Battle of Chausa') and forced to flee to Kabul. The Suri Empire now held sway over Delhi and India.

With the death of Sher Shah Suri in 1545, the usual internal wars began within his sons, weakening the Suri Empire. Humayun seized his moment to reoccupy Delhi and Agra in 1555, and once again it was Mughal rule over Delhi. But a few months after his victorious return, Humayun was dead, in January 1556, after a freak fall down a flight of steps in the Purana Qila.

With his death, a 13-year-old Akbar was hastily crowned Emperor of India in a simple ceremony at Kalanaur (near Amritsar). But he was Emperor only in name. The real power lay with his regent Bairam Khan, a man with a domineering and imposing personality.

The Afghans had been pushed towards Gwalior and Adil Shah Suri, a weak, pleasure-loving king, presided over the remnants of the Suri kingdom. Yet the entire functioning was in the capable hands of his Chief Minister, Hemchandra – or Hemu – one of the most charismatic figures of Indian history. The son of a humble shopkeeper from Rewari, he had risen up the ranks of the Afghan court to become Adil Shah's most dependable general and administrator. He had won 22 consecutive battles and his political and tactical skill was legendary. With the death of Humayun, and the political chaos that followed, he realized that the time was ripe to occupy the throne of Delhi.

When Humayun presented his plan to reoccupy Delhi, Adil Shah's response was predictable. He left the entire functioning and execution to Hemu and continued with his life of pleasure-mongering in Gwalior. Hemu meanwhile built up an alliance of Afghan and Rajput Chiefs and gathered an army of 50,000 troops, 1000 elephants, 51 cannon and 500 musketeers. He marched out in August 1556, rapidly capturing the Mughal outposts of Bayana, Etawah, Shambad and Narnaul and by the end of September had captured Agra, the heart of the Mughal Empire. Here he consolidated himself and in end of October began his march to Delhi.

Akbar and the bulk of the Mughal army were away on a campaign against rebels in Jullandhar and the defense of Delhi was entrusted to its Governor, Tardi Beg Khan – a seasoned veteran of many past campaigns. He had a force of around 30,000 cavalry, and though outnumbered by Hemu, each of his generals was a seasoned veteran and his men were well-trained and battle hardened.

The armies met on 06 Oct 1556 on the outskirts of Delhi with the ramparts of the Tuglaqabad fort in the background. The imposing outline of the Qutub Minar could be seen just six kilometers away, and it stood almost as a symbol of Delhi itself. Both armies arrayed themselves as per the traditional doctrine of the times – with a strong center, two flanks, a vanguard and a reserve. The Mughal lines had Tardi Beg himself in the center with Haider Mohamed commanding the right flank and Iskander Beg on the left. In the vanguard was Abdullah Uzbeg, with a strong contingent of cavalry. Hemu deployed similarly, but even as he was moving his force into their battle formation, the Mughals attacked.

The Mughal vanguard and their left flank with a combined force of around 10,000 heavily armed cavalrymen launched a furious pre-emptive strike that tore through Hemu's right wing, killed over 3000 men and captured over 400 of his prized elephants. As Hemu's right flank began withdrawing in disarray, the Mughals chased them furiously reaching right up to Hemu's camp. Then, as was their custom, many of the soldiers stopped the battle and began looting and plundering the camp, thinking that victory was already theirs.

Imagine the scene. We have Hemu's center and left flank intact, his right flank broken and around 10,000 Mughal cavalry looting his camp around 3–4 miles to his rear. His position was precarious. He could have chosen to wheel back to contest the Mughal cavalry behind him, but he did just the opposite. He realized that the Mughals too were vulnerable with their cavalry away and decided to attack the Mughal lines bang in the center.

Using 300 of his elephants and around 3000 of his best cavalry, he charged into the Mughal left flank and center. The attack was bolstered by the timely arrival of the Afghan Chief Haji Khan coming from Alwar who swooped down the Mughal lines from a flank while Hemu hit them from the center. The combined assault broke the Mughal lines who fled in panic leaving behind over 8000 dead. Tardi Beg himself fled the battlefield and this set off a panicked rout.

Hemu could have chased the retreating Mughal forces and decimated the army, but he did not. He chose to consolidate his position, knowing that

Mughal Cavalry was still in his rear. By the time the Mughal Cavalry returned from looting his camp, Hemu had already gained control of the battlefield. They too slipped away from a flank, caught up with the rest of the withdrawing forces and went on towards Punjab to rejoin Akbar's main forces. Hemu's failure to decimate Tardi Beg's forces would make a difference when the two armies met again just a month later.

The Coronation of Hemu

Hemu entered Delhi in style. He shook off his allegiance to his ineffectual ruler, Adil Shah Suri, and had himself coroneted as Samrat Hemchandra Vikramaditya – the king of kings. The sounds of Vedic chants and hymns reverberated around the Purana Qila as Hemu took over as the first Hindu king to ascend the throne of Delhi after almost 400 years (the last being Prithviraj Chauhan in 1192). He would also be the last and his brief reign lasted just 22 days. Barely had the sounds of the celebrations died down, when Hemu once again marched out for an even more decisive confrontation with Akbar and the Mughal army which was now returning from Punjab and was poised near Panipat to contest him. His next battle – the Second Battle of Panipat – (see 'The Cusp of Victory') – would be the only battle he ever lost, and unfortunately would also be the most decisive.

9

05 November 1556
THE CUSP OF VICTORY

Second Battle of Panipat

Hemu did not have much time to enjoy the throne of Delhi. Just three weeks after his victory at Tuglaqabad (see 'The Outskirts of an Empire'), he would march out once again to face the vengeful Mughal Army, now returning in strength from their campaign in Punjab. He would confront them just around seven kilometers South East of the spot where the first battle of Panipat was fought (See 'An Empire Forged through Cannon Smoke') and from where Babur carved his Empire. Here near a village called Saundhapur, the Second Battle of Panipat would decide the fate of India.

Hemu

Akbar was camping with his army in Jullandhar when the remnants of his force at Delhi reached him with news of their loss at Tughlaqabad. The 13-year-old was just a titular head. The real power lay in the hands of his loyal, if overbearing Bairam Khan. Alarmed by the defeat at Tughlaqabad, most of his Generals were of the view that they should withdraw to Kabul. It was the domineering personality of Bairam Khan that curbed any defeatist talk. To drive home his point, he had Tardi Beg executed for his failure to defeat Delhi (though that had more to do with personal enmity than any stratagem) and promising the same fate for any man who wavered, he prepared the army to move back towards Delhi for battle with Hemu.

Shaken out of their despondency, the Mughal Army marched towards Delhi under the command of Ali Quli Khan, the *'Sar-e-Lashkar'*. Akbar himself took no part in the battle wisely leaving it to his father's veteran fighters. The army reached Panipat on 04 November and there it deployed. Arriving early at the battlefield gave it a considerable advantage. And fortune conspired to give it another decisive advantage.

Hemu left Delhi on 02 November and moved towards Panipat on hearing of the advance of the Mughal army. During his advance march itself, he made an uncharacteristic error. He sent his entire field park of 51 guns ahead with his advance guard. The Advance Guard was ambushed on 04 November with a force of around 10,000 Mughal Cavalry who routed them, and worse captured the precious cannon. Even before the battle had begun, Hemu was bereft of his fire support. That would prove crucial during the battle.

Yet, Hemu shrugged off the loss and reached Panipat on the night of 4 November. As per some reports, that night – the last night of his life – he had a dream. He saw himself being yanked from his elephant by a chain of arrows – a dream his pandits interpreted as a sign that he would be defeated and captured. That dream would prove prophetically true.

Hemu lined up his army at dawn the next day. Hemu was numerically stronger with around 30,000 Rajput and Afghan warriors and 500 prized elephants. He himself was in the center atop his war elephant Hawai – with a force of around 12,000, with two wings of 10,000 each on either flank, the right commanded by the Afghan general Shadi Khan Kakkar and the left by his nephew Rammaya. Around three kilometers opposite him were the Mughal army in a mirror formation, but with one major difference. Ahead of their positions were their cannon – now reinforced by Hemu's own captured guns – which could pour a devastating torrent of fire on the enemy.

Hemu made the first move, even though his troops had arrived just around midnight the night before, while the Mughals had been awaiting them for two full days. At dawn, both his flanks launched a violent attack on the Mughal positions. Yet the Mughal cavalry, instead of retreating, wheeled to the sides and began pouring arrows from the flanks, and slashing at the weaker legs of the heavily armoured elephants from the sides. Hemu's attack was further stalled by a large ditch, whose presence his troops were not aware of. Hemu's initial attack paused and around 6000 heavily armed Mughal cavalry tore through his left flank and killed the commander. Hemu, seeing the gravity of the situation, now led a counter attack, forcing the Mughal cavalry to retreat, and managed to salvage the situation.

By noon, the battle hung in balance. Hemu led another coordinated attack, using his center and left flank, on the Mughal positions and slowly the battle tilted in his favour. Both wings of the Mughal army were falling back under his onslaught and Hemu himself led the attack straight at the enemy center. The Mughal lines were crumbling and it seemed any moment now the troops would break and run. Then the arrow came.

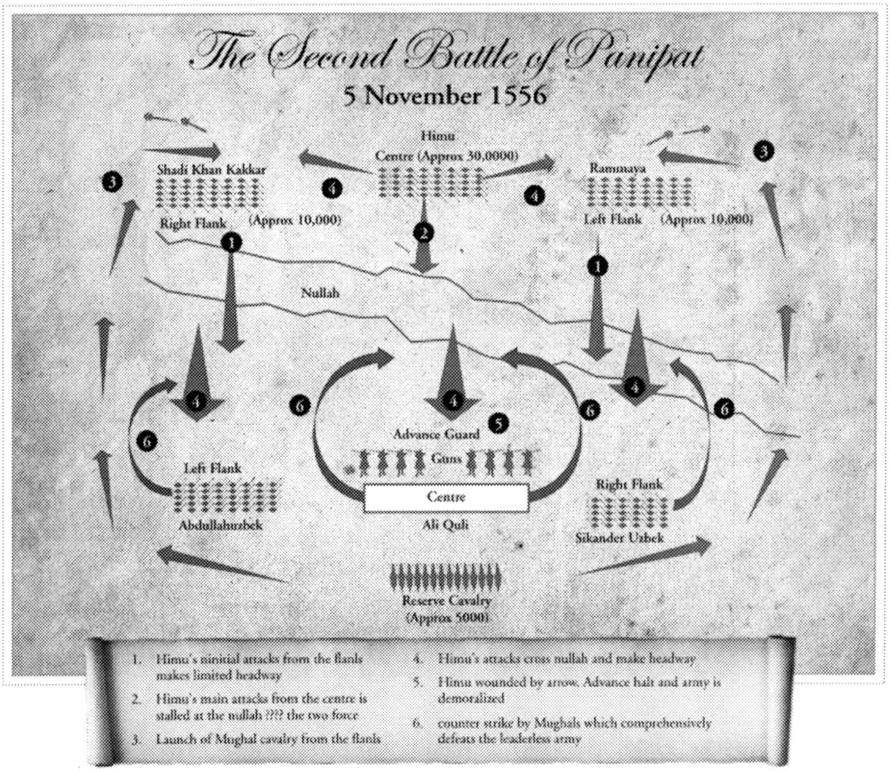

The Battle

Hemu's imposing presence atop his ornately armoured and heavily bejeweled elephant Hawai was the rallying point of his men. Yet the Mughals had nominated a screen of archers who were specifically tasked to fire at Hemu, knowing that his fall would change the battle. In the shower of arrows that came towards him, one found its way through his body armour, face mask and helmet to strike his only exposed part – his eye.

Dazed and badly injured, Hemu still pulled the arrow out, bandaged the wound with a scarf and tried to continue, but the shock and loss of blood took its toll and he swayed and collapsed in his *howdah*. Seeing their leader fall, the army which was on the cusp of victory lost heart. His men halted and without any one to direct their actions, began withdrawing. The Mughals seized the moment and launched their final counterattack with all the cavalry at their disposal, attacking along both flanks. Hemu's mahout tried to take his master back to safety, but was intercepted, captured and led back to Akbar, with Hemu still unconscious in the howdah.

By then the battle was lost. Over 5000 of Hemu's men lay dead with many more killed while fleeing. Bairam Khan urged Akbar to kill Hemu, which Akbar refused – and an enraged Bairam Khan decapitated him with his own sword. His beheaded body was placed on a gibbet in Delhi and Akbar himself entered the city in triumph two days later. The stage was now set for Mughal rule in India which would go on for another 250 years.

All because of a fateful arrow!

10

23 January 1565
THE 'CITY OF VICTORY'

Battle of Talikota

The Ruins of Hampi – where the 'City of Victory' once stood

Two centuries before the clash between the Afghans and the Marathas in the Third Battle of Panipat (see 'The Blackest Day in India's History'), another cataclysmic clash took place between Hindu and Muslim armies with distressingly similar results. This battle – named The Battle of Talikota, by some, and the Battle of Rakshasi–Tangadgi by others – has been largely ignored by historians, but it caused more casualties than all the three battles of Panipat put together, destroyed the powerful Vijayanagara Empire, and brought the curtain down on Hindu rule in Southern India.

Established in 1336, the Vijayanagara Empire had for over two centuries been the most flourishing empire state of South India. A hub of commerce, culture and arts, it had a thriving trade with Persia, Arabia and the Far East. It was a bastion of Hindu culture and philosophy which held its own in a sub-continent fast coming under Islamic rule. Its capital city of Vijayanagara (meaning the City of Victory) was acclaimed as the most beautiful city of South India and perhaps all of India. It had reached the pinnacle of its power during 1520-1560, first under Krishna Deva Raya (1509-1529) and then under his son-in-law Rama Raja Raya. At its peak, the Vijayanagara Empire encompassed all of Southern India.

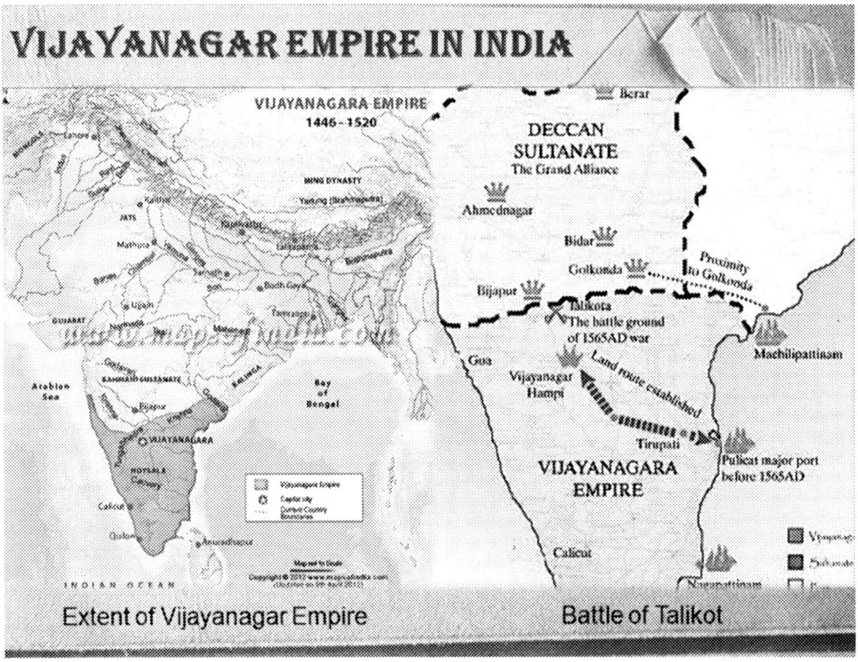

Rama Raya was himself a very capable military leader and an able administrator. However, he had taken over the throne after imprisoning most of the royal family and declaring himself the ruler – an act which lost him the support of most nobles. He removed most of the earlier faithful officials from the administration and military and replaced them with members of his own family. He hired Muslim mercenaries from the armies of the Sultan of Bijapur and appointed two of them, the Gilani brothers, Noor Khan and Bijli Khan as generals leading independent divisions. This was done in spite of warnings from his own advisors. As he expanded his empire, he reached the banks of the Godavari. Flush with power, he began interfering with the affairs of his neighboring states of the Deccan Sultanates – the states of Bijapur, Ahmadnagar, Golconda, Berar and Bidar – and came into conflict with each of them. These states came together under Ali Adil Shah of Bijapur to form a Muslim confederacy against the Vijayanagara Empire.

The joint armies of the Sultanates put aside their past rivalries, cemented the alliance with marriages between each other's families and began preparations for a joint assault on Vijayanagara. News of their activities reached Rama Raya and so around Dussehra in 1564, he began mobilizing his own forces. He had over 100,000 infantry and around 40,000 cavalry against a combined force of around 110,000 which the Sultanates had assembled. But the numbers don't tell it all. His *force de main* were 1000 war-elephants on which the army depended heavily. His infantry had no body armour and fought in turbans and loin cloth. Their six-foot-long spears and short swords were no match for the 16-foot-long spears of the Sultanates' armies. Their unwieldy bamboo bows were out-ranged by over 70 yards by the composite bows and metal arrows of their opponents. The small country-bred ponies of their cavalry did not have the strength or the mobility of the Arab steeds of the Sultan's arm. The clincher lay in the artillery. Although Rama Raya had around 200 cannon and rockets, they were yet a generation behind the batteries of the 600 latest cannons held by his opponents, manned by expert Turkish and Persian gunners. And there was the leader himself. Rama Raya was in his 70s, and his brothers and other generals equally aged. Though they led from the front, they just did not have the energy and vigour required for battle.

'Malik-e-Maidan' – One of the Cannons used in the Battle

The Krishna River formed the dividing line between the Vijayanagara Empire, and Rama Raya had deployed large forces to guard its crossing. On 27 Dec 1564, the combined armies of the five Sultanate states reached the main crossing place at Tangadgi. The crossing was held in strength by Rama Raya's brother Tirumalla, but was crossed easily using an age-old stratagem. The Sultanate forces moved eastwards, ostensibly trying to find another crossing place and their move was shadowed by the defending forces on the opposite bank. Then one night, a strong covering force of cavalry wheeled back to Tangadgi, crossed the River and secured the far bank. Over the next three nights, the rest of the army crossed the Krishna and were in Vijayanagara territory.

Rama Raya had been waiting behind with his main force and the two armies made contact. Over the next three weeks or so, frequent clashes erupted between the two armies, in which the Sultanate armies suffered crippling losses, which almost broke the alliance. Ali Adil Shah, the architect of the alliance also sent message to Rama Raya professing neutrality, a ploy which prevented his forces from being attacked by the Vijayanagara army. In the period of wait, the Sultanate's emissaries made contact with the two mercenary generals of the Vijayanagara Army – the Gilani brothers, Noor Khan and Bijli Khan – who agreed to switch sides at an opportune time in the battle.

The main battle took place on 23 Jan 1565 in a wide area south of the Krishna River between the villages of Tangadgi and Rakshasi. Rama Raya was in the Center with the main force and his brothers Tirumalla and Venkatadri on the right and left flanks. The army was deployed in an all-arms formation with the guns and rockets ahead to give them clear fields of fire. The opposing Muslim formation had Hussain Nizam Shah and his Ahmadnagar forces in the center, the army of Bijapur under Ali Adil Shah on the right wing and the armies of Golcunda and Bidar under Ibrahim Qutb Shah on the left. They were deployed in a classic Turkish formation with a screen of light cavalry ahead, the main force in a defensive layout, light cavalry on the flanks and heavy cavalry in the rear as a central reserve. Their artillery park of 600 modern cannon was kept centrally to bring down maximum volumes of fire.

The forces lined up in the morning with the firing of guns and rockets, none of which did any major damage. Around midday, Rama Raya's brothers

Tirumalla and Venkatadri launched spirited attacks on both flanks which pushed back the left wing of the Deccan armies. This initial success was not exploited and the attacking force was pushed back by showers of arrows from the agile cavalry who charged, fired and wheeled away. Venkatadri and his son were wounded and carried away and the attack weakened.

A Tapestry of the Battle

With the battle not going well, Rama Raya decided to launch an assault with the bulk of his forces from the center. He was old and had to be carried to the battlefield on a *palki* and then hoisted atop an elephant where he sat with trays of gold coins and jewels to be given to those who fought well. Under his urging, the Vijayanagara armies launched a desperate attack. The attack was repulsed by the combined fire of all 600 of the Sultanate guns which had been kept primed and filled with bags of copper coins which scythed through the attacking ranks like shrapnel. In spite of heavy casualties, the attack was making headway, when the two Gilani brothers – acting on a predetermined signal – changed ranks and began attacking their own forces from the rear with their two divisions. This attack took the Vijayanagara forces completely by surprise. Faced with attack from the Muslim divisions of their own army from the rear and the Sultanate forces from the front and flanks, they gave way and broke ranks.

Rama Raya's elephant was hit by a cannon shot and fell. As he was being carried away on a *palki,* he was overtaken by the Sultanate's officers who beheaded him and mounted his head on a lance for display. This shattered the morale of troops completely leading to a rout. What followed was a general massacre of the once magnificent Vijayanagara army.

Worse was to follow. Rama Raya's brother Tirumalla Deva Raya fled to Vijayanagara and instead of defending the capital, fled with the royal treasury mounted on 1550 elephants. Three days later, the Sultanate's armies descended on Vijayanagara. Over a period of six months they destroyed the city, killing over 500,000 civilians. "With fire and sword, with crowbars and axes, they wrought their work of destruction. Never in the history of the world, has such havoc been wrought on so splendid a city, teeming with wealth and prosperity one day, seized and reduced to ruins, the next."

Vijayanagara, 'The City of Victory' virtually vanished, with the center of arts, culture and heritage passed on to history. The 200-year-old Vijayanagara Empire limped along for another few decades as its limbs were slowly torn into pieces and annexed into neighboring kingdoms. What remained of that magnificent empire are just the ruins of Hampi – on the site of the old city of Vijayanagara – which are a stark reminder of what once was and of what could have been.

11

21 June 1576
THE PASS OF BLOOD

The Battle of Haldi Ghati

Few battles have captured the collective imagination of Indians as much as Haldi Ghati. Though nowhere in the scale of the titanic struggles at Panipat, Talikota, Plassey or Tarain, it still had a lasting impact and stands out as a tale of Indian valour in the face of overwhelming odds.

Akbar, the grandson of Babur had expanded the Mughal Empire from Kandahar to Bengal and upto Gujarat in the south. Most rulers had either acceded to his sovereignty or had been won over by marriages. Yet Mewar, the strongest Rajput kingdom, refused to submit to his authority and held on steadfastly.

Akbar launched a campaign to subjugate Mewar by force and in 1567 he marched out at the head of a large army to capture Chittor, its capital. The Rana of Mewar, Raja Uday Singh was urged to leave the besieged fort and take refuge in the hills of South Rajasthan. After a five-month-long siege, Chittor finally fell on 25 Feb 1568 and almost each of its defenders was killed. Akbar also ordered the slaughter of over 20,000 innocent civilians of the fort in an orgy of vengeance that went on for a week after its capture. This remains a lasting blot on his legacy.

The loss of their capital did not curb the zeal of the Mewar rulers. Rather it inflamed it. Uday Singh formed a new city of Udaipur and established his capital in Gogunda, in the Aravali Hills. With his death in 1572, his son, Rana Pratap took over the mantle and the struggle continued.

Akbar tried to make peace with the defiant ruler of Mewar, even sending his emissaries to Rana Pratap, in an effort to win them over. But Rana Pratap refused to yield till his capital Chittor was handed back to him. Finally in the spring of 1576, Akbar dispatched a large army under the command of his own brother-in-law Man Singh – himself a Khushwaha Rajput – to bring the rebellious Rana to his knees.

Man Singh's army had around 5000 of his own Khushwaha Rajputs and around 5000 Mughal and Afghan troops along with 100 elephants. No cannon or heavy cavalry were carried because of the problems of transporting them across that difficult terrain.

Rana Pratap received news of Man Singh's move and moved out of his capital Gogunda to take up positions at Haldi Ghati. The narrow, two-kilometer-long pass permitting only one horseman to pass through at a time and its forested hills made it a strong defensive feature. The soil and crumbly rocks around it were pale yellow, perhaps due to high sulphur content, giving it its name – Haldi Ghati. The yellow soil around the pass would soon be stained red with blood, earning it another name, *Khooni Ghati*, or the Pass of Blood.

Rana Pratap had a force of around 3000 Sisodiya Rajput warriors and a contingent of 500 Afghan horsemen under Hakim Khan Suri. Around 1000 Bhils, local tribesmen who knew the area intricately and were skilled archers, also joined him. Though outnumbered by around 1:2.5, the Rana was in a strong defensive position on the pass. The rugged terrain of Haldi Ghati nullified the numerical superiority of the Mughal forces.

The Pass as it must have been in 1576 **And today**

Man Singh's forces reached the vicinity around mid-June and camped in the flat ground short of the pass near Khamnor Village and the Banas River. He did not attack, but waited for Rana Pratap to make the next move. For a week or so, the two armies remained static in their positions, raiding and skirmishing without decisive combat. Finally on 21 June 1576, Rana Pratap left his positions on Haldi Ghati and advanced down to engage the Mughal forces.

It is not clear why Rana Pratap chose to leave his strong defensive positions for an open ground where the Mughals would be at an advantage. Some say it was intended to be just a raid that went awry. Others say the Rajput concept of a 'fair fight' led them out, prompted by calls of cowardice from their Rajput kinsmen on the other side. Whatever the reason, the Rajput army moved out to the sound of drums, *ranbankuras* and war cries and arrayed themselves at the mouth of the pass in the traditional order of *Haraval* (vanguard), *Chandawal* (rear guard) *Vam Parshwa* and *Dakshin Parshwa* (left and right wings). The Rana himself was in the center, in his distinctive white tunic atop his war horse *Chetak*, who would himself acquire a kind of immortality in the lore of Indian warfare.

The Mughals arrayed similarly. But Man Singh's advantage of numbers enabled him to maintain a reserve *(Iltimish)* of around 1000 cavalry. These reserves would save the day.

The Rajputs attacked first at around 8 am from the left flank as around

1000 Rajput and Afghan horsemen slammed through the Mughal vanguard and hit its right flank. On the right, a similar attack was launched with equal ferocity. The combined weight of the attacks on both flanks forced the Mughals to give way and the troops began breaking ranks. It was only the Sayyids of Barhi on the right flank who held on and prevented a complete breakthrough.

With his formation about to break, man Singh launched his *Iltimish* of 1000 cavalry to stabilize the situation. As the cavalry moved forward, amidst the troops running in panic, Mihtar Khan, the Commander of the reserves, shouted out, "The Emperor is coming. Akbar Badshah himself is coming." The pronouncement did the trick. The ranks stopped their withdrawal and beefed up with the timely arrival of their cavalry, held their positions, preventing any further breakthrough by the Rajputs.

It was now around 11 am and the Rajputs had been fighting for over three hours. Exhaustion and heat were taking its toll and slowly the Mughals (or more appropriately, Man Singh's Khushwaha Rajputs) were getting the better of the situation. Rana Pratap had only one reserve, the small pool of elephants which he launched to charge the Mughal lines. The Mughals countered by bringing up their own elephants. Elephants of both sides clashed on the battlefield, cheered on by their respective soldiers. In an epic clash, *Lona,* the

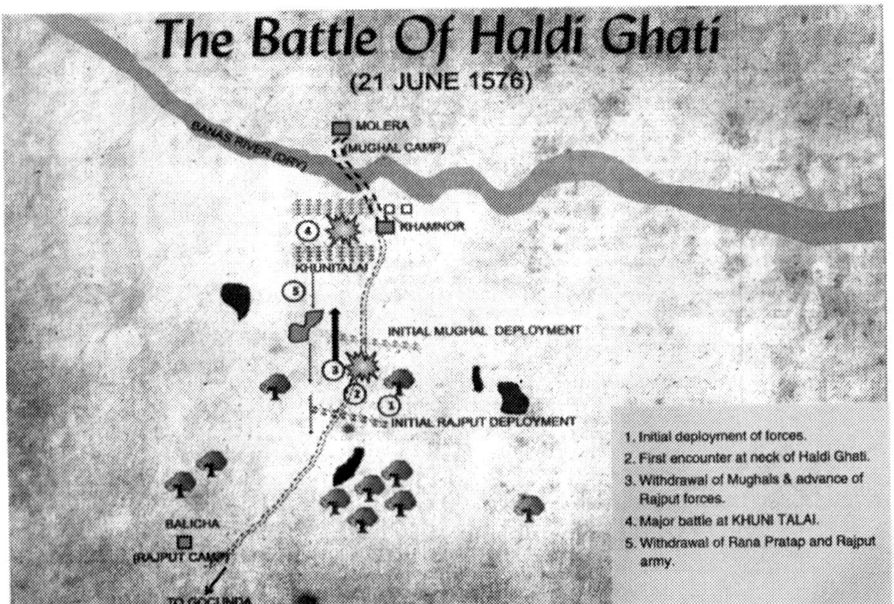

Rajput war-elephant slammed with *Gujmukut*, the Mughal champion, goring each other with their tusks, till *Lona* fell of his wounds and was captured. One by one, Rana Pratap's elephants were killed or captured and he lost his final card.

With the situation so critical, Rana Pratap launched a final attack directed at Man Singh himself. He charged full tilt atop Chetak (Chetak had a leather snout affixed to his head. It was a standard practice, since the short-sighted elephants would mistake the smaller horses for their young and often hesitate to attack them) slashing his way through the Mughal ranks till he reached Man Singh's elephant. As he closed in, Chetak rose on his hind legs, giving his master a clear shot. Rana Pratap hurled his spear which went through the mahout, and slammed against the armoured *howdah*, barely missing Man Singh. Before Rana Pratap could strike again, Man Singh's guards converged on him.

At this point, Bida Mana, a Jhala Chieftain placed Rana Pratap's *Chattri* (royal umbrella) over his head proclaiming that he was Rana Pratap. The ruse worked. The body guards rushed towards him, while the wounded Rana was carried away by Chetak, pursued by Mughal officers. Chetak, who had been badly wounded during the attack, raced away, and made a final leap across a

The death of Chetak

wide crevice which his pursuers could not cross. He took his master to safety, but died at that spot of sheer exhaustion and loss of blood. A cenotaph still marks the spot where he fell.

The Rana and the rest of the Rajput army withdrew to the safety of Haldi Ghati, their withdrawal covered by the arrows of Bhil archers. Man Singh did not follow up the pursuit – an act which earned him the wrath of Akbar when he returned. Around 500 Rajput warriors fell in the "Thermopylae of Mewar" with around 250-350 of Man Singh's Khushwahas and Mughal soldiers on that day.

But who really won at Haldi Ghati? Tactically, yes, it was a victory for Man Singh, but it achieved none of Akbar's long-term strategic goals. Rana Pratap remained unbowed and recovered to continue his struggle, pushing back three other expeditions that Akbar launched to subjugate him. His guerrilla war continued for two decades till his death in Jan 1597 and with his passing, India lost one of its noblest sons – one unbowed and undefeated till the end.

12

29 May 1658
THE THRONE OF BLOOD

The Battle of Samugarh

Few figures in Indian History evoke as much revulsion as Aurangzeb. This sixth and last great Mughal Emperor was perhaps the reason for the Hindu–Muslim split that rose during his time and exists even today. His bigotry paved the way for the eventual dissolution of the Mughal Empire.

But this third son of Emperor Shah Jahan was not even due to be the Emperor. That honor was to go to the eldest son, Dara Shukoh – whom Aurangzeb defeated and eventually killed in the Battle of Samugarh and then waded through the slaughter to the throne. That battle was not only one of succession between Shah Jahan's sons, Dara Shukoh and Aurangzeb. It was also a battle between ideologies. Unfortunately, the wrong son won, and the wrong ideology prevailed.

Dara Shukoh

Aurangzeb

It was the year 1657. Emperor Shah Jahan fell grievously ill in 1657 and named his eldest son Dara Shukoh as his successor. That triggered off a war of succession between Dara and his three other brothers – Shujah, Aurangzeb and Murad Bakshi. Shujah was in Bengal, Aurangzeb in the Deccan and Murad Bakshi was in Gujarat when Dara was declared as Shah Jahan's successor and the three brothers – each of whom felt he was the rightful claimant to the throne – marched towards Agra to stake their claims to the Peacock throne.

Dara, the liberal elder son, was a lover of poetry and culture. He had translated the Upanishads from Sanskrit to Persian and had written the excellent treatise *Majma-ul- Bahrain* (The Confluence of the Seas) in which he tried to find common ground between Islam and Hinduism. He was also a patron of the arts and a lover of music. His liberal views were frowned upon by his brothers and even some of his Muslim subjects who looked upon his tolerant ideology with suspicion.

Dara had little experience in warfare and was largely used to the comfort of Agra. Aurangzeb, however, was a seasoned campaigner who had spent most of his life under canvas and had won a string of victories for the Mughal

Empire. The other two brothers Shujah and Murad Bakshi too were experienced warriors. As the three brothers marched towards Agra, Shujah from Bengal, Murad from Gujarat and Aurangzeb from the Deccan, Dara sent his ablest troops under his eldest son to contest Shujah's advance. Shujah was defeated, but Dara's force was unable to return to Agra for the more decisive battles ahead. Another force under Maharaja Jaswant Singh was sent to contest Aurangzeb and Murad Bakshi, who had joined hands and were now advancing together. This force was decisively defeated by Aurangzeb in the Battle of Dharmat and withdrew to Jodhpur taking no further part in the action. Even before the main battle was joined, over one third of Dara's force was frittered away. Yet he still had with him a formidable Rajput and Mughal army of 100,000 cavalry, 20,000 infantry and 80 guns. Yet, many of his Muslim generals were against his liberal views and had loyalties towards Aurangzeb. They could defect at any stage.

After Aurangzeb's victory over Raja Jaswant Singh in the battle of Dharmat, the joint forces of Aurangzeb and Murad advanced towards Agra. Dara had selected his main defenses along the line of the Chambal River and had deployed his guns on the banks to prevent a crossing. Though Aurangzeb was temporarily delayed, he was able to discover a crossing place near Dhaulpur. His army waded across the river even though over 5000 men and horses were swept away in the crossing. In two days, Aurangzeb's entire army was across the Chambal River and had established a bridgehead on the other side.

With their defenses outflanked, Dara's forces on the Chambal River hastily retreated towards Agra leaving behind almost all their cannons and heavy stores. These precious cannons were thus denied to Dara for the decisive battle that lay ahead, when their firepower would be sorely required.

As the combined forces of Aurangzeb and Murad closed in on Agra, Dara marched his army out and deployed around 13 kilometers east of the city. It was the hottest time of the year in an unbearably hot Indian summer and men and horses – especially those in armour – were collapsing and dying of heat stokes. Dara's forced march with his army was the first of the many mistakes he would make during the battle.

The two armies met on 29 May 1658 in an open plain near Samugarh. Both armies deployed in the conventional pattern of the times, with a strong center, two flanks and an Advance Guard. Dara had positioned himself in the Center with Rustom Khan on his left wing and Khalil Ullah Khan, a general of dubious loyalties, on his right. His son Sipah Shukoh commanded the Advance Guard with around 12,000 Rajput and Mughal troops. Both armies faced off, and Aurangzeb, the seasoned campaigner, realized that in this wilting heat, the side that attacked would be at a disadvantage. He remained on the defensive and bided his time, and waited for Dara to attack.

Dara's impatience got the better of him and he ordered his son Sipah to attack Aurangzeb's Advance Guard. The attack met with initial success, but Aurangzeb, who had positioned himself at a vantage point and was following each move of the battle closely, sent forward his reserves and stabilized the situation.

Here is where Dara's inexperience showed. He decided to take personal control and led an attack from the center with around 20,000 of his personal troops. He moved obliquely, thus blocking the fire of his own guns. He also came under heavy fire from Aurangzeb's advance guard, which deflected him further and made him lose contact with his main forces. His Rajput and Mughal forces were exhausted in the heat but advanced valiantly towards Aurangzeb's left flank held by his brother Murad Bakshi.

Dara and his personal troops – mostly Rajputs – were now engaged in a pitched battle with Murad Bakshi's forces. He was out of contact with the rest of his force. Now came the crucial moment of the battle. Dara's right wing under Khalil Ullah Khan chose this moment to desert and slipped away to join Aurangzeb's forces – something that had evidently been planned and pre-determined before. Dara was in the midst of Aurangzeb's forces, without any support whatsoever. Each inroad made by his exhausted forces was countered by Aurangzeb sending up fresh troops, and by around midday, his forces were spent. He also made the mistake of dismounting from his elephant and mounting a horse. Seeing his empty howdah, his men thought their leader had fallen, and as had happened so often before, they panicked and fled. His faithful Rajputs, who did the bulk of the fighting, suffered terrible losses. Dara himself was carried away to safety leaving behind all his guns, baggage and equipment on the battlefield over which Aurangzeb held complete sway.

Aurangzeb reached Agra three days later and entered the capital with the grandeur of a conquering emperor. His father, Shah Jahan was imprisoned in Agra fort where he would spend the rest of his life, pining away and gazing at his beloved Taj Mahal. Dara who had fled Agra was pursued and captured near Multan and then beheaded on Aurangzeb's personal orders. His brother Murad Bakshi, who had fought valiantly by his side, met the same fate as Aurangzeb eliminated all future competition. On 31 July 1658, Aurangzeb took over as the Sixth Mughal Emperor of India. His reign would unleash a wave of intolerance and bigotry that would eventually lead to the fall of the Mughal dynasty and bring about the divide in Indian society that remains even today.

Aurangzeb seeing the head of Dara

What if Dara had won? He would have definitely been a tolerant, liberal king who treated all subjects equally. Perhaps he could have even got about a peaceful co-existence of the two religions that would enable them to live in harmony. But he did not. It was the wrong son that won, and the wrong ideology that prevailed.

13

04 February 1670
"GAD AALA PAN SINH GELA"

The Capture of Sinhgarh Fort

Shivaji has been rightly considered as one of the greatest Indian heroes of all times. His life reads like a story book. He captured his first fort when he was just 16, waged a three-decade-long war against Aurangzeb and carved a Maratha Empire against all odds. Yet few of his exploits have gripped public imagination as much as the capture of Sinhgarh Fort – or to give it the name it had then, Kondhana Fort.

The fort of Kondhana stands 25 kilometers away from Pune, on the highest point of the Sahyadri ranges. This triangular fort with its two-mile-long perimeter wall has the natural defenses of a 40-feet-high cliff on three sides and is only accessible from two gates – the Kalyan Darwaza in the South East and the Pune Darwaza at its North East. It was considered virtually impregnable, and by its strategic location in the center of a string of other forts – Raigad (Shivaji's own capital), Purandhar and Torna – was considered to be the linchpin in the defense of the Deccan.

Sinhgarh Fort

View from its Gates

The fort has an ever-changing history. It was built 2000 years ago by the Koli dynasty, which held on to it till its capture by Mohammed Bin Tughlaq in 1328. It then came under the control of the Nizams of Bijapur. In 1647, as Shivaji began his campaign for Independence, he gained control of the fort, only to lose it in 1649. He regained it again in 1656 and in spite of concerted attacks by Mughals in 1662, 1663 and 1665, held on to this prized possession. In 1665, Aurangzeb sent his best general, Mirza Raje Jai Singh, to curb Shivaji's rise in the Deccan. In a year-long campaign, he inflicted a series of reverses on Shivaji, forcing him to sign the Treaty of Purandhar. Amongst the terms of the agreement, Shivaji had to hand over 23 of his forts, keeping just 12 for himself. One of the forts handed over was Kondhana, which was soon garrisoned by Mughal troops.

In the five years following the Treaty of Purandhar, an uneasy truce existed between the Marathas and the Mughals. Then in 1670, Aurangzeb once again decided to bring the Deccan under his sway. He attacked the Deccan and tried to imprison Shivaji, who escaped just in time. With the truce broken, Shivaji gave the order, "Take the Forts." As he set about recapturing the forts held by the Mughals, his first target was the strategically vital Kondhana fort.

Folklore says that one morning Shivaji's mother, Jijabai, was combing her hair in her fort at Pratapgarh, when her eyes fell upon Kondhana (Kondhana, by its location was visible to both Raigad and Pratapgarh and dominated both). The thought that this prized fort was occupied by the Mughals infuriated her and she summoned Shivaji, ordering him to recapture the fort. Shivaji wavered, but then succumbed to his mother's wishes and sent for the only person who would be capable of the task – Tanaji Malusure.

Tanaji, Koli chieftain of Umrathe village in the Konkan, was engaged in the preparations for his son's marriage when Shivaji's summons reached him. Putting off his son's marriage, he gathered a force of 1000 Mavala soldiers and accompanied by his brother Suryaji and uncle Shelar set off for Raigad. He was a veteran of many campaigns with Shivaji and widely respected for his ingenuity and courage. He knew the import of the task and swore that he would capture the fort or die in the attempt.

The fort was occupied by around 1700 Mughal, Afghan and Rajput troops under the command of the renowned warrior, Uday Bhan Rathod. Tanaji kept his troops some distance away. He then dressed as a commoner and mingled with the local Koli people, seeking out information. He discovered that the fort had one weakness. There was one spot in the West, known as the Dongri Cliff from where its walls could be scaled.

Tanaji reconnoitered the area himself and the next night – on 04 Feb 1670 – moved his army in small groups toward the Kalyan Gate, moving them along different routes to avoid detection. Guided by two of the locals, he moved to Dongri Cliff with 300 men and began the silent, arduous climb along its walls. Legend has it that he used a giant monitor lizard to scale the wall, tying a rope to it and sending it scurrying up the walls and onto the other side. But in all probability, it is just a legend. 'Ghorpade' – as these lizards are called in Marathi – is a common Maratha name and it is likely that the first person who climbed the wall and then threw a rope ladder down was named Ghorpade. That individual is lost in history, but the story of the lizard remains.

Using the rope ladder, Tanaji and the rest of his men scaled the walls, their swords gripped between their teeth. They were undetected, but when around 50 men had climbed up to the ramparts of the fort, the rope broke. Tanaji and his small band were on their own inside the heavily defended fort.

Scaling the Fort

Tanaji kept his nerve and silently led his party towards the Kalyan Gate, where they killed the guards and tried to open the massive gates. As they were doing so, one of the guards raised an alarm and the party was soon surrounded by angry, vengeful Mughal guards.

The small band of Marathas held their own against immense odds, and to break their ranks, the War elephant Chandravati was launched against them. The elephant had been fed copious amounts of opium before its attack and perhaps its senses were dulled. It was killed, either by a spear throw, or by a Maratha warrior who managed to mount it and kill it with a sword thrust into its brain.

Yet, this was a small victory. The party was hemmed in and came under repeated attacks by the Mughal garrison, first by Sidi Hillal, the Second-in-Command of the fort, and then by Uday Bhan Rathod himself. Uday Bhan attacked Tanaji and a furious duel ensued. Uday Bhan's powerful thrusts broke Tanaji's shield and he wrapped a cloth over his left hand and used it to parry the thrusts. Another powerful slash severed his hand, but in a final desperate lunge he hurled himself at Uday Bhan killing him with a blow to his head. Then weakened by the loss of blood from the many wounds he had suffered, he fell dead to the ground.

Seeing their leader fall, the Marathas were on the verge of collapse when Tanaji's brother Suryaji with around 200 other warriors clambered over the wall with another rope ladder. Suryaji rallied the wavering troops and led them on a fresh counterattack which kept the Mughals at bay and also enabled them to open the gates of the Kalyan Darwaza. The 700 Marathas waiting outside poured in and routed the defenders, killing most. Many of the defenders hurled themselves across the walls to their deaths below, and the rest were taken in as prisoners. By daybreak, the fort was in their control and a thatched hut was set ablaze, as a signal of success.

The Death of Tanaji

Shivaji saw the plumes of smoke from his fort at Raigad, indicating the capture of Kondhana. He rushed to the fort and entered through its gates, now held by Marathas. But there was no jubilation amongst the victorious Mavalas. They stood silently around the body of their fallen leader. Shivaji himself wept at the loss of his friend and comrade and said *"Gad aala, pan Sinh gela"* (The fort has been gained, but the lion is lost).

Kondhana was renamed Sinhgarh after the lion-hearted Tanaji Malusure and even today his bust stands at the spot where he fell. With Sinhgarh under his control, Shivaji soon captured the adjoining forts of Purandhar, Moholy, Kurnalla and Lohgarh and reached as far as Bhiwandi and Kalyan. With the critical forts forming the crux of his defenses, he launched a skillful guerrilla campaign in the rugged valleys of the Deccan that repulsed successive Mughal offensives for over a decade. On 06 June 1676, he was coroneted at Raigad as Chattrapati, and with this act asserted his complete independence from Mughal yoke. Over the next few years, he carved out the Maratha Empire fighting both the Mughals and the Nizams of the Deccan, till his death in 1680. His legacy was carried forward by the Peshwas who followed and extended Maratha rule virtually till Afghanistan (see also 'The Battle of Maneuver –Palkhed') till their eventual eclipse in the Third Battle of Panipat (see also 'The Blackest Day in India's History' – Third Battle of Panipat).

Sinhgarh remained in the hands of the Marathas till it was recaptured by Aurangzeb in 1703, only to be retaken three years later. The fort remained in Maratha hands till 1818 when it was eventually captured by the British after a three-month-long siege. Although the fort changed hands often, one thing about the fort remained constant. It retained the name of the lion that captured it – SINHGARH.

14

28 February 1728
THE BATTLE OF MANEUVER

The Battle of Palkhed

Baji Rao I – one of India's greatest warriors – has swept into public consciousness after 'Bajirao Mastani', a movie that celebrates his passionate love for the beautiful Mastani, a Muslim Princess of Bundelkhand whom he married against all opposition. Yet, few remember the fact that he was a master of maneuver warfare, who carried Shivaji's legacy (See *Gad Aala, pan Sinh Gela* – The Capture of Sinhgarh fort), and helped consolidate the Maratha Empire. He remained undefeated in forty battles and the secret of his victories was simple. He travelled light, moved fast, hit the enemy where least expected, and then disappeared to surface elsewhere.

Baji Rao I took over as the second Maratha Peshwa (Prime Minister) after his father Balaji Vishwanath died in 1720. He was just 20 at that time, and his appointment as Peshwa by Chhatrapati Shaju met with much resentment from the elders of the court who eyed the coveted position. Yet, as time would prove, Shaju's choice was wise. Baji Rao took the Maratha Empire to great heights even reaching the doorsteps of Delhi.

In his twenty years as Peshwa, he re-developed the Maratha Army on the concept of nimble, fast-moving cavalry that travelled light, with no excess baggage whatsoever. They lived sparsely, carrying just enough to sustain them for the campaign. Each man had a cloth pouch containing two half-baked *chapattis*, a packet of salt, a handful of parched gram, two or three chilies, an onion and maybe a lump of jaggery. These were the standard daily rations for each man, General to Sowar alike. The army had no encumbrances, no camp followers or baggage trains and moved fast on their agile Deccan ponies – three between every two horsemen – appeared out of nowhere, struck hard and retreated. Following the classical tenets of maneuver warfare, they extended the Maratha Empire not only across the Deccan, but northwards as well into Madhya Pradesh and Gujarat.

Maratha Horseman

Baji Rao's campaigns were studied by General Montgomery who applied the same principles in his tank battles two and a half centuries later. The battle that most aptly brings out his skillful use of maneuver is the Battle of Palkhed, in which he encircled and defeated the much superior army of the Governor of Mughal Deccan and forced him to surrender virtually without a fight.

The Battle of Palkhed

The fledging Maratha Empire had taken root under Shivaji, but had fallen into disarray after his death in 1680. Shivaji's son Sambhaji was tortured and killed by Aurangzeb, and his grandson Shaju imprisoned in Delhi to curb any future Maratha ambitions. Shaju's escape after the death of Aurangzeb in 1707 began the revival of the Maratha Empire.

Shaju was appointed 'Chhatrapati' – the Emperor – and guided by able Peshwas, first Balaji Rao and then Baji Rao I, the Maratha Empire began rebuilding. They were granted a right by the Mughal Emperor to claim *Chauth* (or one fourth) and *Sardeshmukhi* (a 10% surcharge) in the areas controlled by them. This included the six provinces of the Deccan: Aurangabad, Ahmadnagar, Berar, Khandesh, Golcunda and Bijapur.

The rise of the Marathas was viewed as a direct threat to Nizam-ul-Mulk, the Governor of Mughal Deccan. The Maratha claims of *Chauth* and *Sardeshmukhi* was a blow to his own power and revenues. In December 1726, he set out with a large army comprising around 80,000 cavalry and infantry and over 100 heavy guns and cannons. In August 1727, he burst through Northern Maharashtra and entered Maratha territory.

At that time, Baji Rao was campaigning in Karnataka with the bulk of the Maratha Army. He was hastily recalled by Chhatrapati Shaju to counter the threat. He reached Pune in mid-Oct 1727 and immediately moved northward towards Ahmadnagar towards the border between the Nizam's and Maratha territory.

The Nizam was waiting for Baji Rao in the area between Ahmadnagar and Aurangabad. In those open plains, his large army and heavy artillery would have a distinct edge in close battle. Yet, rather than engaging the Nizam's army, Baji Rao bypassed it and entered the Nizam's territory, first attacking the town of Jalna, 40 kilometers away. He then moved to Washim, another 30 kilometers ahead, then Mangilpur and Hathgam, and ransacked the area. From here, he made an obvious and deliberate move towards Burhanpur, the most prosperous town of the Mughal Deccan, forcing the Nizam to move to counter him. But the Nizam's ponderous army, weighed down by his heavy guns and a vast administrative train, could not keep pace with Baji Rao's fast maneuvers. As the Nizam's army approached, Baji Rao moved further westwards towards Gujarat, crossing the Tapi River and then the Narmada and moved towards Bharuch to threaten the Mughal ports in Gujarat.

Over the next three months, from October to December 1727, Baji Rao moved from place to place. He knew he could not counter the Nizam's much superior army in a pitched battle and wanted to exhaust him by making him follow his maneuvers. By crossing rivers repeatedly, he hoped to force the Nizam to shed his heavy guns – which could not make a river crossing easily. And he refused to engage his opponent in a pitched battle, choosing instead to exhaust him and then lure him to a place where his own mobility could be best exploited.

The Nizam himself changed his strategy and in January 1728, he turned south towards Pune, the principal Maratha town. He surrounded the town and forced Chattrapati Shaju to take refuge in Purandar fort. He also used the internal rift between the Marathas by placing Shahu's cousin, Sambhaji of Kolhapur, on the Maratha throne. He gambled that this threat to Pune and the seat of Maratha power would force Baji Rao to reverse his steps and draw him to battle in the open area around Pune.

Baji Rao did not take the bait. Rather, he turned towards Aurangabad – the greatest city of Mughal Deccan named after Aurangzeb himself. By mid-February, he was prowling the outskirts of Aurangabad and Burhanpur. It was a war of nerves as both sides threatened the cities of their opponent, and the Nizam cracked first. He withdrew from Pune and rushed to counter the threat to Aurangabad. He moved with as much speed as he could muster towards Palkhed where the Maratha army was deployed.

To reach Palkhed, the Nizam's army had to cross the Godavari River at a place called Puntambe. An advance guard crossed over the river first on 25 February and selected a camp site. They were followed by Banjara civilian traders who accompanied the army and set up a bazaar to sell supplies and provisions. After them would come the main army and finally the heavy guns and rear guard.

By the time the Nizam's advance guard crossed the Godavari and reached Palkhed, Baji Rao had already deployed his forces around the village in a horseshoe formation. His force of around 25,000-30,000 cavalry was led by Malhar Rao Holkar, Ranoji Shinde, Pawar and other seasoned generals. In a series of skirmishes, they defeated the Advance Guard, and also routed the Banjara traders forcing them to flee, leaving their supplies behind.

Hearing of the encounter, the Nizam crossed the Godavari with his main body. However, to gain speed he had to leave behind all his guns and heavy equipment – just what Baji Rao wanted him to do. As the main body moved towards Palkhed, Baji Rao sent his cavalry on their flanks and rear. A strong detachment also blocked the way to the Shiv Nala in the North which was their only source of drinking water. Maratha cavalry patrolled around the Nizam's vast army, cutting them off from their supplies and drinking water. Baji Rao was in the center with the bulk of his forces, blocking the route to Aurangabad. One wing of Maratha cavalry blocked the Godavari River ensuring that Nizam's guns could not cross. The Nizam was without his most potent weapon as his guns remained powerless and impotent on the other side of the river.

Encircled and hemmed in from all sides, the Nizam was unable to fight or maneuver. Fast running out of water and supplies and losing men in daily skirmishes with fast-moving Maratha raiding parties, he finally capitulated on 28 February. On 6 March 1728, he signed the Treaty of Moongi-Paithan in which he agreed to return all the territories his armies had overrun. He also agreed to allow them to collect *chauth* and *sardeshmukhi* over all his territories in the Deccan, thus acceding to the Marathas' main demand.

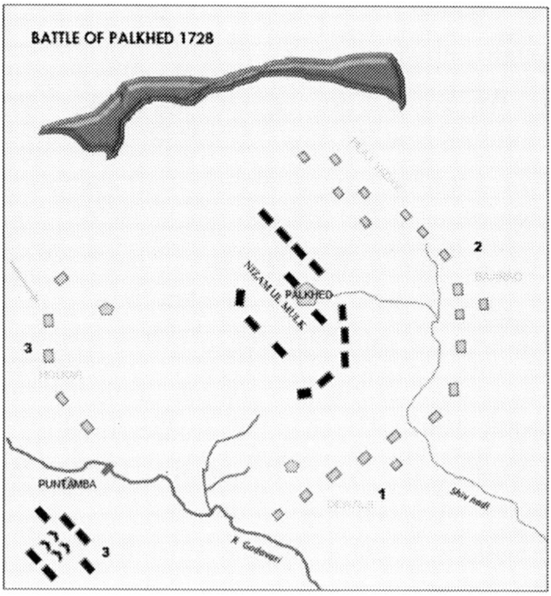

The Marathas had overcome a force almost thrice their size, through a series of maneuvers and with hardly any fighting. Throughout the campaign, Baji Rao resisted Shaju's entreaties to go on the defensive, insisting that, "To cut a tree, you do not need to cut off the branches and trunks – the best way is to strike at the roots." He struck when the time was right, and lopped off the very roots of Mughal power in the Deccan.

In 1737, the Nizam tried again to destroy Maratha power. His vast army of 80,000 men was encircled and trapped around Bhopal – in a battle which was a virtual re-run of Palkhed.

Palkhed was just one of Baji Rao's battles. Using the same principles of mobility, he expanded the Maratha kingdom across the Deccan and Malwa. He had promised to take Maratha power up to Attock, but it was a promise he could not keep. On 28 April 1748, at the age of just 40, he died on the banks of the Narmada River, after a sudden fever, most probably brought about by a sun stroke. He died as he had lived, out in the open with his men in the midst of another campaign.

In 20 years, Baji Rao fought 40 battles, remaining undefeated in each. His key to success was simple: move light and fast. It is ironic that the Marathas would forget these very tenets. His wife Kashibai had been deeply hurt by his love and marriage to Mastani. (Baji Rao was given the hand of the beautiful Mastani while out on a campaign. His passionate love and marriage to her scandalized and enraged Maratha society.) After his death, she passed a decree stating that in future, Maratha soldiers would be permitted to take their families with them – so that they would not get beguiled by other women when out on long campaigns. That decree had fateful consequences. The Maratha Army now became encumbered with women and children and they would lose their greatest asset – their mobility and speed. Just sixteen years after his death, a Maratha Army – slowed down with over around 30,000 women and children – would meet a crushing defeat in the Third Battle of Panipat (see 'The Blackest Day in India's History'). The Maratha Empire was established and consolidated on the principles of speed and mobility. When they lost sight of these principles, their decline began.

15

23 June 1757
A TRAITOR'S BATTLE

The Battle of Palashi

One of the advantages of winning battles is that the victor gets to write its history. Unfortunately, Indian rulers have won few of their battles and the versions we receive of them are from the other sources. When the British won at Palashi, they even changed the name to an Anglicized version. This momentous battle has thus gone down in history as the Battle of Plassey, one which helped establish Imperial rule in India.

The East India Company made inroads into India by the mid-18th century. They successfully ousted the French, the Dutch and Portuguese in the Carnatic Wars of 1850s and became the largest trading power of Peninsular India. As their power grew, so did their ambitions and they turned their eyes to Bengal, India's richest province.

Bengal was ruled by the 19-year-old Nawab Siraj-ud-Daulah, a young inexperienced prince who had been abruptly thrust on the throne after the death of his father. Yet, he proved to be surprisingly firm. The East India Company had established settlements in Hoogly and Calcutta and had slowly secured a monopoly of all trade, even refusing to pay taxes and tariffs to the state. Siraj-ud-Daula clamped down on their depredations, made them stop building fortifications, refused to grant them any further concessions, and earned their ire.

As the tensions were building up, the British, under Robert Clive, were making plans to remove him. They had got in touch with his Commander in Chief, Mir Jafar promising to put him on the throne if he agreed to help them. Mir Jafar – whose name has since then been synonymous with treachery – agreed willingly and also roped in two senior commanders, Rai Durlabh and Yar Latuf Khan with him. The trio promised Clive that they would take no part in the battle and help in the defeat of their Nawab.

The young monarch was unaware of these machinations when he marched out of his capital of Murshidabad in mid-June with a force of around 35,000 infantry, 18,000 Cavalry and 50 pieces of excellent French-manned artillery. Clive too left Calcutta with 600 European and some 2400 native soldiers and a small artillery park of six field guns and two small howitzers. His plan to defeat a force almost ten times his size hinged on the fact that Mir Jafar, Yar Latuf Khan and Rai Durlabh had been won over and would defect at a crucial stage of the battle.

Clive's force reached Palashi, a small village on the banks of the Bhagirathi River around midnight on night 22 June. He deployed his forces in a large mango grove with his guns ahead in a brick kiln from where they could fire effectively. Around three kilometers away Siraj-ud-Daulah's vast, if disunited army, was encamped and sounds of singing and music wafted over from there. The next morning, 23 June 1757, his army moved out and formed a large crescent shaped deployment around the British force (see map). The traitors with their divisions were in the South flank and Siraj-ud-Daulah, with his one loyal General Mir Mardan, was in the North. As events would show, the Southern flank took no part in the battle, and it was only Mir Mardan and his division that fought.

At around 8 in the morning, the battle began with furious cannon firesing from each side. Both sides launched tentative attacks which could not move forward because of enemy fire. By around noon, it seemed a stalemate was emerging and then something happened that dramatically changed the situation.

It began to rain.

It should not have been such an unexpected situation. After all it was mid-June when the monsoons traditionally erupts over North India. But with inexcusable negligence, the Nawab's gunners had forgotten to carry tarpaulins to cover their weaponry. In the torrential downpour, the gunpowder got wet and their cannons were rendered ineffective, unable to fire.

Tarpaulins enabled the British to fire their cannon in spite of the rain

When the rain stopped an hour later, Mir Mardan, Nawab's only loyal general, launched his attack, thinking that the British guns would be similarly affected. The British had covered their guns – their gunpowder was dry. The attack was met with musket and cannon fire, but with Mir Mardan himself leading the charge, the attack pressed on and came dangerously close to the British positions in the grove.

Then came the turning point of the battle. Mir Jafar, Rai Durlabh and Yar Latuf Khan had not moved their divisions and Siraj-ud-Daulah himself came to Mir Jafar's tent pleading him to move. Rather than supporting his monarch, Mir Jafar actually proposed that Mir Mardan's attack be halted and they would launch a coordinated assault the next morning. The inexperienced Nawab gave in and ordered Mir Mardan to halt his attack and move back to the camp.

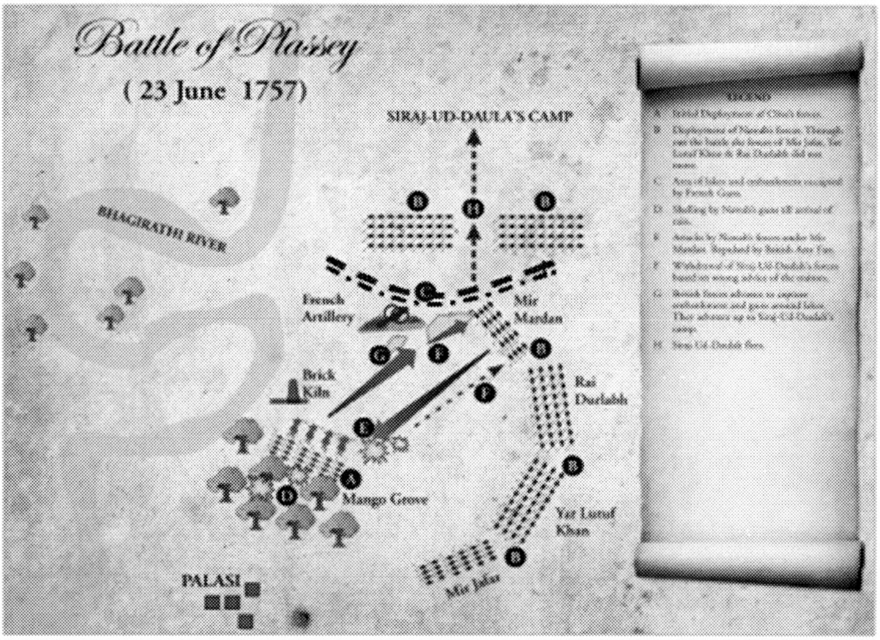

The Battle

The order caused nothing but confusion. His troops which were closing in began withdrawing and Mir Mardan himself was killed. The withdrawal became a retreat and then a rout, with British guns taking a heavy toll and their own guns unable to provide covering fire. Mir Jafar also passed message to Clive about what he had done, and seizing the moment, the British attacked, pursuing the troops back in their camp. Throughout the battle, the traitors with their three divisions of around 45,000 men stood impassively watching the defeat of their comrades which they had helped engineer.

By nightfall, Clive and his men had taken over Siraj-ud-Daulah's camp, routing his troops. Siraj-ud-Daulah fled on camel back towards Murshidabad, but was overtaken and brutally put to death on the orders of Mir Jafar. Mir Jafar himself met Clive the next morning who greeted him with, "Hail, Mir Jafar, Emperor of Bengal, Orissa and Bihar" and presented the new Nawab with a ceremonial tray of gold coins. The British had succeeded in putting their own puppet on the throne.

Mir Jafar became the Nawab of Bengal and allowed the British to loot India's richest province dry. Their victory at Palashi gave them a grip which allowed them to continue their depradations across the country. More than that, it established a psychological supremacy that lasted generations. But it was not British supremacy that won them the battle. It was the treachery and deceit of our own.

And the fact that they forgot to carry tarpaulins for their guns.

16

14 January 1761
'THE BLACKEST DAY IN INDIA'S HISTORY'

Third Battle of Panipat

14 January 1761 – the auspicious day of Makar Sankranti – was the 'Blackest Day in Indian History.' On this day, 50,000-60,000 Marathas fell during the Third Battle of Panipat. Another 20,000-30,000 women and children were captured and taken as slaves, and the Maratha Empire received a death blow from which it could never really recover.

The roots of the battle can be traced to the rise of the Maratha Empire and which brought it into conflict with the Durrani Empire of Ahmad Shah Abdali in Afghanistan. By 1755, the Marathas were the dominant power of the sub-continent. Its influence encompassed the Deccan, most of Northern India and even Calcutta. In 1759, a Maratha expeditionary force had reached Kandahar in Afghanistan and they had established garrisons in the major cities of Punjab.

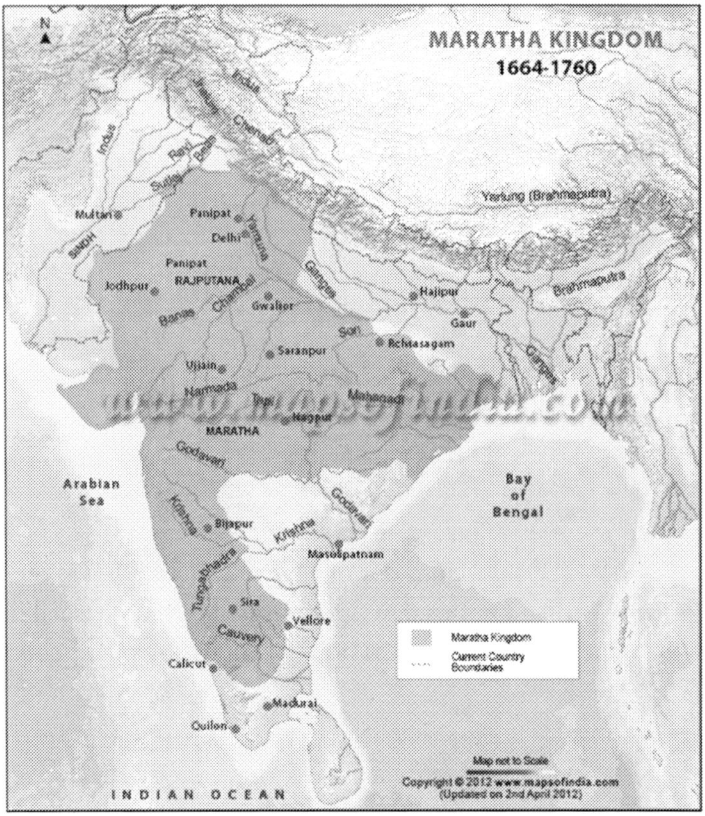

The rise of the Marathas was viewed with fear by the Muslim rulers of North India. Led by Najib-ud-Daulah of Rohilkhand (modern-day Western UP) and Siraj-ud-Daulah of Awadh, they invited Ahmad Shah Abdali to wage '*jehad*' against the Marathas. The call was sweetened by a purse of Rs 2 crores and after his initial hesitations, Abdali decided to come to India to contest the Marathas.

Abdali entered India through the Khyber Pass in January 1960. His armies brushed aside the Maratha garrisons in Punjab and forced them to withdraw. He then moved his armies to Anoop Shahr (around 70 kilometers east of Delhi near Saharanpur), in the kingdom of his ally Najib-ud-Daulah, and camped there awaiting the Marathas.

The arrival of Abdali and the defeat of their garrisons had worried the

Marathas and in March 1760, Peshwa Nanasaheb decided to send a large expeditionary force under his most capable general, Sadashiv Rao Bhau, and his own son, the 17-year-old Vishwas Rao to contest Abdali.

The Maratha army left Udgir (near Nashik) on 7 March 1760, with around 40,000 cavalry, 15,000 troopers and around 200 pieces of artillery. It was joined along its advance by forces from the Holkars of Indore and the Scindias of Gwalior. Yet in spite of its size, it was ill-equipped and lacked administrative support. The army was told to live off the land as it advanced, a strategy that led to looting and pillaging of the countryside over which it advanced and earned it much antagonism in its northwards move. The army was also encumbered by the presence of around 15,000-20,000 ladies and children and camp followers, which slowed the advance of the army as it moved slowly over three months, before it reached Delhi on 21 July.

Maratha and Afghan Warriors

The Marathas captured Delhi easily and ransacked it, camping there for over three months. The army of Abdali and his allies were in Meerut–Saharanpur, the two armies separated by the Yamuna River. Though patrols and skirmishes were frequent, no major clash of arms took place as yet.

Then in end of October, Sadashiv Bhau led his army out of Delhi and moved towards Kunjpura, a fortress on the west bank of the Yamuna which was a major supply hub of Abdali. Kunjpura was strongly held with over 10,000 Afghans but was captured in just two nights after an intense attack using artillery and cavalry in close coordination. Abdali and his army were on the opposite bank of the river and though Abdali could see and hear the plight of his men, he was unable to cross the flooded Yamuna to aid them.

Kunjpura fell on 18 October and was the last major success of the Marathas. They now had access to Abdali's supplies and better still were in a position to block his return to Afghanistan. Bolstered by this success, the Marathas moved further towards Kurukshetra hoping to block Abdali's return route completely. Then Abdali launched his master stroke. On a rain-swept night on 25 October, he crossed the swollen Yamuna River. Even though over 200 soldiers were swept away, his entire army got across over two nights completely taking the Marathas by surprise. The tables were now turned. Abdali was now behind the Marathas and had cut off from their route back to Delhi and the Deccan.

With their escape routes blocked, the Marathas established a camp in the vicinity of Panipat. For three months, the Marathas remained besieged within their camp. Disease and starvation was rampant as they were cut off from their supplies. Skirmishes took place almost on a daily basis causing heavy casualties on both sides. Worse, winter was setting in and the Marathas were ill-equipped and unprepared for the North Indian winters.

With their strength weakening, Sadashiv Bhau called for a meeting of his Chiefs on 12 January and the War Assembly decided that rather than remaining besieged, they would make one concerted attack to break through the Afghan positions and make their way back to Delhi and thence the Deccan. Ceremonial *paan* was served as a gesture of farewell, the Quartermaster was ordered to distribute the remaining food amongst the troops and the chieftains went to prepare their men for battle. The die was cast for the most decisive battle in India's history.

The Bloody *Makar Sankranti*

At dawn on 14 January 1761, the Maratha army moved out of its camp to the sound of conches and *ranbakuras*. Around three to four kilometers opposite them, the Afghans had arrayed in battle formation with a force of around 60,000 cavalry, infantry and artillery. Yet more than the numerical superiority of over 20,000 which the Afghans enjoyed, what made the difference was that Abdali's army was a well-knit, cohesive force with the disparate chiefs held together by the iron personality of Ahmad Shah Abdali. On the other side, the Marathas were riven by dissension, with their chiefs often at loggerheads with each other. The divisions would come to the fore as the battle progressed.

Abdali's army on the move

The Marathas attacked first from their left flank – an attack led by Ibrahim Khan Gardi, a Muslim chief who would be one of the heroes of the battle. It was an ordered, disciplined attack with nine battalions, with one moving forward as the other gave fire support. The attack made slow, but gradual progress, and inflicted heavy casualties on the Afghan right flank opposing them. Then the Marathas made their first mistake.

As per plan, Gardi's musketeers were to establish a foothold in the Afghan lines and then the Maratha cavalry was to attack from the flank. Yet even as Gardi's troopers were inching forward, the cavalry attacked pre-maturely moving ahead of Gardi's infantry and preventing them from firing. The cavalry assault which should have given a decisive edge in the initial stage of the battle petered out, but in spite of that, a breach was made in the Afghan right flank by around noon.

Simultaneously with the attack of his left flank, Sadashiv Rao Bhau had launched the main attack with around 20,000 crack troops – the Huzarat – directed at the Afghan center. He led the attack himself and its sheer force and momentum tore through the Afghan center causing them to break in disarray.

Around midday, the Marathas were well poised. They had broken through the right flank and the Center. Their right flank, under Holkar and Scindia, was to have attacked after the Afghan lines were breached, but inexplicably they did not move. They remained static even though Sadashiv Bhau sent a personal message to Holkar. The reluctance of their right flank to attack cost the Marathas dear. It gave time for Abdali to position his military police to round up all who were fleeing the battle and send them back to the front lines (with a few summary executions of those who refused). He also sent around 10,000 of his reserves to reinforce the crumbling lines. By around 2 pm, the Afghan lines were steadied and any hope of a Maratha breakthrough vanished.

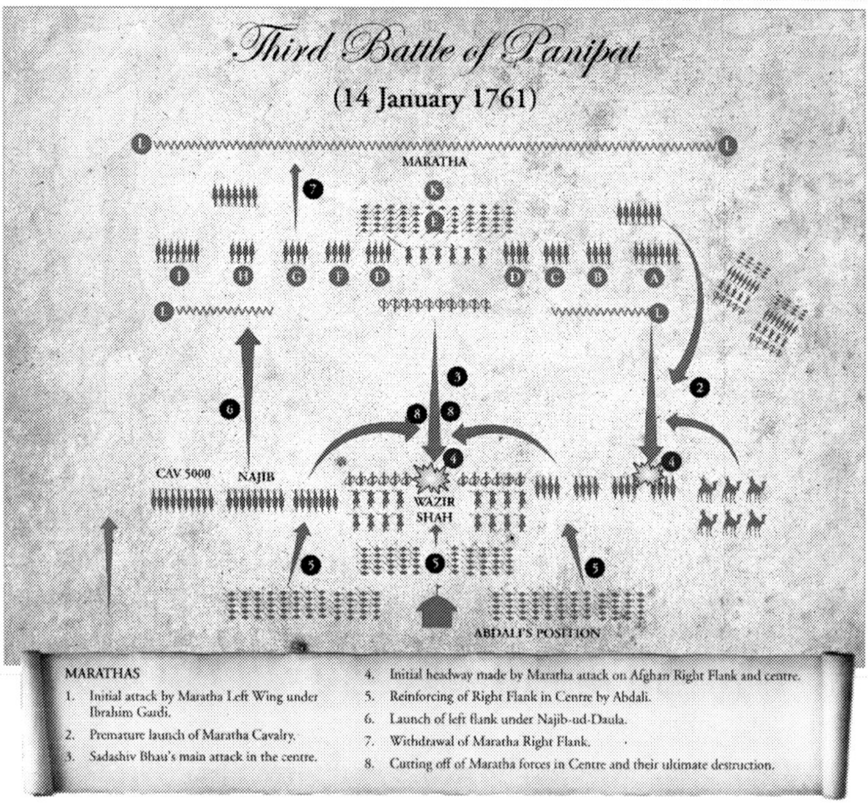

The Battle

The Maratha attacked petered out and Abdali launched a counterstroke from his own left flank behind the Marathas. His cavalry and '*Zamburaks*' – camel-mounted swivel guns – poured a relentless stream of fire on the Marathas, who were gradually being compressed in a tight knot ahead of the Afghan positions. Afghan bullets took a deadly toll on the bunched Maratha infantry and one of the bullets hit Vishwas Rao, the Peshwa's son on the head killing him instantly.

The death of Vishwas turned the battle dramatically. Seeing him fall, the troops lost heart. Sadashiv Bhau himself dismounted from his elephant to come to see Vishwas and without his rallying presence, the Marathas troops panicked and began fleeing the battlefield. In the unruly chaos that followed, Abdali launched another attack with the rest of his reserves that swung in from the rear and sides of the beleaguered Marathas.

What followed was slaughter. Weakened after the day-long fighting, they were cut to pieces as the Afghan cavalry tore into them and bullets rained upon them. Their right flank under Holkar and Scindia took no part in the fighting and melted away from the battlefield, moving to Delhi and then their home bases. For the rest it was carnage, as they battled desperately in isolated pockets. Over 30,000-40,000 Maratha soldiers fell that day alone (another 20,000 had been lost in the skirmishes of the preceding months). The vengeful Afghans, who had lost around 30,000 of their own, ran amok in the Maratha camp, slaughtered the menfolk and took the women and children as slaves. That night, the moon was full and the fleeing Marathas were chased and cut down in the open fields around Panipat. An estimated 60,000-70,000 lives were lost in that one day which has often been called 'The Bloodiest Day of the 18th Century.'

Of the estimated force of 70,000-80,000 that set out, only around 15,000 or so succeeded in making their way back to the Deccan. Abdali left back for Afghanistan soon after the battle, receiving a hefty compensation from the Muslim rulers. The Peshwa died of shock after the disaster and Maratha power now waned. Its decline set the stage for Imperial rule in India. Devoid of any major challenger, the British consolidated their position and established British rule in India that would last 200 years. That perhaps was the greatest tragedy of the battle.

17

23 October 1763
ESTABLISHING IMPERIAL RULE

Battle of Buxar

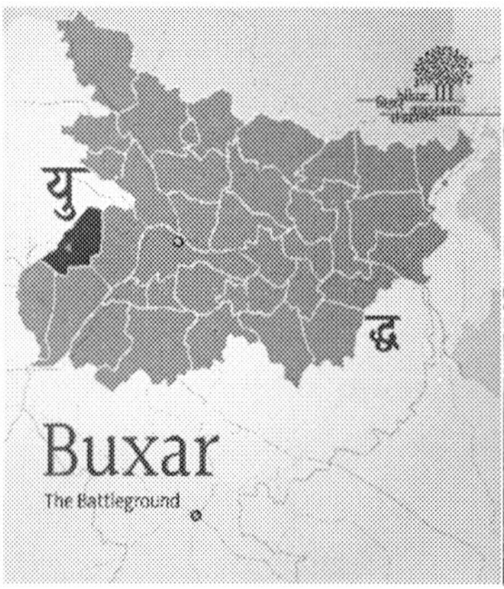

The British, or more appropriately the East India Company, established their supremacy over the Eastern Provinces by their victory over the Nawab of Bengal Siraj-ud-Daulah in the Battle of Palashi in 1757 (see 'A Traitor's Battle'). They had established *de facto* sway over the Province – aided in large by the concessions they had extracted from the pliant rulers they foisted on the thrones of the Provinces they had subdued. They took over all trade, refused to pay taxes or tariffs and generally did as they pleased. After years of unbridled loot of their provinces, Mir Qasim, the Nawab of Bengal, Shuja-ud-Daulah of

Awadh and the Mughal Emperor Shah Alam II got together in an uneasy alliance to evict the British and put an end to their depredations.

Coat of Arms of the East India Company

The three Nawabs cobbled together a force of over 40,000 infantry and cavalry with around 200 pieces of artillery. Yet, their large, unwieldy force was a heterogeneous mob of Pathans, Awadhis, Mughals and Europeans with little common training or doctrines. The differences between them ensured that it was at best an uneasy alliance. The British, under General Hector Munro, had assembled an army of 12,000 combatants composed of 2000 European and 10,000 Indian troops. It was a well-drilled and trained force, held together by the iron discipline which was the hallmark of British armies. As was the norm, they tried to first break the Indian alliance by turning one against the other and promising rewards for those who defected. Fortunately, the Indian alliance held and the stage was set for a clash that would determine British rule over the subcontinent.

The two armies met at Buxar in modern-day Bihar in October 1757. Shuja-ud-Daulah, the Nawab of Awadh, was appointed as the overall commander of the force and had deployed his vast army in an open plain, with the Ganges on his right and the fast flowing Tora Nala on his left. The bulk of his own troops, around 15,000 strong, were placed in the center with eight battalions in line with the gaps covered by field artillery. On the flanks were Awadh infantry – largely levies whose fighting qualities were suspect. Around 12,000 Afghan and Rohilla cavalry was on his right flank from where he hoped to launch his major attack on the British positions. His heavy artillery was deployed in a grove on the left flank from where it could most effectively deliver fire. His plan was to deliver a heavy artillery fire and then follow it up with an attack with overwhelming numbers to swamp the British positions.

The British force under Hector Munro reached Buxar on the night of 3 October and after an extensive reconnaissance, took up camp around three miles south of the Indian positions. For two weeks, the armies sized each other up, each waiting for the other to make their move. Then on 23 October 1757, Shuja-ud-Daulah moved his armies out of his camp and deployed in battle order. The British forces too formed up in a well-rehearsed battle array, deploying in two compact lines with British troops in the center and two Indian battalions on either flank. The entire frontage was covered by artillery fire. Munro himself was in the rear where he had established an efficient communication system to rapidly transmit orders and coordinate the actions of his forces.

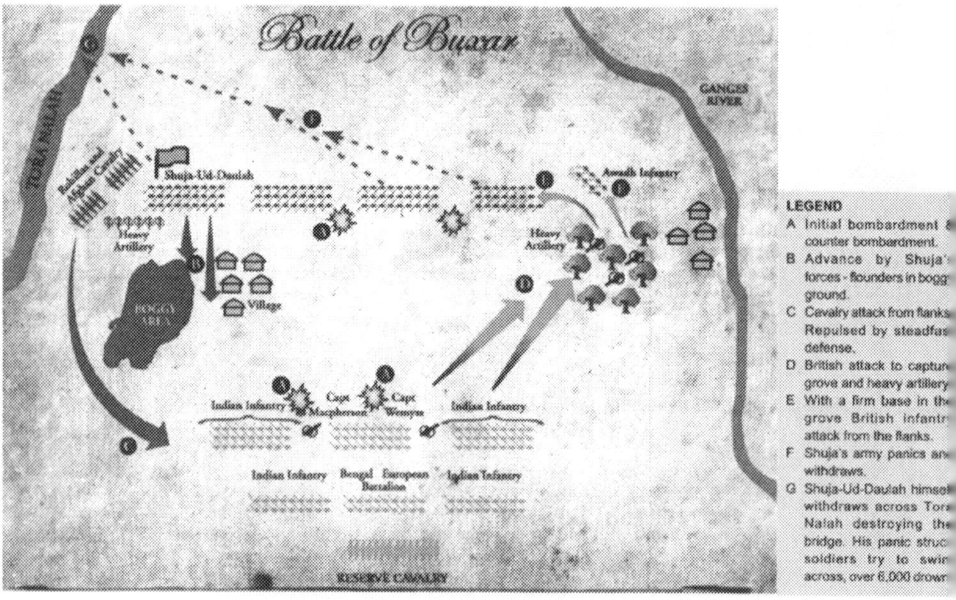

The Battle

Shuja-ud-Daulah launched his first attack at around 9 in the morning after a long preparatory bombardment. He used his own infantry for the initial attack, which made initial headway, but was halted by steady volleys of musket shot and artillery fire, before it could even close in on the British positions. Shuja then launched his Afghan and Rohilla cavalry from the right flank. The cavalry attack floundered in a patch of swampy ground ahead of the British lines and could not make headway. Two such attacks were beaten back and by noon, Shuja-ud-Daulah had shot his bolt. His forces were unable to make any

The British Attack

penetration against the compact British lines that held firm with iron discipline and superb fire control.

Munro now ordered his own ranks to attack. The British lines advanced in a well-rehearsed and drilled maneuver, with one battalion advancing while another gave it covering fire. With by short bounds of 150-200 yards, using the time-honored principles of fire and move, the assaulting forces advanced steadily. The Nawab's artillery took a toll but discipline held and slowly the British ranks closed in on the Indian positions. Munro now ordered one battalion to attack the grove on the flank, where the artillery guns were deployed, and in a swift move they succeeded in capturing all 27 of the heavy artillery guns there. The guns were now turned around and their fire directed towards the Indian lines. Seeing the British forces so close to them and faced with a hail of fire from their own guns, the Indian ranks broke and battalion after battalion began leaving their positions running towards the Tora Nala hoping to cross it and flee. No order could be maintained, and in anger, the Nawab ordered the destruction of the bridge of boats on the nala to halt the rout. It was of no avail. The soldiers jumped into the stream and over 6000 were swept away by the fast-flowing waters – more casualties than were caused by British fire. The Indian lines had simply disintegrated.

By 3 in the afternoon, it was all over. Though outnumbered by over 4:1, the British still won a decisive victory, but at a high cost. Over 1800 were killed and 2000 wounded – a high casualty figure dismissed callously by Munro as "being mostly blacks."

Buxar was even more decisive than Palashi. It consolidated the foundations for Imperial rule, which Palashi had laid and established it firmly in India. Its sun would now continue its ascent over the subcontinent for almost two centuries more.

18

January 1767 to May 1799
THE TIGER OF SRIRANGAPATNAM

The Anglo-Mysore Wars

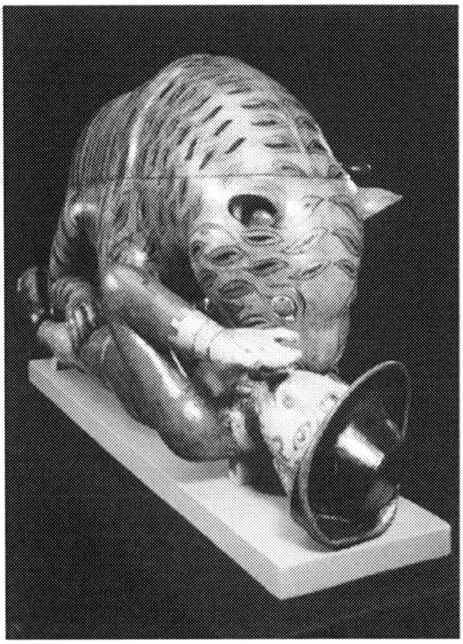

Few figures have been as distorted or as misunderstood in Indian History as Tipu Sultan. He has been painted as a bigot, a religious intolerant who persecuted Hindus and Christians and as a cruel and vengeful ruler. He did have shades of all these. But more importantly, he was also the ruler who fought the longest and most sustained battle against British Imperialism. Perhaps had other Indian rulers supported him in his three-decade-long struggle, instead of joining arms against him, the cancer of British rule in India would have been curbed and India would have been spared the devastations that followed.

Tipu Sultan, born Fateh Ali Sahab Tipu, was also known as the Tiger of Mysore – a name he acquired after killing a tiger with his dagger while on a hunting expedition. The Tiger became his leitmotif and formed the emblem on his banners, arms and weapons. His own sword had an exquisite silver tiger on its hilt. Tigers roamed his palace grounds and by some accounts, those unlucky to offend him were thrown to the fierce beasts. He even had French engineers build a mechanical figure 'Tipu's Tiger' which showed a life-sized wooden tiger mauling a British soldier. An intricate mechanism inside made the two figures move realistically and even emitted wailing sounds and roars. This figure symbolised his implacable hatred for the British.

Mysore's long struggle with the British began when Hyder Ali, the Commander-in-Chief, took over the throne of Mysore from the Wodeyar rulers and appointed himself as Sultan. His rule was fraught with battles between the Marathas, the Nizam of Hyderabad and the British, the dominant powers of Southern India. In addition, the French and Dutch were also vying for influence in India. The period of the 18th century saw the powers jostling with each other and subtle maneuverings by the British successfully pitched one Indian ruler against the other. In fact, more often than not, Tipu Sultan had to fight on two or more fronts – against the British on one hand and the Marathas or the Nizam on the other.

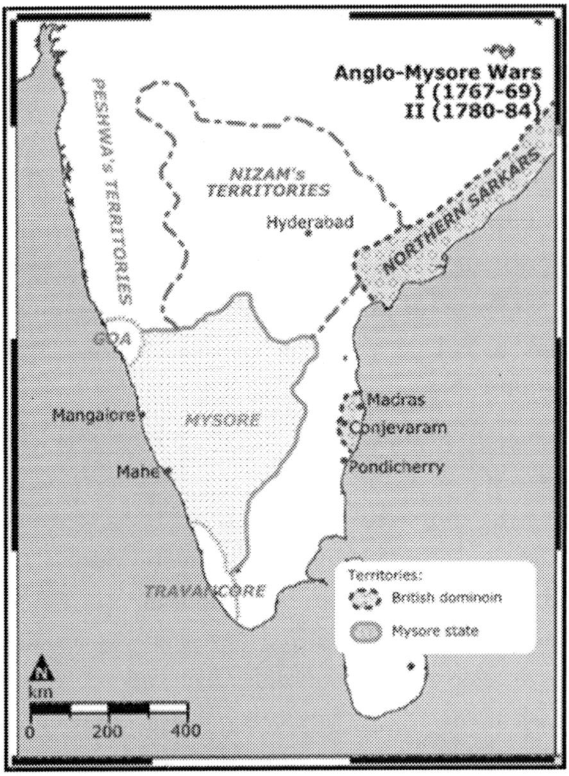

The Deccan

The First Anglo-Mysore War (1767–69) was the first of the four wars fought over 30 years right till Tipu's death in 1792. Here, Hyder Ali's Mysorean forces successfully kept a large British force at bay and even audaciously attacked Madras, the Headquarters of the British East India Company, forcing them to sue for peace.

Yet the gains of the First War were short-lived. An uneasy state of no-war-no-peace existed between Mysore, the Nizam of Hyderabad, Marathas and the British. Added to that was the rivalry between the British and the French whose ongoing war in Europe was spilling over in India. The French were allied to Mysore, and provided them with the bulk of their artillery, military hardware and expertise. In 1779, the British seized the French port of Mahe. Mahe was of strategic importance to Hyder Ali since he received all his imports through it. He marched towards Mahe, captured the British settlements in the Carnatic and laid siege to the fort of Arcot. A large British column sent to relieve the siege was intercepted by Tipu Sultan, volleyed mercilessly with rockets, and nearly decimated in the Battle of Polilur. It was the most crushing defeat suffered by a British army in India followed by a series of major skirmishes at Tanjore, Chitture, Bednore and Mangalore in which the Mysorean army came out trumps.

Then in the summer of 1782, Hyder Ali passed away due to cancer, forcing Tipu Sultan to rush back to Mysore where he was coroneted king. The battles continued, but after four years the British realised that they could not defeat Tipu. Tipu too realised that he could not defeat a force that held dominance over the seas and both sides entered negotiations in March 1784 in which they agreed to a status quo. Yet even before the ink was drying, the British were already making plans to repudiate the treaty and remove Tipu Sultan whom they considered as the greatest hurdle to their expansionism in India.

After an uneasy peace for five years, things came to a head again in 1789 when the British acquired the Circar of Guntur, a long swath of land along the East Coast that got them close to Tipu's territory. The British also formed alliances with the Marathas, the Nizam of Hyderabad and the Raja of Travancore in a mutual defence pact where each was obliged to come to the aid of the others in case of an attack.

Tipu had been isolated by the Indian rulers of Southern India, but in a way, he had himself to blame. He had alienated his subjects and his neighbours by his high-handedness, destruction of churches and temples, forced conversions and circumcisions of entire communities. He was an able administrator who had helped develop the economy of his state and introduced far-reaching reforms, but resentment against him was growing. In 1789, a rebellion broke out in his Southern territories adjoining Travancore. He marched against it and when the rebels sought refuge in Travancore, they entered the state as well. This gave the British the excuse they needed to launch war against him.

The British were aided by the Marathas who advanced from the North and the Nizam of Hyderabad who attacked Mysore from the East. The combined threat forced Tipu to withdraw to his capital at Seringapatnam – or to use its correct name, Srirangapatnam. From here, he launched a series of attacks directed at British supply lines and communications. He embarked on a scorched earth policy, destroying the countryside to deny any provisions to the British. That act was tactically correct, but it further alienated the population against him. What made it worse was that his only allies – the French – were wrapped in the French Revolution sweeping their country and in no position to help him.

For two years Tipu waged war single-handedly. Then in the summer of 1791, a large Maratha army of around 30,000, an additional British force with 25,000 cavalry and a large ponderous force of the Nizam of Hyderabad converged towards him. By January 1792, he was besieged in his capital. He rained down rockets upon his besiegers but they could only stave off the inevitable. Tipu's rockets had ranges of over two kilometres and which were mounted on metal rods for greater destructive power. They were designed to explode overhead or plough through the enemy ranks in a curving, haphazard trajectory that scythed all in the path. His rockets were his prime weapon and later even adopted by the British. But they were of no avail.

Slowly the noose around Srirangapatnam tightened and eventually in March 1792, Tipu was forced to sign the Treaty of Seringapatnam. In this, he handed over half of his territories, paid over 3 crores as war damages and even handed over two of his sons to Lord Cornwallis as a guarantee that he would keep his part of the Treaty. It was a humiliating end to the Third Anglo-Mysore War, but the worst was still to come.

The loss of half of his kingdom and almost all his revenues hurt the Mysore state deeply. What made it worse was that Tipu Sultan was completely isolated, and he turned to the French. He reached out to Napoleon who promised to help and even raised a force to be deployed in India. Yet once again, the French were defeated in Europe and no troops could be spared for their colonies in India.

Tipu's overtures to the French alarmed the British and in end 1798, they launched the Fourth Anglo-Mysore War. Aided by the Marathas and the Nizam of Hyderabad, three large British armies – one of them commanded by Arthur Wellesley, the future Duke of Wellington – advanced towards Srirangapatnam once again. Tipu's small force was outnumbered by almost 2:1, and though they fought a series of delaying battles, they could not prevent the British reaching the outskirts of the city on 5 April 1799. They crossed the Cauvery River – then only around four feet deep – and laid siege to the capital.

The British had brought over key officials of Tipu's court. The Chief Minister Mir Sadiq had been in correspondence with them and was passing key information about the state of affairs and the weaknesses of the fort. Tipu refused to see the emissaries sent asking him to surrender, perhaps hoping to gain time. On 2 May 1799, the British armies launched the assault on the North Western walls which they knew were the weaker walls. Their advance was halted by a stream of rockets, but by nightfall they had made a breach in the outer walls. Tipu had laid mines between the outer and inner walls to be detonated when the assaulting force came in the area. These mines went off pre-maturely, perhaps hit by a stray rocket and further aided the breach. By the night of 3 May, the breach had been widened sufficiently for an all-out assault.

Mir Sadiq had been in touch with the British officers and advised them to attack at noon the following day – a time when he withdrew all the troops from the walls, on the pretext of distributing their pay. With the ramparts depleted, British forces poured in under a heavy covering fire and in just 16 minutes clambered up the walls. They then wheeled right and left and spread out across the city.

Tipu Sultan was last seen in the defence of his city, firing his hunting rifles at the advancing force. By some accounts, he was finely dressed and kept firing his rifles which his servants loaded and passed to him. He was severely wounded and finally shot by a British officer whom he himself killed in a final, desperate sword lunge. He fell along with hundreds of his soldiers, but it was a futile, though gallant defence. By nightfall the city was in British hands. Tipu's body was found beneath a heap of bodies near one of the gates with multiple wounds on his person. In a final mark of respect, the body was washed and then permitted to be ceremoniously buried by his remaining followers next to his father's tomb. A stone plaque still marks the spot where he fell.

The last moments of Tipu Sultan

The British did not occupy the city, but handed it over to the Wodeyar Dynasty, who had ruled Mysore before Hyder Ali took over the state. It was a puppet government, whose every action had to be approved by a British 'Adviser.' With Tipu's death, the last opposition to British exploitation in South India disappeared. The field was now open to them.

And what of the Tipu's Tiger and his famed sword. Like much else, it was looted and taken to London where it was placed in the Victoria and Albert Museum, till it was purchased by the Indian government and returned to India. Tipu Sultan too received belated recognition. In spite of his mixed legacy, he was the one ruler who had continually opposed the British, perhaps sensing the dangers they posed to the country. Had he used diplomacy in his dealings with the other powers of the time – the Marathas and the Nawabs- and had Indian rulers presented a combined front against British rule, we may have been spared the 190 years of Imperial rule.

19

01 January 1818
THE VICTORY PILLAR

Battle of Bhima Koregaon

On the Pune–Ahmadnagar highway, just 19 kilometers North East of Pune, stands an imposing monument on the banks of the Bhima River. This well-maintained granite obelisk commemorates the battle of Bhima Koregaon where some 800 British-led troops of the East India Company put up a resolute defense against the Marathas. The daylong skirmish saw the large Maratha force withdraw after being unable to overrun its much smaller adversary and marked the ascendency of the British power in the Deccan.

The Battle had its roots in the Anglo-Maratha battles during 1770–1817 for the control of the Deccan. The Marathas were defeated in a series of battles and the Peshwa, Baji Rao II, was forced to concede large tracts of his territory to the East India Company. The resentful Marathas were confined around Pune and rose again in revolt in mid-1817; however, they were defeated in the Battle of Khadki in November 1817. The defeat forced the Peshwa to flee towards Satara with his army and the Company troops took control of Pune.

The Peshwa was pursued by a large British force under General Smith while Pune was defended by a small garrison under Colonel Burr. As the Peshwa fled from his pursuers, he retraced his steps towards Nashik and then moved back towards Pune, hoping to recapture his capital. Colonel Burr hearing of the arrival of the Marathas asked for help from the Company's troops stationed at Shirur. Around 500 troopers of the 2nd Battalion of the Bombay Native Infantry, 300 horsemen of Poona Auxiliary Horse (later Poona Horse – one of India's most illustrious Armoured Regiments) along with a contingent of artillery, with two six-pounder guns, left Shirur at 8 pm on 31 Dec 1817 under the command of Lieutenant Francis Staunton, to reinforce the Poona Garrison. Marching all night, they reached the village of Koregaon where they saw the advance guard of the Peshwa Army across the Bhima River.

Koregaon, on the banks of the almost dried up Bhima River was a small hamlet of huts surrounded by a low mud wall with almost no defense potential. Rather than withdrawing back to Shirur, Stanton chose to stand and fight there. He deployed his infantry and cavalry in a concentric pattern around the village and placed one of his guns to cover the crossing place across the Bhima River and the other to guard the road from Shirur.

Although the Maratha army camped in the vicinity, had around 20,000 cavalry and 8000 infantry, only its advance guard, of around 2000-3000 infantry were tasked to clear the village. The Peshwa and the bulk of his army remained at Phoolsheher (near modern-day Pulgaon) while the attack on Koregaon was led by the chiefs, Bapu Gokhale, Appa Desai and Tribakji Dengle. At around 8 am on 01 January, three parties of 500-600 Maratha troopers (comprising Arabs, Gosavis and Marathas) crossed the Bhima River at three different places, supported by cannons and rocket fire. Another force launched a feint attack along the Shirur–Pune road. Although outnumbered, the defenders of Koregaon held on grimly. The first two attacks were repulsed, but the third gained a foothold on the outskirts of the village. From there they launched an attack towards a small temple (which still stands even today) where the British six-pounder gun was deployed. They killed all eleven gunners, including the British officer Lieutenant Chisholm and captured the gun. The same gun was now turned around to fire at the British positions inside the village.

It was now around noon, and the force inside Koregaon were hungry, thirsty and exhausted. Morale cracked and some of the troops suggested a surrender. However, the British officers refused, and instead launched a counterattack on the Maratha foothold led by the 6 feet 7 inches Lieutenant Pattison. His spirited attack pushed the Arab and Maratha troops out of the village and they recaptured their gun. The decapitated bodies of Lieutenant Chisholm and the gunners were also recovered and displayed to the wavering troops saying that they would be accorded the same treatment if they surrendered.

The troops, though denied food or water all day, held on. Some contingents of the Maratha forces managed to enter the village and fierce hand-to-hand fighting took place in the congested lanes. The British-led infantry, supported by its small cavalry contingent held strong, counterattacking fiercely against any breach. As night fell, the fighting reduced and by around 9 pm, even the Marathas who had entered the village withdrew and moved back. Nightfall also permitted the defenders to creep up to the river and get some much needed water.

The Marathas did not attack at night, even though the defenders were exhausted, and one more spirited attack could have well overrun the village. Rather, the Peshwa was apprehensive that the bulk of the British forces would return to attack his forces and went on the defensive himself. Seeing a lull in the activity, Captain Staunton decided to vacate Koregaon and at nightfall on 02 January, the remnants slipped away from the village, carrying their dead and wounded.

They reached Shirur after marching all night. The move was undetected and the Marathas did not attack the column, even though that was the time they were most vulnerable. Of the 834 troopers who had set out three days ago, 275 were dead, wounded or missing. The Marathas too suffered grievously, losing 500- 600 men in just a day of battle. Worse, the British gained the psychological ascendency they would never relinquish.

The British Counterattack

The Peshwas withdrew from Koregaon that same night and the next day, a large British column under General Smith reached the village. The village was deserted, its streets littered with dead men and horses, most of them from the attackers who had succeeded in penetrating the village. The Peshwa's forces were relentlessly pursued away from Poona and suffered a series of reverses at Nashik, Satara and Astha. Finally in June, with most of his trusted lieutenants killed and his army dispirited, the Peshwa surrendered to the British. The Deccan now came under British sovereignty giving them unfettered access to continue their loot and plunder of the sub-continent.

To commemorate "one of the proudest triumphs of the British Army in the East", a large victory pillar was erected at the site, with the names of the dead inscribed. Indian units that participated in the battle were given awards and titles. The victory pillar featured on the badge of the Mahar Regiment (created by the British, composed of lower castes) and was replaced by a crossed machine guns insignia only after Independence. Most of the men who fought under British arms at Koregaon were local Dalits. They initially wanted to be recruited in the largely upper caste Maratha army but had been rudely refused. The British willingly accepted them into their army where they served with discipline and courage. The staunch defense of Koregaon is projected as Dalit valour, though the defending force was a homogenous mix of all castes. The roll call of the dead shows 22 Mahar, 16 Marathas, 8 Rajputs, 2 Muslims and 2 Jews, along with 11 European soldiers and two British officers – a toll which was described with typical British callousness as, "fortunately, largely natives". Perpetuating the divide between castes and religions in India to further their own aims was standard British practice. And as this battle shows they succeeded very well in this. This victory pillar, which commemorated the victory of a foreign power against a local ruler, unfortunately began to represent the victory of oppressed Dalits against the upper castes of the Maratha army and became a symbol of the class struggle. And yet, this battle was not a victory of any caste or race. Rather it was a collective defeat of all Indians.

20

11 December 1845 to March 1846
BLOOD IN THE SUTLUJ

Anglo-Sikh Wars

In the early years of the 19th century, the Sikh Empire under Maharaja Ranjit Singh had expanded rapidly covering most of Western Punjab (modern-day Pakistan) as far as Afghanistan. Its rise had unnerved the East India Company which had by then taken over most of North India. Punjab with its riches still remained out of their reach.

However, with the death of Maharaja Ranjit Singh in 1839, his stately court descended into petty squabbling. Numerous claimants arose for the throne and finally Jind Kaur, his youngest widow took over as Regent on behalf of his son, Dilip Singh. Others also vied for power. One was Lal Singh, the vizier, and Tej Singh, the Commander of the Army. Both aspired for the throne and it was in their interest to weaken the Empire, and especially the army which was getting increasingly assertive and emerging as an independent power center in itself. Many historians feel that Lal Singh and Tej Singh conspired the defeat of the Sikh Army to weaken Jind Kaur and

Maharaja Ranjit Singh

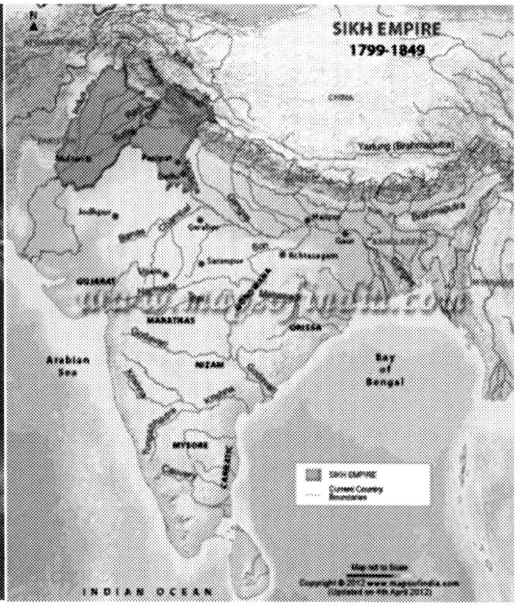

Sikh Empire at its Prime

promote their own interests. They had been in secret talks with the British and were continually passing inside information of the State right from the days preceding the wars.

The British exploited the self-serving ambitions of Lal Singh and Tej Singh in much the same manner they had used Mir Jafar and the other traitors to defeat the Nawab of Awadh in the Battle of Buxar (See 'Establishing Imperial Rule – Battle of Buxar'). Seeing the dissensions in the Court, they moved up a strong force of around 15,000–20,000 troops from Ambala and Meerut towards Punjab. This augmented the division of around 7000 men already located at Ferozepur. With the movement of British troops towards their border, the Sikhs moved their own army of 22,000–25,000 troops and 192 prized guns towards the Sutluj, the river which marked the boundary between the Sikh and British Dominions. The two forces were evenly matched. What would tilt the scales would be the ineptitude and treachery of the Sikh Commanders.

The two armies faced off across the Sutluj River and on 11 December 1845, the Sikhs sent a small detachment across the river to occupy the village of Moran. (As per Sikh accounts, the village legitimately belonged to them and they were moving into their own territory.) This was the trigger of outbreak of hostilities and set off the first Anglo-Sikh wars.

Cannonading began across the river and both sides moved aggressively towards the other. The Sikhs made the first move and crossed the River in strength heading towards Ferozepur. A large division under Tej Singh closed in on Ferozepur, and though the British division there was unprepared and exposed, Tej Singh did not attack – perhaps deliberately. This would be the first of the many blunders the commanders made. Another force under Lal Singh moved to engage the large British force which was advancing from Ambala under Sir Hugh Gough. The British force was encountered around 30 kilometres from Ferozepur, near the village of Mudki, where the first major battle of the war was fought. The Sikhs attacked the British who had encamped within the village on the night of 18 December. Sikh cavalry – their skilled *Ghorchurras* (or horse riders) – charged from the flanks but the British force recovered and halted the attack by cannon fire. The British infantry then advanced towards the Sikh position at night – an unexpected move as usually no fighting took place after nightfall. Even though casualties were caused in the confused fighting, by around midnight the Sikhs were driven off from the village leaving behind their guns. It was a battle which they could have easily won. But their commander Lal Singh fled and though the leaderless Sikhs fought gallant individual actions, they could not match the disciplined and well-coordinated British moves.

Sikh Ghorchurras

Infantry in Defense

Flush with their initial – and somewhat unexpected – victory at Mudki, the British advanced towards Ferozeshah on 21 December where the bulk of the Sikh army was deployed. They made contact in the morning but waited till additional troops joined them from Ferozepur around noon. Reinforced, they attacked the Sikh positions around 3.30 pm. Under cover of an intensive artillery barrage, three battalions of Bengal Infantry and one British Infantry battalion advanced towards the Sikh positions. Half the attacking force was wiped out, but by nightfall they succeeded in making a breach in the Sikh positions.

All night, fierce fighting raged around the village. It became a series of skirmishes as Sikh and East India Company soldiers fought hand-to-hand battles in the congested lanes of the village. When dawn broke, the British had captured most of Ferozeshah and the Sikhs were pushed out of their stronghold and 71 of their prized guns had been captured.

As the exhausted British were regrouping, Tej Singh's fresh army appeared on the horizon. An attack now would have wiped out the remnants of British and Bengal troops. General Hugh Gough was expecting to be defeated and even sent a message to the rear to burn all official documents. That is when a quirk of fate occurred. With their artillery out of ammunition, a British officer ordered the Artillery train to move back to Ferozepur with a strong cavalry escort, to replenish. Tej Singh viewed this as an outflanking move being carried out by their cavalry and even though his troops were keen on attacking, ordered a general withdrawal. It was an inexplicable act, and reeked of treachery.

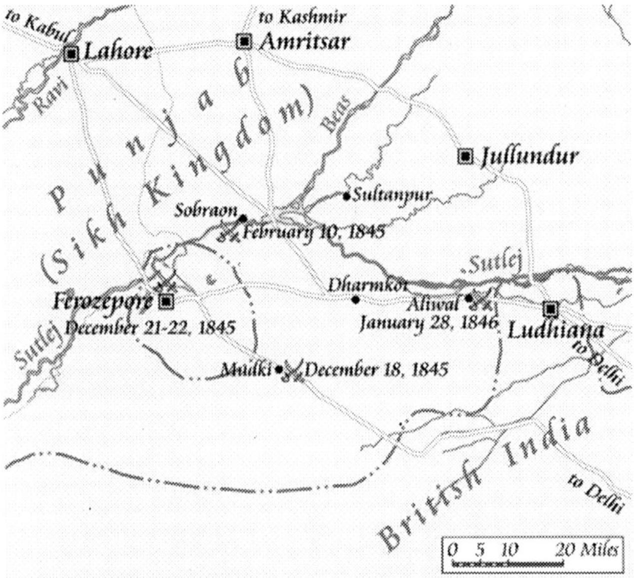

Battles of the Anglo-Sikh Wars

After their unexpected defeat at Ferozeshah, the Sikh army was demoralised. The actions of their commanders had not gone unnoticed. Maharani Jind Kaur came from Lahore to exhort her army and reportedly even flung her *chunni* at the commanders – an insult which implied that they should be wearing women's clothing. The morale of the Sikh army was bolstered with the arrival of capable commanders such as Ranjodh Singh Majitha and Sham Singh Attariwala and they gradually prepared for a fresh offensive.

On 21 Jan 1846, the Sikhs.crossed the Sutluj and established bridgeheads near Aliwal and Sabraon. Sikh cavalry began attacking British supply lines and made forays as far as Ludhiana. The Sikh bridgehead was around seven kilometres long along a ridge near the village of Aliwal, with the Sutluj just behind them. That protected their flanks but also reduced their space for manoeuvre. Realising the danger of the bridgehead, the British launched a concentrated attack on 28 Jan with an entire Cavalry Brigade. Two Indian and one British Cavalry Regiment (16 Lancers) charged towards the Sikh positions as artillery carried out an incessant barrage of fire. The Sikhs formed a square to meet the attack – the time-honoured tactic of countering a cavalry charge – but were overrun and forced to retreat. By the end of the day, they were forced back across the Sutluj losing over 2000 men and 67 valuable guns.

With the Aliwal Bridgehead eliminated, the British turned their attention to Sabraon. The Sikh contingent at Sabraon was led by Sham Singh Attariwala – a respected veteran and a courageous general. Unfortunately, the overall command still rested with Lal Singh and Tej Singh who were conspiring for the defeat of their own army. They were in touch with the British and passing on key information to them. The Sikh bridgehead was connected by a single pontoon bridge on the Sutluj. The river was in flood after three days of continual rain and the bridge was considerably weakened.

The British built up their forces before launching their attack on Sabraon. Another division arrived from Ludhiana; 35 heavy howitzers were also brought up to pound the Sikh positions. Then on 10 Feb 1846, one division launched a feint attack from the left, while two divisions launched the main attack on the right of the bridgehead. Here the defences were of soft sand, lower and more vulnerable – information that had been helpfully provided by Lal Singh to the British. The intensive bombardment collapsed the fortifications and

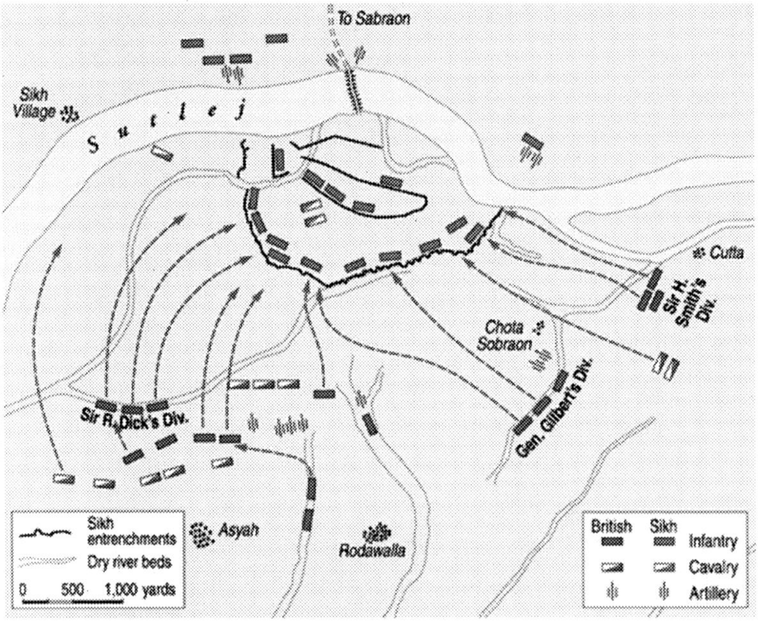

Battle of Sabroan

the British attack made an initial foothold. In spite of repeated counterattacks, the British held on and through the breach, Infantry and Cavalry poured in. The Sikhs fought bitterly, launching repeated counterattacks, but were forced to retreat. Tej Singh fled the battlefield and ordered his guns on the other side of the Sutluj to fire on the Pontoon bridge – seemingly to prevent the British from using it. As fleeing Sikhs were racing across the bridge to the safety of the other side, the bridge collapsed and 20,000 men were trapped on the other side.

The Sikhs, led by Sham Singh Attariwala, fought on grimly to death. Some tried to cross the river but were swept away. British guns lined on the flanks poured a relentless fire on them and by the end of the day over 10,000 Sikh soldiers perished on the battlefield.

The next day, the British crossed the Sutluj and by 13 Feb reached Lahore, the seat of the Sikh Empire. Here the Treaty of Lahore was signed in which the Sikhs were forced to concede the valuable territory between the Beas and Sutluj Rivers. They also had to pay an indemnity of 1.2 million pounds and because they could not pay the amount, Kashmir was taken from them.

It was a crushing defeat for the Sikh Empire and with it the last challenge to British rule in North India disappeared. Yet in April 1848, the resentment at the defeat and the harsh terms of surrender erupted again in the Second Anglo-Sikh Wars. Here in the battles of Ramnagar and Chillianwala, the Sikhs inflicted much damage on the British, but unfortunately lost the Battle of Gujarat which was the most decisive battle of the war. With this, the Sikh Empire finally disintegrated. Maharaja Duleep Singh signed away his claims to the throne and Punjab was annexed by the East India Company. Area from Multan, Peshawar, Lahore, Ludhiana, Jullandhar and right up to Kashmir came under British yoke. The fabled Kohinoor diamond was carried away to England and became one of the jewels on Queen Victoria's crown – and India became the prime jewel of the British Empire.

The Sikhs were acknowledged as the finest fighters the British had encountered and were gradually amalgamated in the East India Company. Ironically for all their ferocity in fighting the British, the Sikhs would be instrumental in helping them during the First War of Independence. Sikh battalions were used against the rebellious battalions of the Bengal Infantry – the same battalions which had fought them in the Anglo-Sikh Wars (see 'The First Fires of Independence'). Using this card, the British ensured their loyalty and with the time-tested policy of divide-and-rule maintained their hold on India for over a hundred years more.

21

10 May 1857 to 20 June 1858
THE FIRST FIRES OF INDEPENDENCE

India's First War of Independence

The Spark

On 29 March 1857, a 29-year-old sepoy of the 34th Bengal Native Infantry put on his uniform, loaded his musket and walked out to the Barrackpore parade ground, near Calcutta. He took position near the saluting base and called out to his fellow sepoys, urging them to join his revolt against the British. When the Sergeant Major and the Battalion Adjutant approached him, he fired at them injuring them. His calls must have struck a chord, yet none of his comrades joined him. In frustration, he placed his musket against his chest, yanked the trigger with his toe and tried to take his own life. His uniform burst into flames and he suffered a severe chest injury, but he survived to face a court martial and was hanged to death just a week later. His act was not futile. Mangal Pandey had just fired the first shots of India's First War of Independence.

Mangal Pandey

The reasons for the resentment that Mangal Pandey and hundreds of thousands of Indians felt are not hard to find. Ever since their victory in the battles of Plassey in 1757 (see 'A Traitor's Battle') and then Buxar in 1764 (see 'Establishing Imperial Rule'), the East India Company had extended their tentacles over most of the country, subjugating local rulers and looting and exploiting at will. Anger had also been brewing amongst the 300,000 strong Indian soldiers of the British Indian Army against the gradual erosion of Indian values and systems, the subtle introduction of Christianity and British culture in India and interference in their religious beliefs. The final spark came from an innocuous source. In 1856, a new Enfield P–53 rifle was issued to the troops. To load this weapon, the firer had to bite the cartridge, releasing the gunpowder which was then rammed in the breech. The cartridge was suspected to be greased with beef and pork fat – offending both Hindu and Muslim sensibilities. Although the British tried to allay the suspicion, many units simply refused to fire the weapon. The harsh, officious methods used by British officers created further resentment and across the barracks in Calcutta, Agra, Kanpur, Meerut, Ambala, Punjab, Awadh and Bundelkhand, the disquiet rose till it found expression in Mangal Pandey's act of open rebellion.

The Outbreak

The news of Mangal Pandey's act spread, as did his call to revolt. The simmering resentment came out in the open in Meerut – one of the largest military cantonments with over 2500 Indian and 2000 British troops stationed there. On 9 May 1857, 90 men of the 3 Bengal Light Cavalry refused to perform firing drills; 85 of them were court martialed and sentenced to 10-year imprisonment. The soldiers were stripped of their uniforms, placed in shackles and paraded in front of the entire garrison – harsh even by British standards. The next day – Sunday, 10 May 1858 – Indian solders broke into Meerut jail, freed their imprisoned compatriots, and attacked British officers and their families. Crowds also attacked British soldiers in the bazaar. It was a spontaneous move in which years of resentment erupted.

The troops then marched to Delhi and reached the palace of Bahadur Shah Zafar, the aged Mughal Emperor. Even though the Mughal Empire only existed in name, he was still venerated as the *de facto* Emperor of India. From beneath the ramparts of the Red Fort they called out to him to lead the revolt. Bahadur Shah wavered, but urged by his advisors, he held court the next day and gave his blessings and countenance for the battle against the British. Three battalions of Bengal Native Infantry who were stationed in Delhi joined the revolt and now turned against British officers and men. They were hunted down and killed and the remnants fled the city towards Karnal and Ambala.

Bahadur Shah Zafar – The Last Emperor

The movement spread across the country as Indians rose spontaneously against the British forcing them to flee from their garrisons. Meerut, Kanpur, Lucknow, Ambala, Allahabad, Benaras, Fatehpur, Agra and a host of towns were taken over by the sepoys and the British inhabitants either killed or pushed out. Punjab and South India though were unaffected by the movement, with most troops choosing to remain loyal to the Empire. Seeing the scale of the movement, additional troops were shipped in from England. Battalions in Persia and Crimea were also diverted to India. By June, relief columns were formed – composed of British, Sikh, Gurkha and other loyal troops – which began marching towards Meerut and Delhi. Ironically, Sikh troops did not join the revolt. The rebellious troops were largely from the Bengal Native Infantry, battalions which had fought them in the Anglo-Sikh Wars of 1846 (see 'Blood in the Sutluj' – Anglo-Sikh Wars) and their resentment against them was cleverly used by the British to ensure their loyalty.

By end of June, they reached Delhi and established themselves around the area of Delhi Ridge. A three-month-long siege of the capital began which extended from 01 July to 21 September. Both sides suffered heavily in a series of attacks and daily skirmishes. Then on 15 August, three additional battalions of British, Sikh and Pakhtoon troops arrived to reinforce the besiegers on the ridge. Heavy siege guns were also brought up and the city was subjected to heavy fire. Finally, on 15 September, the city was stormed through Kashmiri Gate and after a week of heavy fighting, British troops reached the Red Fort. Bahadur Shah Zafar and his sons were captured. His two sons and grandson were executed at Khooni Darwaza and their heads presented to the old emperor. Bahadur Shah was exiled to Rangoon where he died and was buried in an unmarked grave. The last of the line and the symbolic head of Mughal India was quietly erased.

British troops ravaged the city committing unimaginable atrocities. Civilians were massacred and the town looted. They then moved to Agra where another force of East India Company soldiers were besieged in Agra Fort, relieved them and took over the city. They then moved towards Kanpur and Lucknow, two of the major fires of the battle.

In June, sepoys from the garrison of Kanpur (then Cawnpore) had risen against their British officers and men. The European soldiers along with their women and children were offered a safe passage to Allahabad and were taken to the Ganges River to be evacuated by boats. An altercation broke out between the enraged sepoys and the British officers. Firing broke out and most of the British soldiers were killed; 5 men and 205 women and children survived the carnage and were imprisoned and later killed in a bungalow called *Bibighar* (literally 'House of the Ladies') and their bodies dumped in an adjoining well. The killings in Kanpur set off a chain of reprisals by the British and have often been used to justify their atrocities.

British forces retook Kanpur in August 1857 and then focused on Lucknow where around 1700 Europeans (including loyal sepoys) had occupied a position inside the Residency compound. For 90 days, they were besieged there. Indian sepoys rained down artillery and musket fire, but were unable to assault and overrun the position. The defenders were down to around 350 British and 300 sepoys when they were reinforced on 15 September by a relief column that fought its way from Kanpur and entered the city. This force reinforced the defenders and helped them hold on till they were finally relieved by a large force that entered Lucknow on 18 November 1857.

However, the Indians under Tatya Tope continued to hold Lucknow and it was only in March 1858 that a large army under General Campbell defeated the Indian force and reoccupied the city. With this, the British regained control of virtually every garrison town of North India.

The unyielding holding on of the British garrison at Lucknow has often been cited as one of the British hallmarks of the battles. Here too, the British force could have been eliminated much earlier, but the Indians were let down by poor tactics and lack of cohesive leadership. No central leadership existed to give overall direction to the struggle and the role of Bahadur Shah Zafar was symbolic as best. In different cities and areas, Indians fought isolated battles without an overall strategy. Yet what is significant is that Hindus, Muslims and all races and creeds fought as one against foreign rule. The unification that was revealed then would re-emerge only decades later during our second struggle for Independence.

Central India

The fires of Independence had also spread to Central and South India. In Jhansi, when the Raja of Jhansi died without a biological male heir, his kingdom was annexed by the British under the high-handed 'Doctrine of Lapse' policy – an arbitrary policy that stated that if a ruler died without a legitimate male heir, his kingdom would come under British rule. His widow, the feisty Rani Lakshmi Bai – who would be immortalised as the Rani of Jhansi – insisted that her adopted son would be the heir to the throne. When the War of Independence broke out, she was in the forefront, leading battles with her infant son strapped to her back. Jhansi became the centre of the rebellion and Rani Lakshmi Bai held on till March 1858, when British troops advanced to Jhansi, laid siege and captured her city, forcing her to flee in disguise to Gwalior.

Rani Lakshmi Bai

Tatya Tope

Rani Lakshmi Bai continued her struggle from Gwalior. Unfortunately, she was killed in Gwalior fort on 17 June 1858 after the fort was subjected to a very heavy bombardment. Three days later, on 20 June 1858, Gwalior was captured and with it the last bastion in the struggle for independence had fallen.

In the yearlong campaign, the British succeeded in regaining all the garrison towns and once again cemented their position in India. Unimaginable atrocities were committed. Captured sepoys were blown off with their bodies tied to the mouths of cannons; entire villages were burnt and the male population indiscriminately hanged to death. Loot, plunder and destruction of the reoccupied towns was a norm and Delhi, Meerut, Lucknow, Kanpur, Agra, Ambala and other centres of resistance were virtually razed to the ground. The toll is estimated to be 1,50,000-2,50,000 Indian lives. Another 2,00,000-3,00,000 were killed in the next few years by famine which was deliberately induced. The British Empire continued, only the rule of the British East India Company was now replaced by the Crown. In a different form, the loot and exploitation went on. It went on for 90 years more, till we finally cast off the shackles and attained true independence on 15 August 1947.

22

12 September 1897
THE LAST STAND AT SARAGARHI

Battle of Saragarhi

Exactly 120 years ago, on 12 September 1897, 21 soldiers of the 36th SIKH Regiment (Later 1 SIKH and now 4 MECHANISED INFANTRY) fought an epic battle against 10,000 Afghans in an outpost known as Saragarhi post. This battle, which often has been called the Thermopylae of India, saw each of the valiant Sikh defenders fall at their post.

Saragarhi was a small village in the North West Frontier Province of Kohat – now in Pakistan. The British had been engaged in a yearlong campaign against the restive Pashtoon tribesmen and 36th SIKH had been recently raised to help quell the uprising. The Pashtoons had been repeatedly attacking British outposts, especially Fort Lockhart and Fort Gulistan on the Samana Ridge of the Hindu Kush mountains. Since the two forts were not inter-visible, a small post of Saragarhi was created midway to function as a heliographic communication post to relay signals between Fort Lockhart and Fort Gulistan.

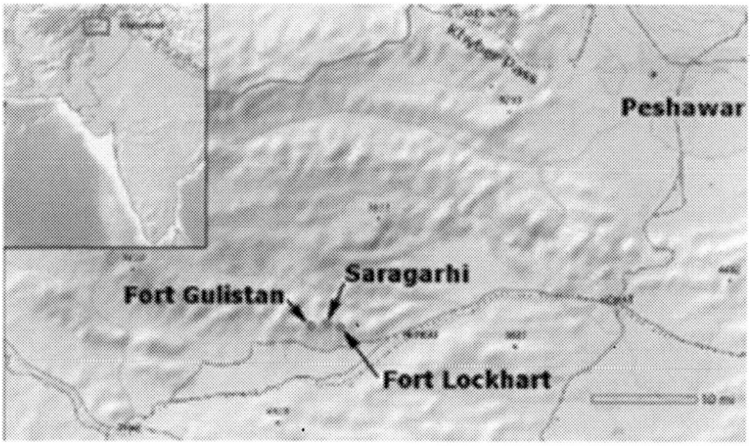

The post was not much, just a small blockhouse and a signaling tower with a mud and stone wall around it on a rocky, wind-swept hill. As the Afghans stepped up their attacks on the British in August–September 1987, they launched repeated attacks on the forts of Lockhart and Gulistan only to be repulsed by the soldiers of 36th SIKH there. They then turned their attention to Saragarhi, hoping to sever communications. Fortuitously, the post had been reinforced just a day earlier and held 1 NCO (Havildar Ishar Singh) and 20 other ranks. On 12 September 1897, around 10,000 Pashtoons of the Afridi and Orakzai clans under their leader Gul Badshah surrounded the post and asked the small garrison to surrender, promising to let them free with their lives if they did. The soldiers conferred together and decided to fight till the last. The Afghan offer was rudely rebuffed.

At around 0900 hours, the Afghans attacked the post. Two attacks were repulsed with heavy casualties. Each action was signaled back to Fort Lockhart, who though aware of the gravity of the situation, could not send any reinforcements there.

At around noon, the Afghans succeeded in breaching the outer wall, and the post commander Havildar Ishar Singh ordered the remnants of his men to fall back into the inner sanctum – the solitary mud and stone blockhouse that contained the signaling tower. He himself remained behind, firing to gain time for his men to withdraw, till he was overwhelmed by hordes of attacking Afghans.

Afridi Warriors

Soldiers of 36th SIKH

The remnants of the post – now down to just a dozen or so – continued holding on inflicting heavy casualties on the enemy, till they were killed, one by one, many of them in hand-to-hand combat. Throughout the battle, signalman Gurmukh Singh continued relaying messages, providing an account of the unfolding battle to Fort Lockhart and Gulistan. In his last message, he sought permission to leave his signaling machine and join his comrades and fell with them when the Afghans finally broke through into the communication tower.

It was only around 1600 hours or so that the last cries of '*Bole Son Nihal, Sat Sri Akal*' and gunfire finally subsided. The Afghans suffered immensely during the battle and lost around 500-600 men. A battle which they thought would be over in an hour had taken all day. The heroic stand of Ishar Singh and his men gained time for reinforcements to reach Forts Lockhart and Gulistan and the Afghan attacks on the forts, the next day, were repulsed. Two days later, on 14th September, Saragarhi fort was also retaken by British reinforcements under cover of heavy artillery fire. Each of the 21 defenders were found dead at their posts. The Afghans had not mutilated them as they usually did, nor were their turbans removed – as a sign of honour, the Afghans accorded them for their courage.

The ruins of Saragarhi

Each of them was awarded the Indian Order of Merit – the highest gallantry award for an Indian soldier at that time – equivalent to the Victoria Cross and today's Param Vir Chakra, the only such instance of collective bravery being recognized thus. To commemorate the battle, two Saragarhi Gurudwaras were constructed – one near the Golden Temple at Amritsar and the other at Ferozepur, where most of the soldiers were from. Saragarhi was a story of collective valour, of men fighting impossible odds, and then, even in death, remaining unbowed and undefeated.

23

27 October 1947
THE RACE TO SRINAGAR

Battle for Kashmir

It was August 1947, but the newly created India and Pakistan were not savouring their hard-won independence. Instead, they were witnessing an orgy of bloodshed that Cyril Radcliff's butcher's knife had unleashed with the Partition of the country. Over 6 million lives were lost in the largest cross-migration in history. Even as the horrors of Partition were unfolding, other problems arose. The Princely states had been given the option of acceding to India or Pakistan, and all had gone one way or the other. However, Jammu and Kashmir, the Muslim majority state ruled by the Hindu ruler Hari Singh, vacillated between India and Pakistan, and even toyed with the idea of remaining independent.

Jinnah was sure that Kashmir would join Pakistan, and as Maharaja Hari Singh wavered, Pakistan decided to annex the state through force. It launched "Operation Gulmarg" – an ingenious plan which came within an ace of succeeding and was only thwarted by the rapid actions of the Indian army in its first battle after independence.

Operation Gulmarg

"Operation Gulmarg", as the Pakistani plan was code-named, was the brain child of Major General Akbar Khan, the then Director of Weapons and Equipment of the Pakistani Army. It involved building up a force of tribesmen from the North West Frontier Province, arming them and sending them to Kashmir to capture the state by force. (Regular battalions of the Pakistani army were not used so as to deny involvement – a tactic they have tried repeatedly even thereafter.) The invaders were organised into "lashkars" of around a thousand tribesmen each and led by officers of the Pakistan Army who would operate in civilian clothing. Each lashkar had a Major as the Commanding Officer, assisted by a Captain and ten Junior Commissioned Officers. Around twenty such lashkars were created, and tasked to storm into

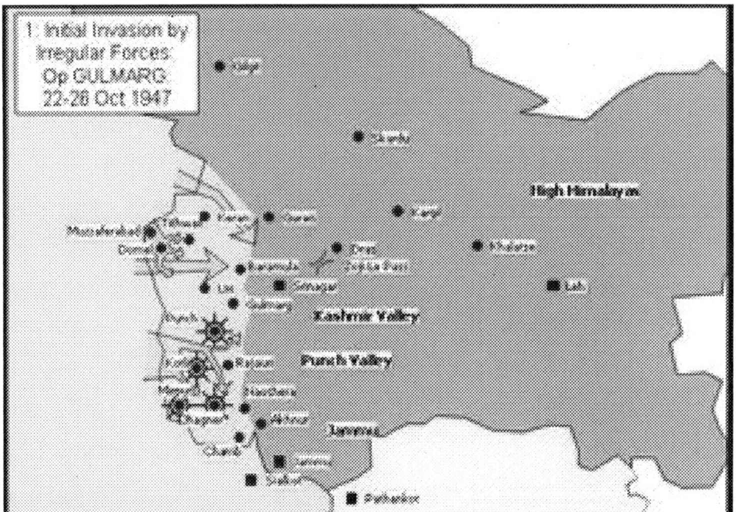

Operation Gulmarg

Kashmir and seize Srinagar – an action which would *de facto* force Hari Singh to accede to Pakistan.

The main offensive was to be with six lashkars advancing along the Muzaffarabad–Srinagar road to capture Srinagar. Two subsidiary thrusts of two lashkars each advanced alongside – one in the Jammu sector to the South, the other towards Ladakh in the North moving towards Leh. Surprisingly, even as this force built up, the government of India or the state of Kashmir received no information till they burst through on 22 October 1947, along the Abbotabad–Srinagar road, entered Muzaffarabad, and routed the single battalion of Jammu and Kashmir state forces there. The town was sacked, plundered and the women taken away to be brutally raped and sold into captivity. The raiders spent one day in the loot of Muzaffarabad and next day advanced towards Uri and Baramula on the way to Srinagar.

The Raiders

Devastation in Baramula

Uri fell on 24 October, and here the raiders were given their first resistance, when Brigadier Rajinder Singh, the Commander-in-Chief of the Kashmir state forces, personally led the delaying action, destroying the iron girder bridge on the road to Baramula. He was killed leading the rear-guard action and later awarded a posthumous MVC. The invaders now pushed forward towards Baramula, just 56 kilometres from Srinagar. The same orgy of violence was repeated here as the town was plundered, the inhabitants killed and the women subjected to inhuman savagery. Even the nuns of the Christian Missionary Hospital were not spared and raped repeatedly and the hospital looted. The ransacking of Baramula delayed the invaders by three to four days, vital time which perhaps saved Srinagar.

The Hindustan Times

KASHMIR ACCEDES TO INDIA

PLEBISCITE SOON ON RULER'S DECISION

SHEIKH ABDULLA TO FORM INTERIM GOVT.

26 October, 1947

The Historic Day

On 24 October, Maharaja Hari Singh, seeing the ravaging of his state, appealed to India for help, but India refused to send troops till the Maharaja formally acceded to India. On 26 October, the Maharaja signed the Instrument of Accession agreeing to join the Indian Union. Kashmir now became part of India and the same day Indian troops were ordered to fly into Srinagar to save the beleaguered state.

Operation Rescue

The unit that received the honour to conduct the first military operation of independent India was 1 SIKH. It was on Internal Security duties in Gurgaon and hastily assembled at Palam airport by 0400 hours on 27 October. Like most battalions, it was not up to full strength, and to make up its deficiencies, Sikh personnel from 13 Field Regiment, who were in Red Fort at the time, were placed under the battalion.

Indian troops arrive in Srinagar

On 27 October at 0600 hours, the first Dakota, with the Commanding Officer, Lieutenant Colonel Dewan Ranjit Rai, on board took off. He was given one set of maps and the Operational Order from Army HQ and was not aware of the exact situation or the fact that Baramula had already fallen. The initial lift only carried the Battalion Headquarters and C and D companies. On the way, one of the Dakotas carrying the Signal Platoon developed a snag and was forced to land at Jammu. It would join them only three days later, and in that time the battalion would be without radio communication at a time it needed it the most. Even as the sorties took off, it was not known if Srinagar airfield was safe or in the hands of the enemy. Rai had been instructed to establish wireless communication with the airfield and land only after receiving confirmation. Else he was to land at Jammu and then move to Srinagar by road. As the Dakotas reached the contact point, the confirming crackle of the wireless message reached Rai and at 8.30 am, the first Dakotas touched down at Srinagar's dusty airstrip. The Indian army had arrived.

On landing, Rai requisitioned whatever transport he could get and sent one company under Capt Kamaljit Singh towards Baramula and one company under Major Harwant Singh to conduct a flag march in Srinagar town to reassure the population. As Capt Kamaljit Singh approached the town, he saw smoke and realised that the town had fallen. He now organised a hasty defensive position east of the town near Milestone 32 on the hills astride the road Baramula–Srinagar. Col Rai also moved toward Baramula along with D company (which had left behind one platoon for the defence of the airfield and one platoon to protect the bridge leading to Srinagar) and joined the force at Milestone 32. On 29 October, the heavily armed raiders launched repeated attacks on his positions and soon outflanked his position. Rai ordered the battalion to move back from Baramula and occupy an intermediate position at Pattan. As Rai was conducting a skilful withdrawal, a burst of enemy fire killed him on the spot. Major Harwant Singh, MC, commanding D coy and the senior most officer with all of six years of service, took over the battalion. He decided to make a stand at Milestone 17, near Pattan, with the four odd platoons he had at his disposal. The position was barely occupied when the leading column of raiders approached and was ambushed with heavy casualties. The raiders launched repeated attacks on the position, but 1 SIKH stood firm and held on grimly for 48 hours. Those 48 hours were vital as they enabled additional troops to be landed at Srinagar airfield, and gave time to coordinate the defences of the town.

It would be fair to say that those 48 hours shaped the map of India. The two other companies of 1 SIKH flew in and joined the battle and the battalion held fast at Pattan preventing the enemy from advancing towards Srinagar. Additional troops of 161 Infantry brigade flew in, and the Indian army built up its defences around Srinagar. A Pakistani attack on Bagdam airfield was repulsed with heavy casualties on 03 Nov (an action that saw Major Somnath Sharma being awarded India's first Param Vir Chakra). Just a week later, Indian troops encircled and destroyed a large concentration of raiders at Shalateng. It then went slowly on the counter-offensive. For over a year the Indian army slowly pushed back the Pakistani army from their captured positions. It was only Nehru's ill-conceived decision to go to the United Nations that prevented the army from recapturing all the lost territory. When the cease-fire finally came into effect on 31 December 1948, Pakistan still held on to over a third of the state. The jagged line dividing Indian and Pakistani positions at the time of the cease-fire became the Line of Control which even today is one of the most volatile areas of the world.

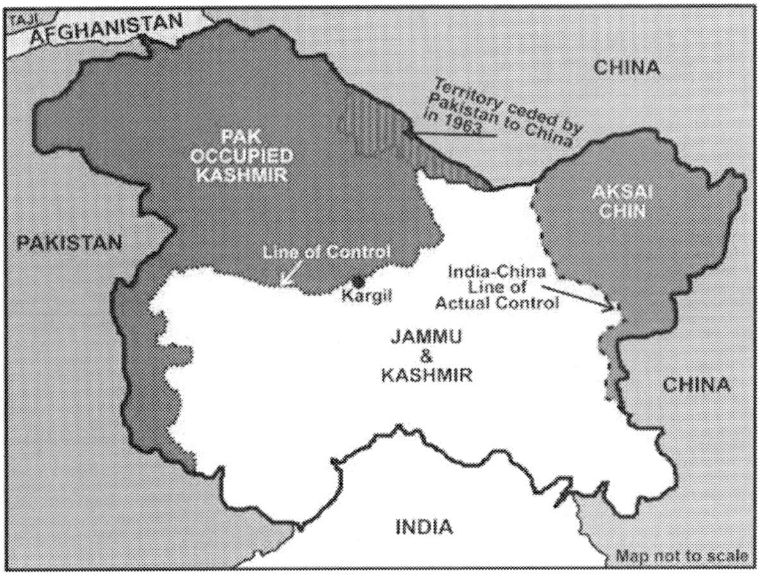

The Line of Control

The actions of 1 SIKH and its gallant Commanding Officer have gone down in history. Lt Col Rai was posthumously awarded the MVC and even today, 27 October, the day the unit landed in Srinagar is celebrated as Infantry Day – the day when the Indian Army saved the valley.

24

October 1947 – December 1948
SAVING KASHMIR

The Indo-Pak War of Kashmir

In August 1947, when India and Pakistan got their bloodied independence, the situation was stark. In an attempt to get Kashmir by force, Pakistan had sent armed tribesmen led by officers of the army to capture the State. As the raiders raped and pillaged their way through the beautiful state, Maharaja Hari Singh acceded to India and the Indian army arrived in Srinagar on 27 October 1947. Their arrival saved the state from falling into Pakistani hands (see 'The Race to Srinagar').

As 1 SIKH, the first unit to land in Kashmir, delayed the invaders on the outskirts of Srinagar, reinforcements flew in. 161 Infantry Brigade under Brig J C Katoch arrived on 29 Oct with 1 KUMAON, 4 KUMAON, 1 PUNJAB and 6 RAJRIF. Its arrival was inauspicious. The commander was wounded on 02 November and Brigadier L P Sen ('Bogie' Sen) took over. At that time, the situation was grave. Srinagar was surrounded by around 10,000 baying tribesmen with around 5000 approaching from Pattan in the West, around 2500 coming in from Sopore in the North and another 1500 or so approaching from Gulmarg in the south. Brigadier Sen decided to keep one battalion (6 RAJRIF) for the defence of Srinagar, 4 KUMAON to defend the airfield and use the other two battalions to deal with the approaching enemy. The arrival of two troops of howitzers, and a troop of Armoured Cars from 7 CAV boosted their meagre firepower considerably.

As the troops were just gearing up for their role, a report was received on 02 November that around 700-1000 tribals were seen near Bagdam villages moving towards the airfield. A force under Major Somnath Sharma was sent towards Bagdam and he occupied a defensive position there with one company by morning of 03 November. By 1500, a force of around 700 tribesmen approached and surrounded the position on three sides. Major Sharma realized that if he withdrew, the way would be open for the city of Srinagar and the airfield. Outnumbered seven to one, the force held on grimly. Maj Sharma, his hand in plaster with a hockey injury he had received even before they had set out, went around the post , galvanizing his men, filling ammunition magazines, firing and encouraging his men to hold firm till he was killed by a mortar bomb that exploded just behind him, his last message to the brigade Headquarters was:

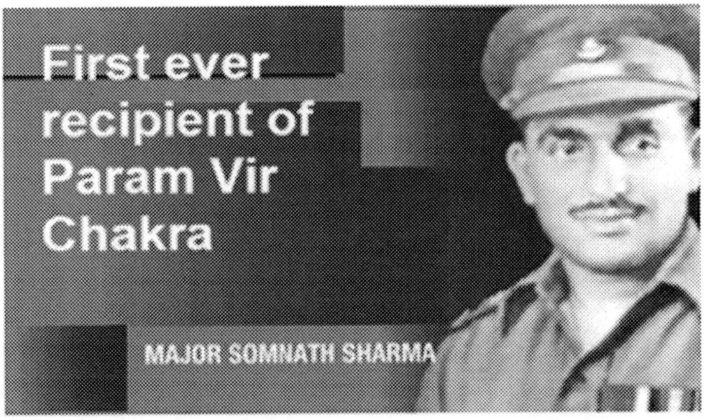

> 'The enemy is 50 yards from us. We are heavily outnumbered, but I will not withdraw one inch but fight to the last man last round.'

Major Sharma's gallant stand inflicted over 200 casualties on the enemy and also injured their leader. It delayed their advance by over 24 hours – valuable time gained to help prepare the defences of Srinagar. He himself became the first recipient of India's highest gallantry award - the Param Vir Chakra.

Srinagar was in peril and Sardar Vallabhai Patel himself flew in to emphasize the urgency of holding on at all costs. Brigadier Sen decided to move his units closer to Srinagar. Meanwhile, an aerial reconnaissance showed a force of around 3000 heavily armed raiders assembling at Shalateng – around 7 kilometers away – with their vehicles parked alongside the road. Brig Sen had two options. He could hold firm hoping that the promised reinforcements would arrive, or he could attack with what little forces he had at his disposal. He chose to attack and that decision shaped the war.

Tribals used by Pakistan

Using one battalion (1 SIKH) to hold the enemy, he encircled the force with two battalions moving stealthily from two directions. A troop of Armoured Cars on a mounted patrol in the vicinity was also called in to close in from the rear of the enemy. Not expecting an attack, the enemy was taken by surprise as they were hemmed in and surrounded by fire on all sides. Caught out in the open in a freshly ploughed field with their vehicles and much of their heavy weapons parked some distance away, the raiders were virtually massacred and the remnants fled back towards Baramula. They were pursued relentlessly, and fired on by air; 472 bodies were recovered at Shalateng and a further 146 on the road to Baramula. The victory at Shalateng now inflicted a decisive defeat on the raiders and brought an end to their offensive towards Srinagar. From now on the enemy was on the defensive and the Indian army rapidly capitalized on this victory. Baramula was recaptured, then Uri and the army was all poised to recapture Domel and Muzaffarabad and push the enemy back into Pakistan.

It was then that a grave situation developed in the South, in the Jammu Sector.

Indian troops Consolidate

The Pakistanis had accompanied their main thrust towards Srinagar with a complementary offensive in the South. A force of around 10,000 Lashkars moved towards the Jammu sector capturing the towns of Mirpur, Bhimber and Mendher in their wake. The same carnage that was witnessed in Muzaffarabad, Uri and Baramula was revisited here, as the raiders went berserk on the hapless citizens of the towns. Poonch, the largest town in the area, was under threat as well. 161 Brigade which was making spectacular gains in the Srinagar sector was now ordered to move towards the South and help reinforce Poonch. One battalion (1 KUMAON under Lt Col Pritam Singh) was sent on foot to enter the town and defend it. Under Col Pritam Singh, Poonch witnessed numerous attacks, and though besieged on all sides was maintained by air and held on for over a year till relieved by an Indian offensive in November 1948.

The Indian situation in the Jammu sector was as perilous as it had been at Srinagar a month ago. The defence in this area was entrusted to 50 Para Brigade under Brigadier Mohammed Usman. (Like so many patriotic Indian Muslims he refused to join Pakistan, even though he was promised the position of Chief subsequently.) The enemy pushed forward capturing Jhangar and Rajauri on the outskirts of Naushera. Naushera held the key to this sector. If it fell, Jammu would be within the striking range. Brigadier Usman placed his battalions on the high ground around the town and his brigade was subjected to frenzied attacks by around 20,000 tribesmen from 5 to 8 Feb 1948. In spite of seven attacks, the brigade held firm, fighting back the enemy in some of the bloodiest close combat battles of the war. When the fighting subsided around 10 Feb or so, the enemy withdrew leaving behind over 2000 dead around the heights of Naushera. This was a major victory and put paid to the enemy's offensive plans towards Jammu.

With the two victories of Shalateng and Naushera under its belt, the Indian army went on the offensive. In the Spring of 1948, Jhangar and Rajauri were recaptured. In the North, the Indian Army moved towards Domel. By now the Pakistani army had given up all pretense of merely using tribesmen and the regular army was occupying most positions. Each hill feature, each town and village had to be won at a high cost, after grim battles. Yet slowly, the Indian army began recovering most of its lost territories. It was poised to move up to Muzafarrabad – the start point of the Pakistani offensive – and push the Pakistanis back where they started when Nehru made the ill-conceived decision to go to the United Nations at a time when the Indian Army was well and truly on the ascendency. On 10 July, the government ordered a halt to our counter-offensive and the guns fell silent. Well almost silent. Firing and sporadic battles erupted for much of the year. The areas held by both sides would become the Line of Control – a violent jagged line that divided the two sides and even today erupts with painful regularity. India ended up with control of two thirds of the State, including the prized valley. Pakistan held on to one third. But the unresolved war of 1947-48 laid the seeds for conflict in 1965, 1971 and 1999 and led to seven decades of mistrust and unrest that continues to this day.

25

01 November 1948
TANKS AT 11,500 FEET

Battle of Zojila

In their grand plan to annex Kashmir by force, during their offensive of 1947-48, the Pakistani army had inducted large columns of tribesmen, led by officers of the army towards Srinagar and Jammu and towards Ladakh in the North. The starkly beautiful region of Ladakh lies to the North East of Kashmir and is connected by a scenic road from Srinagar to Leh which passes through Kargil via the 11,553-foot-high Zojila Pass – one of the highest passes in the world which aptly means, "The Pass of Blizzards". While the Pakistani actions were being contested in Kashmir (see "Race to Srinagar" and "Saving Kashmir"), the Ladakh region saw some equally fierce fighting and in the end was virtually saved by a hair's breadth with the capture of Zojila Pass.

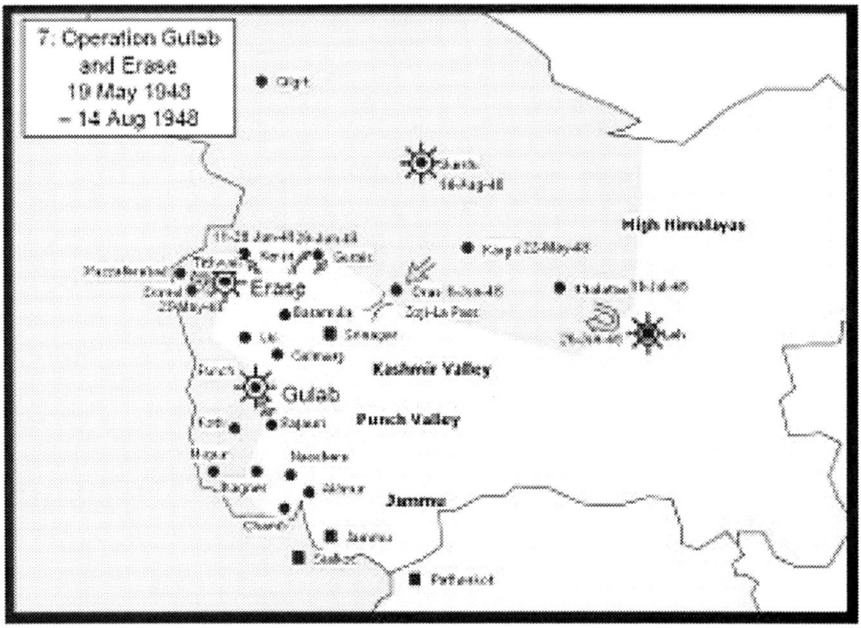

Pakistani incursions up to Leh (June 48)

At the time of partition, the area of Ladakh was lightly held by members of the Jammu and Kashmir State Forces who were strung across in penny-packets across this vast region. Pakistan launched its offensive here in conjunction with its actions in the Kashmir valley. It used its same ploy of having armed tribesmen led by Pakistani army officers to pour into the region in November 1947. Gilgit and Baltistan were lost even before the Indian Army could even react. Ladakh was thrown into panic as the refugees streamed in from the captured Northern Areas, carrying tales of atrocities. Most of the State forces fell back to Skardu, a small town which guarded the approach to Leh. The town was held by a small garrison of around a thousand men under Lieutenant Colonel Sher Jung Thapa. Skardu was contacted by the enemy in early January, but each of its attacks was determinedly beaten back. Besieged on all sides and heavily outnumbered, the garrison would hold on for over eight months before finally capitulating on 14 Aug 1948.

While Skardu was grimly holding out, the enemy bypassed the town, moved towards Kargil and Drass and captured both towns by end of May 1948. Even worse, the enemy captured the crucial Zojila Pass and thus cut off the land link from Srinagar to Kargil-Drass and Leh. With the capture of Zojila, Leh could only be connected by air or the 400-kilometre-long route from Manali. The fall of Leh, and with it all of Ladakh seemed imminent.

As the threat to Leh intensified, it was decided to reinforce the small garrison there. A small detachment of 2 DOGRA under Major Prithi Chand with 70 volunteers marched out from Srinagar and after a monthlong trek through snow storms, avalanches and blizzards reached Leh on 8 March 1948. Each man carried additional rifles and weapons and using the State force personnel already there, they formed a local defence force. A make-shift airstrip was constructed and on 24 May 1948, a single Dakota landed on the highest airstrip in the world. That aircraft was piloted by Air Commodore Meher Singh and had on board General Thimayya, such was the importance of Leh. With the airfield operational, additional forces were flown in and the defences reinforced to withstand an enemy attack.

Dakotas landing at Leh airstrip

Though Leh was reinforced, the town was still effectively isolated as the capture of Zojila Pass had cut off the entire Ladakh region from the valley. The pass had to be recaptured, but it would be a tough nut to crack. It was held by a Pakistani battalion with three main positions: Mukand Ridge and Chabutra Ridge, on the right and left shoulders, and a depth position on

Machine Gun Ridge. At those forbidding heights, it could not be assaulted and the enemy was dug into well-sited positions in the natural caves of the mountain side which were virtually immune to air or artillery fire.

The first attack to recapture Zojila went in on 11 September 48 with 77 Para Brigade. Two successive infantry assaults were launched which failed in the face of heavy fire. The enemy was too well-dug in and air and artillery attacks had no affects. As September was drawing to a close and winter setting in, time was running out. If the pass held for just a month or two more, it would become impossible to capture it in winter and then Leh would have automatically fallen. The entire Indian operations in this sector depended on the capture of Zojila.

Thimayya realised that the only way to eliminate the enemy from their positions would be by using the direct fire of tanks – but then no tanks had ever reached these heights and no tanks had ever operated as such altitudes before. Yet it was decided to take the chance and a squadron of Stuart Mark 6 tanks of 7 LIGHT CAVALRY was moved from Akhnur to Zojila. The turrets of the tanks were removed to reduce weight which would enable them to cross the numerous small bridges en route. Bridges were reinforced, tracks were hurriedly widened, and the tanks trundled up the long difficult climb towards Zojila. An eight-kilometre-long track was widened by cutting into sheer rock face in just 20 days by Engineers of the Madras Sappers. It is a credit to the drivers that not a single tank gave way to mechanical failure or was struck on the slushy narrow tracks, even though the move was made purely by night to ensure secrecy. By 15 October, the squadron was in position, the turrets were refitted and the stage was set for the historic assault on Zojila. Even in the last stage, the tanks had to be physically pushed by jawans along the steep gradient to bring them in position for the final assault.

Operation "Bison", the code name for the attack, was scheduled on 20 Oct, but when all was ready, it began to snow. Zojila lived up to its name. The Pass of Blizzards was hit by raging snowstorms and twice the operation was postponed because of the weather. Finally, D-Day was set for 01 November and with winter worsening, it was literally now or never.

On 01 November, in spite of another raging snowstorm, General Thimayya gave the order to attack. Beneath a leaden sky, with snow flakes swirling all around them, the tanks rumbled across the start line at 10:15 a.m. As the

Tanks and Infantry assault at Zojila

The Capture

tanks roared through, with Thimayya in the leading tank, the infantry attacked from the flanks and on the shoulders of the pass. The poor visibility and atrocious weather actually aided surprise as the enemy did not expect an attack in these conditions. With the infantry moving along the flanks, the tanks sprayed the pass with machine gun and high-explosive fire. The sight of the tanks unnerved them and in panic the enemy fled, leaving behind their dead and dying and vast stocks of equipment. Tanks and infantry swept through the pass, the tanks firing into the bunkers and caves and the infantry clearing the shoulders. By the next evening it was all over and on 02 November, the tri-colour was raised once again on the wind-swept pass.

The appearance of tanks at these heights shocked the enemy and was perhaps the most important factor for the victory. Never have tanks been used at such altitudes – then or after – and it was a masterpiece of innovative tactics. The rejuvenated troops surged forward in sub-zero temperatures in some of the worst terrain imaginable, and on 16 November captured Drass. On 23 November, the leading troops entered Kargil, and the same day linked up with Leh. The long isolation of Leh was over. Leh and Ladakh were saved.

The capture of Zojila was perhaps one of the most important operations of the 1947-48 Kashmir war. Had it failed, all of Leh and Ladakh would have been lost and perhaps Srinagar as well. And it was just in the nick of time. A month later on the night of 31 December, the ceasefire came into being. The ceasefire prevented the Indian army from recapturing Skardu and the Northern areas which were occupied by the invaders, but Leh, Ladakh and two thirds of Kashmir remain in Indian hands. The tanks that rumbled in at 11,500 feet perhaps helped shape the geography of the nation.

26

20 December 1961
GOA'S LIBERATION – AFTER 451 YEARS

Battle for Goa

On 19 December 1961, the Indian Army attained its first major military victory when it liberated Goa from Portuguese rule. This two-day campaign terminated 451 years of foreign occupation and incorporated Goa, Daman and Diu into the Indian Republic.

The Portuguese were the first Europeans to reach India when Vasco Da Gama landed on our shores in 1498. They were also the last to leave. Even after Independence, they held on to their enclaves in Goa, Daman and Diu,

Dadra and Nagar Haveli – collectively called *Estado da India*. Resistance to Portuguese rule had begun way back in 1926 and had picked up momentum after 1947. The Government of India formally entered negotiations to end Portuguese colonization of India – proposals which Portugal rejected outright. Diplomatic talks reached an impasse and at the same time public opinion to integrate Goa with India began intensifying.

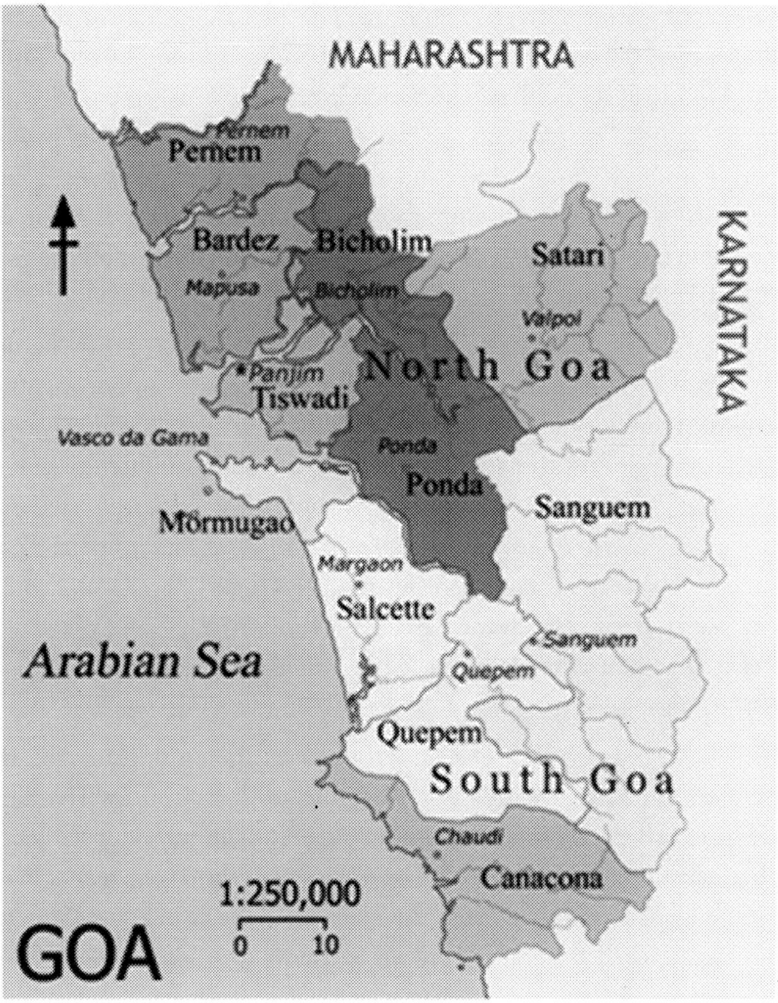

The first major spark came on 15 August 1955, when Portuguese police fired on unarmed Indian activists killing 30. Then on 24 November 1961, Portuguese troops fired on the passenger ship 'MV Sabarmati' – mistaking it for a landing vessel – and killed two crew members. That was the final straw. On 10 Dec, Nehru defied world opinion and gave the go-ahead for military operations to liberate Goa.

The military plan involved a three-pronged advance with 17 Infantry Division, 1 Armoured Division and 50 Independent Para Brigade advancing from the North from Maharashtra into Goa. 63 Infantry Brigade was to advance from the East while a diversionary attack was launched from the South. Simultaneously, the enclaves of Daman were to be captured by one battalion (1 MARATHA LIGHT INFANTRY) and Diu was to be taken by 20 RAJPUT and 5 MADRAS. The IAF and the Navy too had major roles to play. Fighter bombers would soften the targets and also deny the only airbase of Dabolim. Five battleships were to attack from the sea and an aircraft carrier group under the venerable INS VIKRANT was out on patrol 75 kilometers off the coast to stave off any maritime challenge.

Portugal had built up their military strength and inducted three battalions (one each from Portugal, Angola and Mozambique) with supporting units to challenge any military adventure. Two artillery units had also been recently inducted, smuggled in the guise of football teams. No fighter aircraft were available, but the coast was defended by strong coastal batteries with the naval warship '*Afonso de Albuquerque*' and three patrol vessels guarding the port of Mormugao. It was a strong force, but inadequate for the task at hand. The strategy was to delay the advancing Indians for 7-10 days, and prevent them from entering their capital Panaji. That would give time for international pressure to be applied.

Hostilities began on 17 December when an Indian unit clashed with a Portuguese reconnaissance squadron along the northern frontier. The skirmish ended with the Portuguese forces withdrawing pre-maturely destroying bridges and channels along the way and this set the tone for the engagements to come. The next day, 18 December 1961, the main attack went in at 0400 hours and the Indians attacked along three prongs in the wake of intensive air and naval bombardment.

The main offensive moved in to Goa from the North. 50 Independent Para Brigade, which was initially allotted a supporting role, took the lead and moved with three prongs of a battalion each, racing southwards. Supported by tanks, they moved rapidly and by midday had virtually covered half the distance to Panaji. Their advance was met with cheering crowds and more often than not, the Portuguese withdrew – disregarding their orders to fight to the last. The Indians closed in towards Panaji and reached the banks of the Mandhovi River – the major waterway separating the town from the mainland – only to see the only bridge on the river, demolished by retreating Portuguese troops literally minutes before their arrival. The advance to Panaji was halted for the night and Indian soldiers closed in for what was to be the major battle of the campaign.

Indian troops advancing to cheering crowds

Abandoned Portuguese post

In the East, 63 Infantry Brigade advanced in three prongs, wading through rivers and streams as they made their way inwards. The attacks by a single company of 4 Rajput in the South had helped create confusion in the minds of the Portuguese as to the strength and direction of the Indian thrust lines. The Eastern and Southern prongs met near Margao around 1530 hours on 18 December and were now ready to march towards Panaji where the main battle was to be fought. Simultaneously, the attacks on Daman and Diu went in and both enclaves were captured on the first day itself.

As the land offensive moved in, the IAF launched three raids on Dabolim Airbase, using Canberras and Hunters, which damaged the runway and ensured that no reinforcements could land by air. The navy closed in on Mormugao harbor which was strongly defended by coastal batteries and the warship *'NRP Afonso de Albuquerque'*. At around nine in the morning, three Indian frigates led by INS BETWA attacked the 'Afonso' which responded with heavy gunfire of its 120-mm guns. In a naval battle lasting three hours, the 'Afonso' was repeatedly hit and sustained serious damage to its propulsion system. Stricken and out of control, the warship ran aground and the remnants of the crew put up a white flag and surrendered. Independent India's first naval battle came to a close.

The 'Afonso'

By morning on 19 December, Indian troops had concentrated around Panaji and Vasco da Gama. Indian tanks of 7 Cavalry and troops of 2 Sikh Light Infantry crossed the Mandhovi River and approached Panaji, capturing Fort Aguada, the seat of resistance. Around 2000 Portuguese troops had fallen back to Panaji and as per the latest communique received from Portugal, they were to fight to the last there. They were to also adopt a 'scorched earth' policy and destroy Goa before it fell into Indian hands. Fortunately, the Governor General Manuel de Silva disregarded these orders as '*un sacrificio inutil*' (a useless sacrifice) and surrendered at 2030 hours the same day. In a formal ceremony, the Instrument of Surrender was signed and Goa and all Portuguese territories came back into Indian hands. A total of 4668 Portuguese personnel were taken prisoner in a war which cost 22 Indian and 30 Portuguese lives. The two-day campaign brought an end to 451 years of European occupation of Indian soil.

Surrender Ceremony

But this easy victory had its flip side. It gave India's political and military leadership an inflated view of our military capabilities. The shortcomings that this victory glossed over would be rudely exposed just a year down the line as the Chinese waves crashed over the Himalayas in the 1962 Indo-China War.

27

20 October – 21 November 1962
DEBACLE IN THE HIGH HIMALAYAS

1962 Indo-China War

In November 1962, the Indian Army suffered its most humiliating – and only – defeat since independence. It was a body blow to the young nation, then only 15 years old, and left an everlasting impact on the Indian psyche.

To understand the story of the debacle, we must go back to its history and the geography. The problem began in 1950 when China annexed Tibet, and India and China became neighbors. The line dividing the two nations was the

McMahon Line, an unclear, demarcated line between India and Tibet which the Chinese never recognized or accepted.

The Indo-China border runs 3800 kilometers from Burma in the East to Kashmir in the West. In the Eastern Sector, the Chinese claimed the entire area up to Arunachal Pradesh as 'Southern Tibet'. In the Western Sector, they claimed all of Aksai Chin in Ladakh. In spite of this dangerous indication, the government remained blind to the threat, with Nehru pinning his hopes on a *'Hindi-Chini Bhai Bhai'* policy.

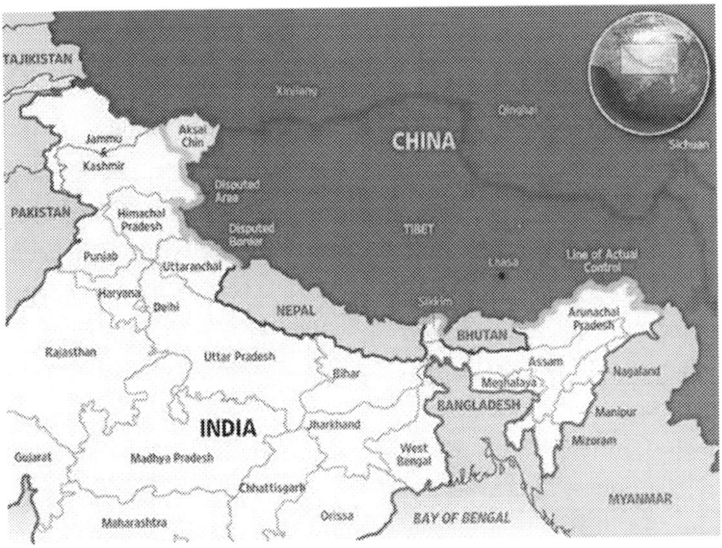

The Disputed Border

Border incidents along the demarcated border had been occurring since 1959. In 1960, to counter Chinese incursions, Nehru, wrongly advised by the Defence Minister Krishna Menon and the Intelligence Bureau, embarked on a 'Forward Policy'. This meant India would establish posts all along the border in the area we claimed as our own. It was a disastrous policy that sent troops in penny pockets, and often cut off, in indefensible positions, without any means of support.

The flash point came in June 1962, when Indian troops occupied a post at Che Dong (which was actually inside Chinese territory). The Chinese responded violently and occupied Dhola Ridge, a feature inside Indian Territory. Unknown to Indian intelligence, the Chinese had been preparing for over two years and had built up 54th Army in Tibet for this operation. Indian strength was woefully short with just one brigade (7 Brigade) holding the area. Worse, the responsibility to defend the area was given to a newly raised 4 Corps under Lt Gen B M Kaul, an incompetent officer, with no battle experience, who was related to Nehru. Indian troops were sent forward towards Dhola ridge, to 'throw the Chinese from Indian territory', as was reportedly said by Nehru. This was the provocation the Chinese were waiting for and on 20 Oct 1962, the Chinese poured out of their concealed positions to launch a concentrated attack in both the Eastern and Western sectors.

The Chinese Attacks

At 5 am on 20 Oct, the silence of the Himalayas was broken by the roar of artillery guns as the Chinese began a two-hour bombardment of Indian positions all along the border. Two Chinese divisions poured down the road from Bum La to Tawang, overrunning the Indian 7 Brigade. This brigade had been ordered to occupy a virtually indefensible position in the Namka Chu Valley and in less than six hours of fighting was virtually wiped out. They now moved forward relentlessly towards Tawang which they occupied by 23 Oct. Ironically, the Indian shortcoming of not developing roads till the border now came to its rescue, as the Chinese were forced to develop a road from the border to Tawang to funnel in supplies. There was a pause in operations as the Chinese built their road, in just 14 days, which provided some time for the Indians.

The Rout

Using the pause in operations, Indian troops were pushed up. But the troops were from the plains, with no knowledge of the area, in summer uniform, with no heavy weapons and just their pouch ammunition. The neglect of the army and in using troops in superfluous activities such as building barracks at the expense of training was showing and the troops were unprepared. They still held on to vintage single-shot .303 rifles since the new automatic rifles had arrived without ammunition. There were no logistics or supplies. The leadership – both military and political – was poor. There was literally nothing but the spirit of the soldier.

On 17 November, the Chinese launched their second phase of operations which outflanked the Indian position at Se La. Se La was strongly held but was ordered to withdraw pre-maturely. In the confused withdrawal, the Chinese attacked. Se La was the worst battle of the campaign which claimed 1800 casualties in just 2 days. The Chinese advanced from Se La to Dirang to Bomdila as the Indian army withdrew in disarray. In each case, they followed a standard tactic of infiltrating behind own positions, attacking from different directions, and cutting off our own troops. They were aided by a poor military leadership that gave no clear directions, and ordered panicked withdrawals when they should have held firm. Then when Chinese were virtually at the foothills of Assam, on 21 Nov, they announced a unilateral ceasefire and withdrew back in to their own territory. The curtain rang down on this tragedy of arms.

The war raged from 20 Oct to 21 Nov 1962, but the actual fighting was for less than seven days. Yet the Indian army suffered 3078 killed, 3018 wounded and 3587 taken prisoner, a grievous loss. The only saving grace was that the army learnt, reorganized itself and focused on training and modernization. In the years that followed, it developed into a more professional and cohesive army that more than held its own in every other battlefield. The lessons of 1962 had come at a high cost. Let us hope that we never forget them.

28

18 November 1962
THE LAST STAND OF 'C' COMPANY: 13 KUMAON

Battle of Rezang La

In the annals of heroism, the stand of C Company of the 13 Kumaon at Rezang La on 18 November 1962 will always be among the more glorious chapters. The monument that stands at Chushul asks, "How can a man die better, than facing fearful odds, for the ashes of his fathers, and the temples of his gods." In the dark days of Nov 1962, the stand by C Company stands out as a saga of heroism, in the Indo-China war of 1962.

The Chinese had attacked on 20 Oct 1962, both in the East in NEFA (modern-day Arunachal Pradesh) and in the West in Ladakh (see 'Debacle in the High Himalayas'). In the first three days of the offensive, most of the forward posts had fallen. Chinese were now poised for the attack on the most important objective in the sector, Chushul and its precious airfield, with an all-weather landing strip, which lay just 15 kilometers from the border.

The Ladakh Sector

Till September 1962, the defence of all of Ladakh was vested with 114 Brigade commanded by Brig TN Raina (later General and COAS). It consisted of just two infantry battalions, the 1/8 Gorkha Rifles and 5 Jat. When the gravity of the Chinese threat began to be realized, 13 Kumaon, which was at Baramula in the Kashmir Valley, was sent in to reinforce 114 Brigade. In the first week of October, the 3 Himalayan (later Mountain) Division was formed for the overall defence of Ladakh and the Chushul sector was entirely left to 114 Brigade. On 26 October, 114 Brigade set up its headquarters at Chushul and braced for the inevitable Chinese attack.

The Chinese could attack along the Spangur Gap – a picturesque gap that led straight to Chushul. Most of 114 Brigade's defences were based facing the gap. There was only one other way to Chushul, through the narrow Rezang La pass, which stood at a height of 16,000 feet, and was around 10 kilometers away from the rest of the defences. C Company, 13 KUMAON was deployed on Rezang La to prevent the Chinese from out-flanking the defences from that direction. Most expected that the Chinese attack would be directed at the Spangur Gap. Instead, when it came, it was launched at Rezang La.

C Company spent a week digging defensive positions in those isolated heights often in full view of the Chinese. The men had come from the plains and were still not acclimatized to those heights. At this altitude, it took hours to bring a kettle to boil for tea and whatever fruit and vegetables that came were frozen hard. In the rarified air, breathing was a problem. Rezang La had a more serious drawback. It was out of range of own artillery support and away from the rest of the defences. It had to fight its battle virtually alone.

Maj Shaitan Singh, PVC

Maj. Shaitan Singh, a Rajput from Jodhpur, commanded C Company of 13 Kumaon. The company was made up of Ahirs, from Haryana and its three platoons were numbered 7, 8 and 9. They held the antiquated .303 rifles with about 600 rounds per head, and between them six Light Machine Guns, and a handful of 2-inch mortars. The Chinese infantry had 7.62-mm self-loading rifles; MMGs and LMGs; 120-, 81- and 60-mm mortars; 132-mm rockets; and 75- and 57-mm recoilless guns to bust bunkers.

The Chinese attack came silently at 4 am on 18 November, even as a light snow was falling. They crept up the gullies hoping to catch the Indians unaware, but were detected. The Ahirs waited till the Chinese came into range and opened up with everything they had. The gullies were soon full of dead and wounded Chinese. Having failed in a frontal attack, the Chinese let loose a murderous shelling. Under the cover of this intense shelling, the Chinese infantry came again in swarms. Yet the company held on in the face of repeated assaults forcing the enemy to bring up 75-mm cannons on wheel barrows to destroy the position though direct fire. In the face of intense fire, the defences slowly gave way and the company fell, fighting virtually to the last man and to the last bullet. Out of the 128 who attended the "stand-to" in the morning, only 14 survived. Shaitan Singh himself was amongst the last to fall. Mortally wounded by a burst to the abdomen, he refused to be carried to safety and continued firing from his position to allow his comrades to withdraw. His gallant stand was immortalized in the Hindi film "Haqeeqat' which reflected the horrors and the rigors of the 1962 War with great accuracy and helped bring home to the Indian audiences the courage of the individual Indian soldiers and the abysmal conditions in which they fought.

Rezang La finally fell at around 1330 hours, but the stand had gained time for the rest of the brigade to withdraw and consolidate itself near Chushul preventing the fall of the vital airfield. The Chinese announced a unilateral ceasefire on 21 November and Chushul remained in Indian hands.

The Final Rites

In the aftermath of the ceasefire and the Indian withdrawal, none really knew what had happened to C Company, 13 Kumaon, for over two months. Then in December, a shepherd passed word to the Indian Brigade Headquarters about the bodies of Indian soldiers lying in the snow at Rezang La. When Indian troops reached the spot, they saw a tableau of death. Each man was dead at this post, with bodies preserved in the cold. The mortar loader was frozen in the act of loading a bomb in his mortar, the Medical Orderly held a syringe in his hand that he was about to administer to a comrade, Major Shaitan Singh's body was found some distance away. Though severely wounded in the abdomen, he refused to be evacuated fighting on till his last breath, as did each man of C Company, 13 Kumaon. The Chinese had covered his body with a blanket in a rare gesture of honour. The other bodies too were untouched by the Chinese, perhaps in acknowledgement of their courage.

Every man had died a hero. A hero of the Thermopylae called Rezang La.

29

25 August 1965
CAPTURED ON GROUND, LOST ON THE TABLE

Capture of Haji Pir Pass

Very few have heard of Haji Pir Pass, fewer even know where it is and why it is so important. But this windswept mountain pass was the site of one of the most notable battles of the 1965 War and a tale of courage and endurance.

Situated 8652 feet high in the Himalayan Ranges, Haji Pir was a vital pass in Pakistan- occupied Kashmir. In the 1947-48 Kashmir War, Pakistani raiders had attacked Kashmir in the hope of capturing it militarily. Though they came to the doorstep of Srinagar, they were pushed back by the Indian Army. When the yearlong war came to a close, Pakistan still retained large swaths of Kashmiri territory which is today Pakistan-occupied Kashmir. Haji

Pir Pass was also held by them. This strategic pass was inside a bulge, which protruded like a dagger inside Indian territory and could be used by them to send in raiders and launch attacks into India.

In 1965, Pakistan was emboldened by India's defeat at the hands of China and also their victories in the border skirmishes in the Kutch desert in April. They decided to launch an ambitious plan to send raiders – military men and tribals in civilian clothing – into Kashmir valley to stir uprevolt, lay ambushes and launch attacks on Indian army positions. Haji Pir was one of the major areas through which the Pakistani infiltrators came in.

In August, the Indian Army decided to attack the very launch pads of these terrorist infiltrators, to cut off their entry routes. Haji Pir was the most prominent amongst them. Although war had not been declared, both sides were engaged in fighting with each other. The Indian plan for the capture of Haji Pir, involved a double pincer: one from the North and one from the

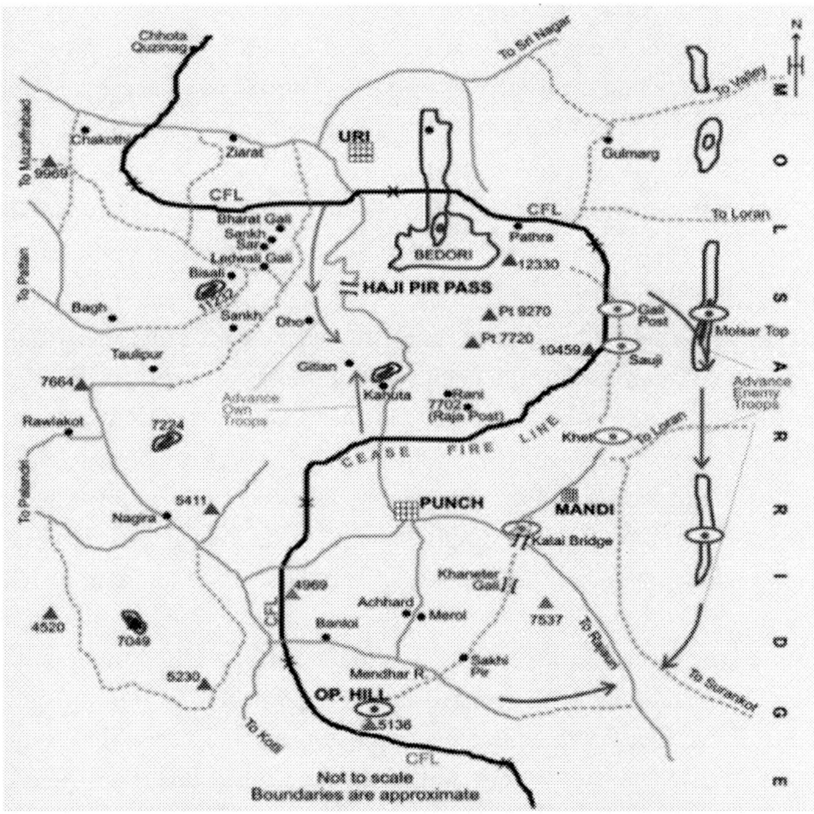

The Haji Pir Bulge

South that would encircle the bulge and capture the crucial pass. Yet the pass would be a tough nut to crack. It was held strongly by a Brigade, reinforced by irregular troops and supported by artillery. The defences were arrayed in layers and before reaching the vital pass, the enemy defences at Bedori, Sank and Ledwali Gali had to be first cleared. The attack was to be launched on 24 August, but bad weather postponed the launch and on 25th night, after much trepidation, the attack went in. The troops moved across the mountains in hail and sleet, and infiltrated unseen through the gaps in the Pakistani positions.

Moving along the treacherous ridges, 68 Brigade slowly approached Haji Pir from the North. As per the initial plan, 1 PARA was to advance along a narrow mountain gully, capture the enemy position of Sank and provide an approach for the subsequent capture of the pass. Another battalion 19 PUNJAB was to move along an equally treacherous ridgeline, and capture Bedori, another preliminary objective guarding Haji Pir. A fresh battalion 4 RAJPUT was to then attack the Haji Pir pass and capture it.

On the night of the 25th, the attacks went in and Sank was captured by 1 PARA after launching three successive attacks. The bad weather actually helped as the Pakistanis did not expect any Indian movement – leave alone an attack in these conditions. Yet on the other side, Bedori, which was to have been captured simultaneously, held on. To make matters worse, the third battalion, 4 RAJPUT, which was to have launched the attack on the Haji Pir pass, was delayed and could not fetch up.

The attack seemed to have ground to a halt, with only one battalion, 1 PARA even approaching the enemy position. This was one of the crucial moments that make or break a battle. At this juncture, 1 PARA volunteered to go ahead alone to capture Haji Pir, since a delay waiting for the next battalion to arrive would have nixed the plan completely. In a calculated gamble, one company under Major Ranjit Singh Dayal (later Lt Gen R S Dayal) made a grueling approach march to the base of the pass, made a circuitous climb along the difficult western shoulder of the pass, and climbed up unseen from a flank of the unsuspecting enemy. By the time they reached the top, it was almost daybreak. They were detected as they approached the summit, and the enemy opened fire. Leaving just a platoon to engage the enemy; the rest of the company moved to the summit and from there rolled down on the enemy positions attacking them from the rear. The surprised defenders fled and by noon, the pass was in Indian hands. The tricolour flew proudly on the pass for the first time since Independence.

With Haji Pir in our hands, the outlying positions soon fell, and the vital pass fell into Indian hands. The bulge through which Pakistani infiltrators came into Kashmir and also their escape route was now cut off. Seeing their plans unraveling, the Pakistanis launched an all-out assault directed at Chhamb and Akhnur which triggered off the 1965 Indo–Pak War (see 'Indo-Pak War – 1965').

The Capture

Haji Pir remained in Indian hands throughout the war, in spite of numerous counterattacks and intensive fire. Yet, the gains made in this operation were lost on the Tashkent negotiation table when India agreed to return Haji Pir and other territory captured during the 1965 War. The vital pass went back to Pakistan, and unfortunately is held by them even today. But the story of its audacious capture, and of the gallant men who engineered it, is one of the hallmarks of India's military history.

30

01-22 September 1965
BLOODY SEPTEMBER

Indo-Pak War 1965

PART I: THE LAND WAR

It was the year 1965. The Indian Army was recouping after a brutal defeat in the 1962 Indo-China War and was in the process of re-organization. Nehru had died in 1964 and the nation was in political turbulence. On the other hand, Pakistan was on an upswing. The army under General Ayub Khan had taken over in a military coup and was in full control of the nation. It had received brand new Patton tanks, artillery guns and Sabre jets from America and was assured of Chinese support. The time seemed right for it to take on a weakened India and seize Kashmir – which it had claimed since Partition – by force.

The 1965 Indo-Pak War is officially said to have lasted for 21 days – from 01 Sep to 22 Sep 1965. In actuality, it began in April 1965 when the Pakistani army began a series of raids in the arid Rann of Kutch claiming the border areas. In a series of bitter skirmishes, they got the better of their Indian counterparts and seized many border posts, including the fort of Kunjarkot. These clashes ended only in end of July when the United Nations brokered a ceasefire and called for the two sides to return to their original positions.

Emboldened by what they perceived as a victory, Pakistan now launched the second phase of their plan called OP GIBRALTER. From July to August, they sent over 20,000 tribals and soldiers in civilian clothing into Kashmir hoping to incite the population to revolt. The infiltrators caused considerable damage, ambushing convoys, blowing up bridges and installations, but the Kashmiri population did not support them and most of the infiltrators were captured or killed. Then, in an unexpected move, the Indian army attacked across the Line of Control to capture the areas through which the infiltrators were pushed in – which included the vital passes of Haji Pir and Kishenganga. The capture of Haji Pir was a feat of great courage and endurance and was a severe blow to the Pakistanis. (see 'Haji Pir – Captured on Ground, Lost on the Table').

Seeing their plans go awry, the Pakistanis now embarked on a full-fledged military offensive directed towards Akhnur in the Jammu sector. This offensive would cut off Kashmir from the rest of the nation and enable Pakistan to take it by military force. Launched on 01 Sep 65, the offensive made major inroads and was within an ace of victory when India launched its own offensive in Punjab forcing the Pakistanis to recoil to meet this new, unexpected threat.

Pakistani Commanders during the Offensive. Third from left is Major Parvez Musharaff

On 06 September, India launched two major offensives in Punjab – with 11 Corps in the South towards Lahore and with the newly raised 1 Corps in the direction of Sialkot further North. This unexpected offensive took the Pakistanis by surprise, more so since they did not expect the Indian '*banias*' to act so boldly and violently. Both offensives made good progress initially. The Indian thrust towards Lahore moved in three prongs and succeeded in crossing the Ichhogil Canal, the British era canal which was the last obstacle on the way to Lahore. Indian troops even reached as far as Bata Nagar, a suburb of Lahore and the US consulate ordered its staff to evacuate from the city. Yet what could have been a major success was not exploited as the Indian troops did not follow up, and rather pulled back across the canal. Then the Pakistanis launched their own offensive.

Pakistan's 1 Armoured Division, with their brand new Patton and Chaffee tanks, had been in the area of Lahore when the Indian attack came and now launched their own offensive towards Indian Punjab. They brushed aside the Indian defenses, captured the township of Khem Karan and began moving inwards hoping to reach the line of the Beas River. A resolute Indian defence delayed them and they were halted in area appropriately named as *Asal Uttar* or right response. Here the Indians had breached the canals and distributaries. The waters seeping out turned the area into a boggy marsh and its tanks were bogged down in the flooded fields. Indian tanks and anti-tank jeeps took a huge toll on the enemy and 97 tanks – most of them in mint condition – were captured or destroyed. Many of them adorn war memorials even today. The Pakistani offensive came to a halt and even the GOC of the division was killed along with most of his staff.

Indian Flag across the Ichhogil Canal

Pak tank burning on the road to Amritsar

The Indian offensive towards Sialkot saw the greatest tank battle in the sub-continent with 100 Indian and 120 Pakistani tanks clashing in the battles of Phillaura and Chawinda. In spite of this titanic clash of arms, neither side could attain its aim and it was at best a stalemate. Finally, on 22 September 1965, after 21 days of intense fighting, a UN-sponsored ceasefire came into being and the guns fell silent, though the sporadic sounds of fire continued for weeks after the ceasefire.

Both India and Pakistan claim victory in the war. Pakistan celebrates 01 September as 'Defence of Pakistan' Day and India commemorates its victory in the war. Yet, neither side really attained their military objectives. India lost 2902 soldiers in the war – the Pakistanis 3800. Over 150 Indian tanks were damaged or destroyed with 220 Pakistani ones. In the air war, the Pakistanis did hold an edge especially in the early days of the war. Yet in the end, India held on to 1528 square kilometers of Prime territory, while Pakistan claimed 544 kilometers, the notable successes being Haji Pir Pass by India and Khem Karan by Pakistan. Both would be returned after the Tashkent Agreement and the two sides would go back to the original positions.

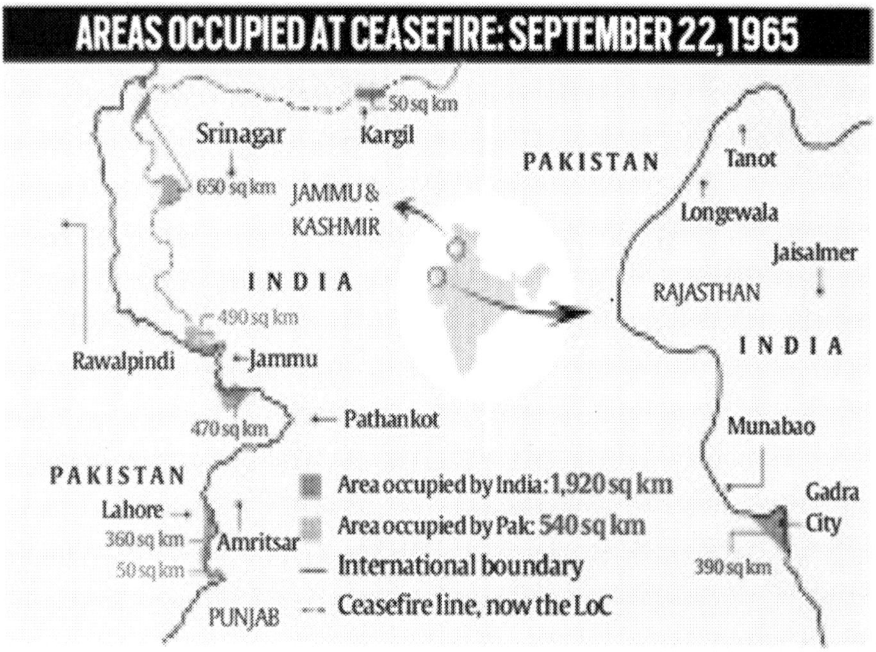

So who really won? I would say, the only true victor was the Indian soldier.

PART II: THE AIR WAR

The 1965 Indo-Pak war started in April with Pak forays in the Rann of Kutch, duly followed up by its incursion in August in J&K as part of the well-conceived Operation Gibraltar Initially the air forces were out of the fray, primarily to avoid escalation. The IAF only came into action on 01 Sep 65 when Pakistan forces launched their offensive in the Jammu sector from Chhamb-Jaurian.

At this critical juncture, Indian Government permitted the use of air force to contain the advancing Pakistan armour in the Jaurian sector on the insistence of its Army and Air Chiefs. Raring to go, the Indian Air Force (IAF) immediately flew its first sortie, in close air support of its ground forces, against Pak ground forces advancing in Chhamb on 01 Sep. When India launched its own offensive inside Pakistani Punjab on 06 Sep, the scale of both the air and the ground war intensified.

On 06 Sep evening, Pakistan Air Force (PAF) attacked Pathankot, Adampur and Halwara airbases in a pre-emptive strike. This caught the IAF off guard and it lost 11 aircraft on the ground at Pathankot. Indian fighters intercepted the Pak aircrafts attacking Adampur and Halwara and both sides lost two aircraft apiece in the first air-to-air operation of the war. The PAF intensified its operations by attacking Kalaikunda airbase in West Bengal on the morning of 07 Sep and again managed to destroy 09 aircrafts on the ground. The loss of precious aircraft on the ground was a huge setback to the IAF at the outset of the war, and the initial victories definitely went to the PAF.

This jolted the Indian Government and it ordered the IAF to undertake air offensive with a caveat of allowing air strikes only inside West Pakistan. It did not permit the IAF to take any offensive action inside East Pakistan. When the air forces joined the war, quantitatively, the scales were in India's favor. However, in terms of quality, Pakistan had a clear edge with its F-86 Sabre jets, F-104 Star fighters and B-57 Martin Canberra, along with better weaponry and radars, in its inventory. The recently inducted Sidewinder missiles in the PAF were also far superior to the cannons mounted on Indian fighter and gave them an advantage of both range and accuracy. Although the Government had authorized the IAF 35 combat squadrons in 1963, it had only 25 combat squadrons as against 11 squadrons of PAF when it joined the war. Of these, it retained over 10 squadrons in the Eastern and Central sectors to ward off the threat from China and East Pakistan. At the start of the war, IAF had 466 combat aircrafts against 203 of PAF, but only 290 were available for the air war in the west. The first-generation subsonic fighters like Vampire and second-generation transonic fighters Mystere, Hawker Hunters and Folland Gnats were a generation behind the Sabres and Star fighters and it is to the credit of the gallant pilots that they still held their own.

After the success of its pre-emptive strikes, Pak planned to destroy the IAF aircrafts on the ground with a bold commando strike by their Special Service Group (SSG). On 06 Sep, they para-dropped 180 commandos in Punjab to launch raids on the bases of Halwara, Adampur and Pathankot. The ill-conceived operation was a disaster. The Indian forces and civil population killed or captured all of them and only 15 of them could make it back to Pakistan. The IAF bounced back with vigor and vengeance to bombard PAF bases at Sargodha and Chaklala immediately and then continued to target more airbases for the rest of the war that included Akwal, Chak Jhumra and Risalwala. Their deepest strikes went against Peshawar and Kohat airbases on the night of 13/14 Sep. Incidentally, both air forces were operating their bombing missions during hours of darkness to take advantage of lack of night interception capability of their fighter aircrafts. Meanwhile, the aerial combat was slowly but surely taking a toll on the PAF where their advanced Sabres and Starfighter jets were slowly losing their initial edge to India's Gnats and Hunters. Though much slower than the Sabre, the Gnat's small size and maneuverability enabled it to close in on the enemy and Pakistani pilots confided that it was 'difficult to see'. Yet, the IAF suffered a major embarrassment when one of its Gnats mistakenly landed on a Pakistani airstrip and was captured as a war trophy.

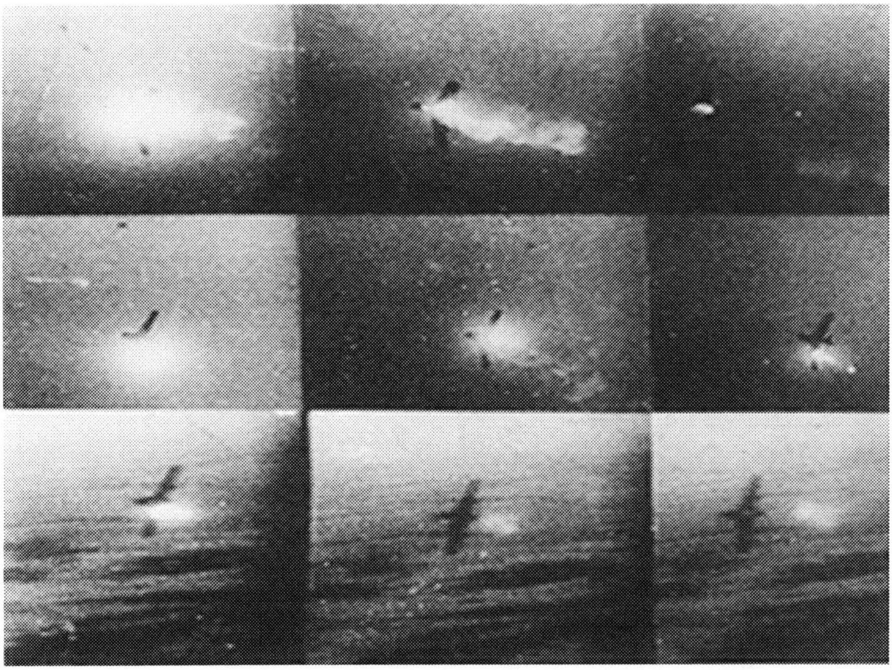

Cine gun camera shots showing a PAF Sabre Jet shot down in aerial combat by an IAF Gnat

As the war progressed, the IAF slowly began gaining the upper hand. The tempo of air operations was gradually increasing and its quantitative superiority was coming into play when the ceasefire was called on 22 Sep. After its initial losses, Indian pilots acquitted themselves admirably, especially in air-to-air combat and received four Mahavir Chakras (India's second highest gallantry award) and 43 Vir Chakras. Also, 23 years later, another Mahavir Chakra was awarded to Squadron Leader AB Devayya, when a British writer, John Fricker, commissioned by PAF, unearthed his heroic tale of how he used his antiquated Mystere fighter against a F-104 Star fighter, and in spite of his aircraft being badly damaged still managed to down the enemy. The two Keelor brothers, Trevor and Denzil, became synonymous with the skill of IAF pilots, when both received Vir Chakras. The credit of the first aerial combat victory of the war went to former while the latter shot down two aircraft in an aerial combat above the Sialkot sector.

The IAF flew 3,937 sorties against 2,364 sorties by PAF and lost 14 aircrafts in aerial combat and 11 to enemy air-defence artillery fire, whereas PAF suffered losses of 18 aircrafts in aerial combat and 25 aircrafts to Indian air-defence artillery fire. Moreover, IAF suffered a loss of 53 aircrafts (36 destroyed and 17 damaged) on ground due to enemy air attacks. The IAF Chief Air Marshal Arjan Singh was widely credited for scripting its success and went on to become the only Field Marshal of the Air Force. The PAF too had their heroes including Squadron Leader M M Alam, credited with shooting down five Indian aircraft, and Pakistani pilots often boasted of how they held off a larger IAF and came out even. Yet, in view of the casualties both sides suffered – both on the ground and in air-to-air combat – their performance was best gauged by John Fricker - the official historian of the PAF – who stated, "The IAF lost the battle on the ground, but won it in the air".

31

07 September 1967
GIVING THE CHINESE A BLOODY NOSE AT NATHU LA

Battles of Nathu La and Cho La

The Chinese are fond of recalling the 'lessons' of the 1962 Indo-China War (see 'Debacle in the High Himalayas'). Perhaps they themselves have forgotten the lessons of 1967.

In September 1967, Indian and Chinese troops stood at heights of 14,200 feet at Nathu La, a strategic pass on the old Gangtok–Lhasa trade route on the Sikkim-Tibet border. Here the opposing troops were just 30 meters away from each other – the closest at any point along the entire 3488-km-long disputed border. This area had seen no fighting during the 1962 war but would erupt in the most violent confrontation between Indian and Chinese troops since the war.

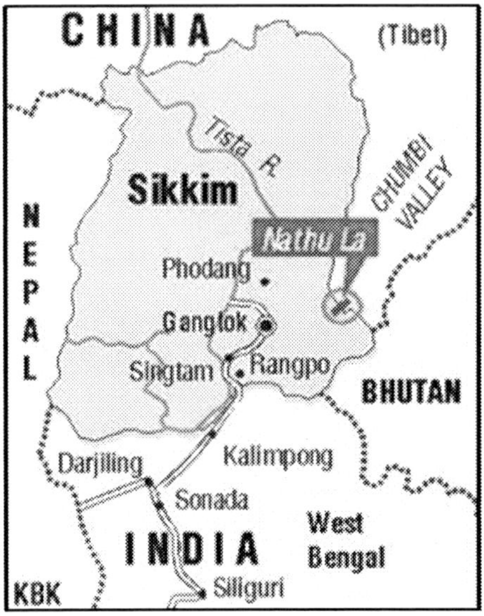

Nathu La

The story actually began in 1965 when at the height of the 1965 Indo-Pak, China issued an ultimatum to India to vacate the posts at Nathu La and Jalep La in the Sikkim sector. Inexplicably, Jalep La was vacated, but at Nathu La, General Sagat Singh, commanding 17 Infantry Division (the Black Cat Division), refused to budge, stating that the post was strategically important. He was supported in his decision, by his Corps Commander Lt Gen J S Aurora and the Eastern Command Commander Gen Sam Manekshaw. The triumvirate would go on to become the architects of the 1971 Indo-Pak War just a few years later. In 1965, after India refused to vacate the post, the Chinese made their usual threatening noises and even advanced upto the border line with fixed bayonets. But the Indians refused to back down and the Chinese withdrew. Their bluff had been called.

Throughout the next two years, the Chinese continued their ploys. Intrusions across the border became frequent; incursions and skirmishes increased. The Chinese installed 27 loudspeakers which sent a non-stop barrage of propaganda across the border and the Indians responded in kind. In August

1967, Gen Sagat decided to mark the border with a three-layer barbed wire fence. Work began on 20 August and though the Chinese protested the laying of the wire and made threatening actions, they did not cross.

On 07 September, the first scuffle took place. The engineers of 70 Field Company were upgrading the fence to a concertina coil, when around 100 Chinese came across asking them to stop. 2 GRENADIERS was deployed in the area of Nathu La and their troops came out. A scuffle broke out in which the tough Jats got the better of their Chinese opponents. The Chinese withdrew and began belting stones, to which the Indians responded in kind. Gen Sagat now passed instructions that the fence was to be completed by 11 September, a day before he was to depart on leave.

That morning of 11 September was bright and sunny, without the fog that usually enveloped the high mountain pass. 70 Field Platoon had commenced work at 05 am as usual. With them was a company of 18 RAJPUT who had been tasked for their protection. 2 GRENADIERS held the positions along the pass. Artillery officers were also deployed on the high dominating positions of Sebu La and Camel's Back. From their positions, the Indians had excellent observation and fields of fire, an advantage denied to their adversaries, and that would prove crucial. True to form, at around 08 am as work was in progress, a Chinese party accompanied by the Political Commissar approached and ordered them to stop work. Lt Col Rai, the Commanding Officer of 2 GRENADIERS came down himself along with his commando platoon and refused. In the altercation that followed, the Political Commissar was roughed up and hurled to the ground. The Chinese withdrew threatening revenge and after a while wire laying resumed.

Minutes later, a shrill whistle from the Chinese positions broke the sounds of hammering pickets. It was followed almost immediately by the staccato of machine gun fire, and murderous fire raked the ground. The jawans of 70 Field Company and 18 RAJPUT were exposed with no cover and mowed down with heavy casualties. Lt Col Rai, who was out in the open, was wounded as well. (He would later be awarded a Mahavir Chakra for his role.) Seeing their Commanding Officer fall, two officers, Capt Dagar of 2 GRENADIERS and Major Harbhajan of 18 RAJPUT, rallied their men and charged the Chinese positions. They succeeded in closing in with the enemy and even bayoneted a few, but were caught in a hail of fire and killed. Major Harbhajan would receive a MVC and Capt Dagar, a Vir Chakra – both posthumously.

Indian troops now began fire from their positions, but the Chinese were in well-fortified bunkers and small-arms fire had little effect. Chinese artillery commenced firing as well, but at Nathu La they were deployed in lower positions and lacked observation. Their fire proved ineffective. Indian artillery observers on the high grounds of Sebu La and Camel's Back now directed effective artillery fire on Chinese positions. We had the advantage of dominating them from high ground and had clear observation of their positions. Accurate artillery fire could thus be brought down on their positions, which continued for over three nights and days, destroying virtually every Chinese bunker and killing over 300 of their troops.

Perhaps the Chinese did not expect this kind of response. On 14 September, they threatened to call in the Air Force, but it was an idle bluff. On 15 September, an uneasy ceasefire was declared and dead of both sides were retrieved. General Manekshaw, Gen Aurora and Gen Sagat were present during this grim exchange. A wounded soldier, still alive after being exposed for four days in the open was also recovered, in what was nothing short of a miracle.

War Memorial at Nathu La

Nathu La was a bloody nose for the Chinese and an indicator that the Indian Army they faced now was different from the Army of 1962. But just

20 days later, on 01 October, another face off took place at Cho La, a pass just nine kilometers to the north. A newly formed unit 7/11 Gurkha Rifles had been inducted in the area and was deployed opposite the Chinese positions just 200 meters across. As the unit was commencing its deployment, the Chinese commander of the post opposite approached the forward platoon and asked them to withdraw. Tensions were still high after Nathu La and as the Commanders got engaged in a heated altercation, the Chinese bayoneted Naib Subedar Gyan Bahadur Limbu, the Indian platoon commander. Seeing their Commander fall, the Gorkhas attacked with open kukris, chopping off the arms of the attacker. The situation escalated into a shooting match, and as it escalated, the Indians did not back down. Rather, they attacked the Chinese positions with two battalions 7/11 Gurkha and 10 JAK RIF pushing them almost three kilometers back to a feature called Kam Barracks. The situation stabilized after three days, but the Indians did not withdraw from the positions they occupied and even today, that is the line of the defensive positions.

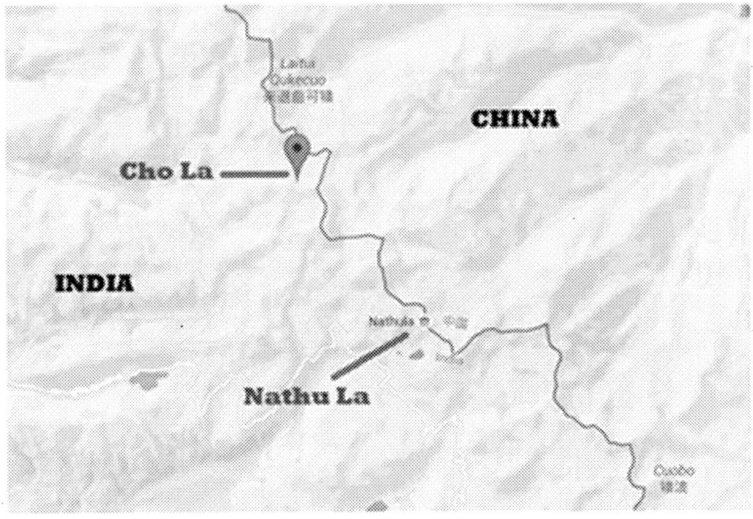

Area of Operations of Cho La and Nathu La

After the two bloody skirmishes at Nathu La and Cho La, the border in that sector has remained peaceful thereafter, till the Doklam stand-off in 2017. That encounter claimed over 300 Chinese soldiers and 65 Indian lives. In comparison, 722 Chinese and over 3500 Indians were killed in the 1962 War. To some extent the ghosts of 1962, if not fully exorcised, were at least put to rest and the specter of Chinese superiority expelled.

32

21 November 1971
THE OPENING SALVOES

Land and Air Battle at Garibpur

Although the 1971 Indo-Pak War officially began on 03 Dec (see 'Creating a Nation in 13 Days'), hostilities had erupted all along the India–Bangladesh (then East Pakistan) border much earlier. Clashes between Indian and Pakistani troops were increasing through all of October and November. Indian troops increasingly accompanied the *Mukti Bahini* in cross-border raids and both sides were preparing for a war that was now inevitable. Yet, the first major confrontation took place on 20-21 November in a major land and air encounter that saw an Indian battalion get the better of a Pakistani brigade and saw three Sabre jets shot out of the skies.

Garibpur lay inside the Boyra Salient, a finger of land that protruded from East Pakistan into India. It had been used by the Pakistanis to launch artillery fire and raids. To prevent the Pakistanis from using the salient, and also to improve our position for the coming offensive inside East Pakistan, 14 PUNJAB (Nabha Akal) along with C Squadron of 45 Cavalry was tasked to capture Garibpur in end of November 1971.

The attack was to be a silent attack, with the battalion moving in stealthily to maintain surprise. On the night of 20 November, a patrol of 14 PUNJAB was sent ahead of the main body to reconnoiter the area. Unfortunately, the patrol clashed with an enemy patrol and now the enemy was alerted of the presence of Indian troops and surprise was lost. Their Commanding Officer Lt Col R K Singh (later Brigadier) ordered his battalion to move forwards feverishly toward their objective and by 3 am on 21 November, the four companies of 14 PUNJAB, along with the squadron of PT 76 tanks, had captured the enemy locations at Garibpur after a fierce fight. The battalion now began readjusting its positions and braced for the enemy counter-attack which they knew was coming.

Pak soldiers in their defences

The Pakistanis reacted violently. An entire brigade (107 Infantry Brigade based at Jessore) along with a 3 Independent Armoured Squadron with Chafee tanks moved down from Jessore, nine kilometers to the North towards Garibpur. Fortunately, a patrol under Capt G S Gill, along with an artillery observer, had been sent ahead and in the cold and foggy morning, his patrol heard the sounds of tanks roaring down the road. The detailed information of the coming counterattack was passed on to the battalion enabling them to adjust themselves to face the impending attack.

The first attack with tanks and Infantry came in at 6 am. The Indian PT 76s, the lightly armed amphibious tanks were much inferior to the Chafees, but they were skillfully deployed and took a heavy toll on the enemy. Squadron Commander Major D S Narang's tank was hit, but the rest of the squadron held firm. 14 PUNJAB held on in spite of three consecutive attacks, the last of which came to within 25 yards of their positions before being beaten back. When the dust cleared and the fog lifted at around 9 am, 11 destroyed Pakistani tanks and scores of dead infantry lay ahead of the 14 PUNJAB positions for the loss of six tanks and 40 of the defenders.

Tank crews being briefed before the battle

One battalion had succeeded in beating back a brigade, but there was more to come. Two airstrikes, with four Sabres each, swooped down around 10 am, strafing the defences and destroying a tank and killing some troops. But NABHA AKAL held on. At 2.30 in the afternoon, three Sabres roared in for another attack only to be intercepted by four Gnats – the diminutive

'Sabre Slayers'. The Sabres had launched one attack and were commencing the dive for the second attack when the Gnats, led by Flt Lt Roy Andrew Massey, struck. Two Sabres were caught at their most vulnerable – when they were pulling out of a dive – and engaged with the 20-mm cannon fire from the Gnats flown by Flt Lt Ganapathy and Flying Officer Donald Lazarus. Both Pakistani aircraft were hit, but both their pilots ejected in time and were later taken prisoner. The third Sabre was engaged by Flt Lt Massey at 700 yards with a burst of cannon fire that hit its port wing. Badly damaged, the Sabre still managed to limp back to its airfield, due to some skillful flying by the pilot.

Sabre kill viewed from the gun camera of a Gnat

The dogfight viewed from the ground by the cheering troops and captured by the gun cameras of the Gnats marked the first aerial encounter of the war. Garibpur was a victory – a decisive one at that – both on the ground and in the air. A battalion had beaten back a Brigade, a flight of Sabres were shot down with no damage to our own aircraft and Garibpur itself was captured in just one night of battle. It would make the offensive into Bangladesh so much easier and set the trend for the coming battles.

There was a footnote. One of the downed pilots Flt Lt Parvaiz Mehdi Qureshi went on to become the Chief of Air Staff of the Pakistan Air Force in 1996. Donald Lazarus, the man who shot him down, sent him a congratulatory letter. To his surprise, he received a reply, thanking him for his wishes and complimenting him for the 'good fight' on 21 November 1971. Perhaps, the Age of Chivalry is not yet dead.

33

3-16 December 1971
CREATING A NATION IN 13 DAYS

1971 Indo-Pak War

The Tribune

BANGLA DESH FREED

UNCONDITIONAL SURRENDER BY PAK TROOPS

INDIA ORDERS UNILATERAL CEASE-FIRE

PART I: THE LAND WAR

Background to War

At 5.45 pm on 03 December 1971, Pakistani fighter aircraft swooped down Indian skies and launched a series of pre-emptive attacks on the Indian airfields of Ambala, Srinagar, Avantipur, Pathankot, Uttarlai and Jodhpur hoping to destroy Indian aircraft on ground and win a decisive victory at the onset of the coming war. They failed. Not a single Indian aircraft was lost on the ground and the IAF responded by launching a series of retaliatory attacks inside Pakistan. The same day, Pakistani troops launched an offensive in the Chamb and Poonch sectors of Kashmir, and the next day Indian troops entered East Pakistan. The third Indo-Pak war had begun.

The roots to the war go back to the flawed two-nation theory that created two wings of Pakistan separated by 2500 kilometers of Indian territory. East and West Pakistan were not only geographically separated from each other. Bound only by religion, the Bengalis of East Pakistan and the Punjabis of the West were also culturally, ethnically and politically different from each other. The Bengalis were considered inferior to their Punjabi and Pathan brethren of the West and the simmering discontent of East Pakistanis was rising after years of exploitation. Then in 1970, the East Pakistani political party, the Awami League under Sheikh Mujibur Rehman, won the General Elections in Pakistan. It meant that for the first time, an East Pakistani would become President of the country.

Atrocities by Pak Army

The flood of Refugees

Yet, rather than accepting the result, the elections were annulled, martial law was imposed and Shiekh Mujibur Rehman placed under arrest. East Pakistanis hit the streets in violent protest, and the Pakistani government ordered a crackdown. Additional troops were flown in, and the uprising was put down brutally. The carnage that the Pakistani army wreaked caused over 300,000 casualties and sent a flood of refugees – over 7 million of them – pouring into India. Alarmed at the situation on its Eastern border and concerned with the influx of refugees, Mrs Indira Gandhi ordered the Army Chief Gen Sam Manekshaw to 'Go into East Pakistan' in April 1970.

Mrs Gandhi and General Manekshaw

In what is regarded as one of the most professional and most courageous military decisions in Indian history, General Manekshaw refused to launch an immediate attack. Instead he asked for time till December when the armed forces would be fully ready, the Chinese passes closed and the weather conditions better for offensive operations. Mrs Gandhi agreed, and the military began preparations for a war that was soon coming. The Bengali militia, the Mukti Bahini were trained and built up, and Indian forces began operating with them. Both sides were preparing and skirmishes occurred with increasing frequency. On 22 November, a major battle took place at Garibpur in East Pakistan, on 22 November involving tanks, artillery and even fighter jets of both sides. The Indian success in that encounter set the tone for the coming battles (see 'The Opening Salvoes: Land and Air Battle at Garibpur'). The situation erupted on 03 December with Pakistan's pre-emptive attack in the West. It gave just the excuse for the Indian Army to enter East Pakistan the next day and go on to create a nation.

The Defeat of Pakistan's Eastern Command

The Indian Army moved into East Pakistan in a four-pronged thrust. 2 Corps with two divisions (4 and 9 Divisions and 50 Para Brigade) advanced from the South West; 33 Corps (30 Division and 71 Brigade) from the North West; 101 Communication Zone with two brigades moved in from the North

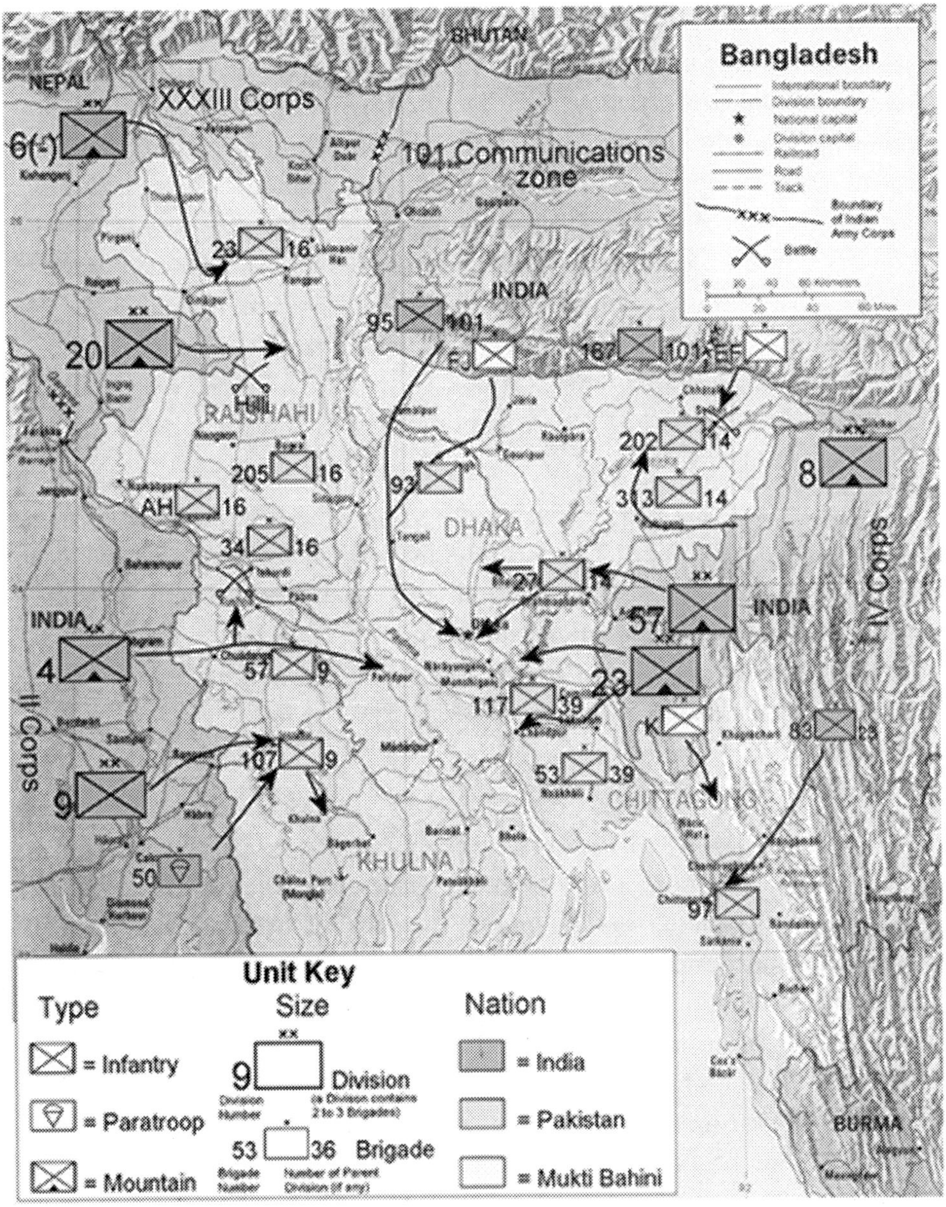

The Plan of Attack

and the main thrust with 4 Corps moved inwards from the East with three divisions (8, 57 and 23 Divisions).

It would not be a cakewalk. General A K Niazi, the General Officer Commanding in Chief, of the Pakistani Eastern Command had almost four and a half divisions, 25,000 para military forces, five squadrons of Chaffee tanks, and around 20 F-86 Sabre jet fighters to contest the Indians. He also had the advantage of geography. The terrain was marshy and crisscrossed with rivers making advance difficult. He chose to deploy his forces in the small towns along the approaches. Each town – Jessore, Jhenida, Bogra, Rangpur, Hilli, Jamalpur, Sylhet, Comilla and Chittagong to name a few – was virtually converted into a fortress and would have to be reduced if the Indian were to advance. Another line of fortresses lay deeper in the second tier. In the center was the capital of Dacca, secure in a bowl behind the Yamuna and Meghna rivers where lay his headquarters. It was felt that if the fortresses delayed the Indians long enough, the Chinese and the US would intervene. All they had to do was hold.

The Indian plan was to advance deep, and capture enough territory to declare Bangladesh. They advanced rapidly using cycles, rickshaws, bullock carts and boats and even moved tanks in the swampy land. They were aided by the Mukti Bahini, who guided and provided invaluable local information. The fortresses of Jessore, Hilli, Bogra, Mymensingh, were captured after fierce battles. But whenever a fortress could not be captured, it was merely bypassed, and the Indian troops moved deeper leaving a small force to contain it. This helped cut off many Pakistani troops who were now unable to withdraw.

In 10 days, the Indian thrust lines moved deeper into East Pakistan. Helicopters and paratroopers were used to insert troops in the rear to cut off retreating Pakistani soldiers and prevent them falling back to Dacca. 2 PARA landed at Tangail and captured a bridge on the Lohaganj River. The para drop which was seen from Dacca first caused jubilation, thinking that the Chinese or American paratroopers had arrived to save them. This jubilation changed to consternation when they realized that Indian paratroopers were behind their positions. A major helicopter-borne operation was launched that ferried one battalion, 4/5 Gurkha Rifles, behind enemy lines to hold a position on the Surma River and cut off Pakistani troops in the town of Sylhet. Although only two companies were initially dropped, BBC reported that an entire Indian brigade had been helidropped and this false news was built up by the Indians as well. Although over a Brigade of Pakistani troops were in Sylhet (built up to over two brigades as withdrawing troops fell into the town), they did not attack the small heli-borne force and the small force of less than a battalion contained the two brigades in Sylhet till its eventual surrender.

The Helidrop at Sylhet

Paradrop at Tangail

Although the US Seventh Fleet led by the aircraft carrier 'USS ENTERPRISE' steamed into the Bay of Bengal, the US and Chinese made no serious attempt to save the Pakistanis. The Indians reached the Meghna River on 12 December and were now within striking distance of Dacca. On 14 December, a conference was held at Government House, Dacca, attended by the Governor, Gen Niazi and senior officials. The information was conveyed by the Mukti Bahini and a flight of two MIG 21s, using tourist maps to guide them to their targets, took off and rocketed the building just as the meeting was underway. This was the last straw that broke Pakistani morale. The Governor resigned, and the next day, Niazi agreed to surrender after being assured of the safety of his troops. The next day, on 16 December at 4.31 pm in Dacca Race Course, Gen Niazi and Gen Aurora signed the Instrument of Surrender in front of a million strong crowd chanting 'Joi Bangla.' A total of 93,000 Pakistani troops – the largest haul of prisoners since World War II – laid down their arms. The war in the East was over. A new nation had been created.

The Surrender

Pak Postage Stamp

Actions in the Western front continued for one more day. Pakistan had hoped to attain gains in the Western theater but here too it lost territory and equipment. Its offensive in this sector did not materialize and on 17 December, Mrs Indira Gandhi declared a unilateral ceasefire. At 2000 hours on 17 December, the guns finally fell silent.

This was modern India's most comprehensive victory and attained through close synergy between the Army, Navy and Air Force. Yet, the gains of the battlefield were given away at the bargaining table. In June 1972, during the Shimla Agreement, Mrs Gandhi agreed to release 93,000 Pakistani prisoners without extracting any concessions for a long-term solution to Kashmir. Pakistan was cut to size, but the problem of Kashmir remained unresolved and continued to haunt the sub-continent for decades thereafter.

PART II: THE AIR WAR

One of the reasons for the complete victory attained in 1971 was the synergy attained between ground, air and naval forces. The 1965 War was largely ground based with the naval not playing any significant role and the Air Force still trying to find their wings. The Navy and Air Force truly came into their own in the 71 War.

The war commenced with a pre-emptive attack by the Pakistani Air Force on Indian airfields at 1630 hours on 03 December 71. But the air war had actually commenced much earlier when 3 Pakistani Sabres were shot down by 4 Indian Gnats over Boyra in East Pakistan (see 'The Opening Salvoes: Land and Air Battle at Garibpur'). No Indian aircraft was destroyed in the Pakistani strike, but retaliation was swift. The next day itself, the airfields of Masroor, Rafique, Sargodha, Mianwal, Murid in the West and Chittagong, Dacca, Jessore and Tezgaon in the East were attacked by Indian fighter bombers.

At that time, the IAF had 34 combat squadrons (including three antiquated Canberra and one An-12 transports) of which 10 were in the East, 4 kept as reserve for defence of important cities, and 20 allotted to the West. The Pakistanis had 19 Squadrons of which 18 were in the West, and a F-86 Sabre squadron with 20 aircraft in the East. The Pakistani strength was boosted with the arrival of F-104 Starfighters, Mirage IIIs and F-86 from Jordan and Chinese F-6 fighters. Technologically, their aircraft had an edge, especially when armed with the lethal US supplied Sidewinder air-to-air missiles. Though India had a clear superiority in the East, it had just a 1:1.2 superiority in the West.

The IAF focused largely on strike operations in the initials days of the war, striking airfields, railway yards, tank formations, dockyards and infrastructure in a continual series of strikes both in the East and the West. In the East, PAF operations virtually came to a halt on 06 December itself when the IAF attacked the airfields of Tezgaon (near Dacca) and Kurmitla, and badly cratered the runway. Three Sabres were shot down as they rushed upwards to intercept the attacking Indians. Their pilots bailed out, but were captured by vengeful Bangladeshis and brutally beaten to death. Two Hunters were also lost, but from that day onwards, the IAF had complete control of East Pakistani skies and conducted raids with impunity.

Attack on Pak Railyard

In the West, the IAF attained its finest hour when Hunters from Jaisalmer decimated a complete Pakistani Armoured Regiment and blunted their thrust at Longewala (see 'Breakfast at Longewala'). The IAF also attacked Karachi and set ablaze the oil tanks in the harbor, in conjunction with the naval raid on Karachi on 04 Dec 71 (see 'Raid on Karachi') causing 'the biggest blaze in South Asia'. Most IAF sorties were directed at ground targets, in contrast to the PAF which focused largely on air interdiction operations. When the PAF did appear to contest Indian fighters, they invariably put up a gallant fight. As the tempo of operations increased, so did the successes. As the war progressed, the IAF maintained its impressive sortie rate, while the PAF sortie generation reduced (perhaps due to lack of spares and trained technicians). Over 4,000 sorties were flown in the West and 1978 in the East as the IAF gained control of the skies.

The newly acquired MIG-21 fighters proved their worth, both in the ground attack and the air superiority role. When confronted with PAF F-104 Starfighters (which had been developed by the US as a counter to the MIGs), they emerged victories in all four dog fights between the two. In fact Pakistan lost 9 of the 20 Starfighters it held, earning it the dubious sobriquet 'widow-maker'. Pakistani Sabres and Indian Gnats were perhaps evenly matched, but Indian Hunters and Sukhoi 7 fighter-bombers suffered disproportionately high casualties because of the high risks the young pilots took to press home their attacks.

F-104 Starfighters

MIG-21s

The last two days of the War were perhaps the best. On the morning of 14 December, a message was received in Eastern Air Command of a high-level meeting in the Governor's House at Dacca. Within 15 minutes, a flight of four MIG-21s, using only tourist maps for guidance, were airborne and bombed the Governor's bungalow with 57-mm rockets, ripping out the roof and shattering Pakistani morale completely. The Governor resigned immediately and two days later, the Pakistani Eastern Command surrendered. The 13 surviving Sabres of the Eastern Squadron were damaged by their own crew, but later repaired and became the foundation of the newly raised Bangladesh Air force. 14 December also saw a momentous action in the Western theater. Flight Lieutenant Nirmaljit Singh Sekhon serving with No 18 Squadron 'The Flying Bullets' was on Operational Readiness Platform at Srinagar Airfield, when it was attacked by a flight of four Sabres. Even as the bombs were falling on the airfield, the Flight Leader Flt Lt Ghuman and Sekhon took off. Flt Lt Ghuman lost contact soon after take-off and Sekhon was left to engage the enemy on his own. Making a tight turn, Sekhon plunged into the enemy formation, which were reforming after their first bombing run and shot down a Sabre with his 30-mm cannon at ranges of just 350-400 yards. He engaged the other firing at long ranges and damaged it badly, leaving it to limp away to its home base, trailing black smoke. Sekhon's aircraft was now bounced by two other Sabres who were flying overhead on Combat Air Patrol for protection of the strike force. He was hit. Advised to return, he banked his aircraft, only for it to flip over abruptly (perhaps the control systems had been damaged). He tried to eject, and his canopy was seeing flying off, but at the low altitude, the parachute did not open. The wreckage of his Gnat fighter was found in the thickly forested hills around Srinagar, but his body was unfortunately never recovered. For his gallantry in saving the airfield and engaging odds of 6:1, he was awarded the Air Force's first (and only) Param Vir Chakra (PVC). Ironically, the Army's first PVC was also earned in defence of Srinagar Airfield by Major Somnath Sharma during the Kashmir war of 1948.

Flt Lt N S Sekhon, PVC and his Gnat

When the war came to an end, the IAF had gained dominance of the skies. But it was at a cost. It lost 56 aircraft, most of them Hunters and Sukhoi-7s. Half the losses were due to anti-aircraft fire and worryingly over 20 percent were from accidents and technical failures. A breakdown of the losses on both sides was as follows:

Combat Aircraft Losses

Description	*Pakistan*	*India*
Air-to-Air	19	19
Ground Fire	15	35
On Ground	29	2
Total	**63**	**56**

But the numbers don't tell it all. At the end of the war, the IAF controlled the skies, and the PAF had virtually ceased to operate. After the war, the Air Chief was publically castigated by Prime Minister Bhutto for the failure of the Air Force in protecting Pakistani airspace.

PART III: THE NAVAL WAR

The 1971 War was the finest hour for the Indian Navy. After a low key role in 1965, it had re-armed and modernized and had acquired new ships, submarines and systems. When the inevitable war came about, it set about its role with alacrity in both the Bay of Bengal and the Arabian Sea, helped blockade East and West Pakistan and inflicted crippling damage in both theaters.

The navy tasted blood early. On the first day of the war, it sank Pakistan's long-range diesel submarine PNS Ghazi off the shore of Vishakhapatnam. Ghazi had been sent on a mission on 22 November (much against the advice of experts who were not sure of the efficacy of the boat) to locate and destroy the aircraft carrier, INS Vikrant, an act which they felt would hit Indian morale strongly in the early stages of the war. Ghazi had however lost contact with Pakistan Naval HQs, around the 26th itself, and no news of its passage was available thereafter. It was only on the night of 3/4th December that the debris of Ghazi was detected and six days later, naval divers detected the sunken submarine in the ocean bed, off the coast of Vishakhapatnam.

By naval accounts, PNS Ghazi had been lured into Vishakhapatnam (INS Vikrant had already left the harbor earlier) by fake transmissions. An elaborate deception plan was made in which extra rations were ordered from naval contractors (presumably to feed the large crew of the carrier) and even a fake telegram was sent by a supposed crew member to fool Pakistani naval intelligence into believing that Vikrant was in harbor. INS Rajput, an old, about to be decommissioned anti-submarine destroyer was the decoy emitting transmission pretending to be Vikrant. On 03 Dec, it noted disturbances in the waters off Vishakhapatnam harbor that could only come from a submarine. It fired two depth charges, one of which hit the boat. The next day a large oil slick surfaced and fishermen detected debris that had come up from the Ghazi. By other accounts, the submarine sank when it hit one of the anti-ship mines it had laid itself around the harbor. Whatever be the truth, the loss of a prime submarine was a severe blow to Pakistan.

PNS GHAZI

The navy followed up this success with a resounding raid on Karachi harbor with its newly acquired missile boats on 04 December, and again on 08 December, sinking six ships and setting ablaze the large fuel storage tanks (see 'Raid on Karachi'). That singular success is celebrated as Navy Day even today.

The navy successfully blockaded both Karachi port in the Arabian Sea and Chittagong and Cox's Bazar in the Bay of Bengal. The Pakistan naval garrison in the East consisted of one destroyer (PNS Sylhet), four gunboats (PNS Jessore, Rajshahi, Comilla and Sylhet) and assorted patrol craft. It was a brown water navy, suitable for offshore patrolling and surveillance and it was soon confined to the harbor and mercilessly pounded both by naval gunfire and air attacks of Seahawks and Alize aircraft launched from INS Vikrant. The destroyer PNS Sylhet was badly damaged, and of the four gunboats – one PNS Rajshahi – managed to escape the naval blockade and slip away to Malaysia. It then rejoined the Pak navy after the war. All others were captured and became part of the newly formed Bangladesh Navy. On 16 Dec 1971, when Pakistan's Eastern Command surrendered, Rear Admiral Mohammed

Sharif, the Commander of Pakistan's Eastern Naval Command formally surrendered to Vice Admiral R N Krishna. As he handed over his pistol, he summed up his predicament saying, "We were both deaf and blind. We had no intelligence and the Indian navy and Air Force pounded us night and day."

The successes were marred by the sinking of INS Khukri, a Blackstone class frigate off the coast of Gujarat on 09 December. Khukri was part of 14 Frigate Squadron which had been sent out to intercept Pakistan submarines which were detected operating in the waters.

On 09 December, as the Khukri was operating along with its sister ship INS Kirpan, it was detected by the Pakistani submarine PNS Hangor. Hangor first fired a torpedo at INS Kirpan, but the torpedo missed. Its second torpedo, launched minutes later, hit the Khukri, just below the oil tanks, and it exploded sinking in less than 2 minutes carrying with it 194 crewmen, including its captain, Captain Mahendranath Mulla, who willingly gave up his life jacket to a sailor and went down with his ship. The Hangor fired again at INS Kirpan, but the torpedo missed again, passing just below the ship. Even though Kirpan fired its depth charges, Hangor slipped away undetected and reached Karachi safely four days later.

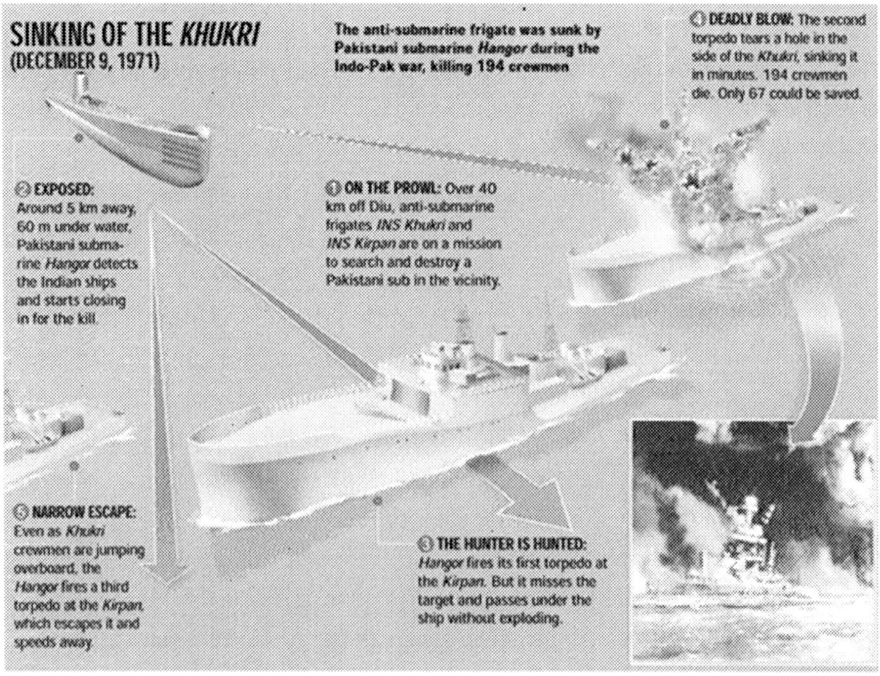

In spite of the loss of Khukri, the navy came up trumps in the war. It enforced an air tight blockade in both the Eastern and Western theaters. It launched attacks on Karachi, Chittagong, and Cox's Bazar and sunk three gunboats, one submarine (PNS Ghazi), two destroyers (PNS Khaibar and PNS Sylhet, with PNS Shah Jahan badly damaged), three patrol craft and eight cargo vessels. Three merchant vessels, 10 smaller craft and 1413 naval personnel were also captured at Chittagong when the Instrument of Surrender was signed. It was one of the most complete naval victories of our times and for the Indian Navy – perhaps its finest hour.

34

04 December 1971
RAID ON KARACHI

The Attack on Karachi

Both during the 1962 Indo-China War and the 1965 Indo-Pak War the navy had not really been brought to bear. In 1971 a modernized navy was itching to go and when war broke out, it played a stellar role. Its finest hour came during the audacious raid on Karachi harbor in the early days of the war.

The audacious raid on Pakistan's largest port was the brain child of the then Naval Chief, Admiral S M Nanda. India had just acquired sleek, fast missile boats from Russia, each equipped with four lethal SS-N-2B Styx ship-to-ship missiles with ranges of over 40 nautical miles (almost 76 kms). These small, fast craft were to be used for a lightning raid on Karachi Harbour. They would strike by night when Pakistani aircraft would be unable to attack, and then speed back.

Three of these Vidyut class missile boats, INS NIPAT, INS NIRGHAT and INS VEER, were to be used. But there was a catch. The small boats did not have the range for the long trip to Karachi and back. Nor did they have long-range radars to pick up distant targets. So two Arnala Class Anti-Submarine Corvettes, INS KILTAN and INS KATCHALL were deployed alongside to tow them towards Karachi and also use their long-range radars to identify and designate targets for them. A tanker INS POSHAK also accompanied the task force, designated as Karachi Task Group under the command of Commander Babru Bhan Yadav of 25 Missile Boat Squadron.

Missile boat firing its deadly Missile

War broke out on 3 December 1971 and next day 'Op Trident' – as this operation was designated – was launched. The strike force had staged forward from Bombay to Okha and moved towards Karachi, with the missile boats towed by the larger Corvettes. The crews had just returned after a yearlong deployment in Russia to take over the boats and were fluent in Russian. All radio transmissions were made in Russian so that even if intercepted would not be understood. (The Pakistanis did intercept the messages, but assumed it must have come from a Russian Task Force operating elsewhere.) At around 2000 hours on 04 December (Pak Standard time), they were in their positions around 80 nautical miles South of Karachi.

Around 10:30 pm, the radar of INS KATCHALL picked up a large target – later identified as PNS KHAIBAR, a Pakistani destroyer – and

INS NIRGHAT was told to engage it. Its first missile hit the right side of the warship and exploded in the boiler room. The second missile was fired minutes later and hit the second boiler room. As per survivor accounts, the KHAIBAR saw the flash of the incoming missile and even tried to engage it with anti-aircraft fire, but was too late. It sank 70 minutes later carrying 222 of its crew with her. Its last message to its fleet HQ was that it had been attacked by aircraft. It also gave its own coordinates wrongly, which hampered the rescue of its crew.

PNS KHAIBAR

PNS SHAH JAHAN

PNS MUHAFIZ

SUNK – SUNK – SUNK

Two other targets were detected at around 11 pm, and INS NIPAT fired two missiles at them. The first missile struck the cargo vessel MV VENUS CHALLENGER, carrying a load of ammunition, and it exploded and sank almost immediately. The other hit the destroyer PNS Shah Jahan, which was badly damaged and forced to be decommissioned later. Simultaneously, INS VEER targeted another ship, the minesweeper PNS MUHAFIZ, which sank even before it could send a distress signal, killing 33 of its crew.

The task force had now closed in on Karachi, and as per plan all three ships were to fire a missile each at Karachi Harbour, targeting its fuel tanks and port facilities. However, at this stage radio contact was lost between them and the Corvettes accompanying them. Also, the Commander mistook the anti-aircraft tracers emanating from Karachi harbor to be enemy aircraft and ordered a withdrawal. He ordered INS NIPAT, which was closest to the harbor, to fire its two remaining missiles towards Karachi port. One of the missiles malfunctioned. The other hit one of the oil tanks in the post. (Though there are conflicting claims about it, the Air Force claims that one of their strike aircraft had hit it earlier in the day.) The force then withdrew, sent the success signal 'ANGAR' to Western Naval Command, and moved back into the safety of Indian waters.

The Pakistanis could not hit any of the ships that participated in the raid, but retaliated with an air strike on Okha port, the next day, which damaged the port facilities and fuel stowage tanks. But fortunately, no naval vessel was in port and damage was kept to a minimal.

Damage at Karachi

The navy followed up the success of Op Trident, with another strike on the night of 8/9 December – codenamed 'Op Python' – to complete the unfinished attack on Karachi. A small force consisting of the missile boat INS VINASH, with two frigates INS TALWAR and INS TRISHUL accompanying it, was tasked for another attack, this time specifically targeting the fuel tanks. On the night of 8 December at around 10 pm (Pak Standard Time), the force approached 12 nautical miles of Karachi and took up firing position. INS VINASH fired all four of its lethal Styx missiles. The first struck the fuel tanks at Kemari Oil Farm in the port. The other hit the fuel tanker SS GULF STAR. A third struck PNS DACCA, a fleet tanker which was damaged beyond repair and the last sank the merchant vessel SS HARMATTAN. With its missiles expended, the force withdrew rapidly to safety.

Damage was extensive. Coupled with the raids by the Air Force on Karachi fuel installations, over 50% of its fuel reserves were lost. Over $3 billion worth of damage was inflicted and Pakistani morale was shattered by this audacious attack into their heartland. The Indian navy had won a major naval victory, with no loss to itself. It had also avenged the raid on Dwarka port by the Pakistan Navy in the 1965 War, (incidentally the Pak Navy celebrates 8 Sep as their own Navy Day) and sank two of the ships – PNS KHAIBAR and SHAH JAHAN – which participated in that attack.

On the return, one of the sailors of the missile boats enthusiastically painted the word 'KILLER' on the now empty missile tubes. The name struck. The missile squadron since then has been called the 'Killer Squadron'. And the day of this victory, 04 Dec, is celebrated as Navy Day throughout the country.

35

04-07 December 1971
"BREAKFAST AT LONGEWALA"

Battle of Longewala

Many of us have seen the Hindi movie "Border" where Sunny Deol and his fearless band of warriors stave off hordes of attacking Pakistanis till the Air Force arrives next morning to deliver the *coup de grace*. That was a highly romanticized rendition of the Battle of Longewala. The truth, though not so dramatic, was equally heroic.

The engagement at Longewala (4-7 Dec 1971) was the first major engagement of the war in the western Sector. 'A' company of 23 PUNJAB, under the command of Major (later Brigadier) Kuldip Singh Chandpuri with

Maj Kuldip Singh Chandpuri – Real and Reel

just 124 men, a jeep-mounted recoilless (RCL) gun, two anti-tank launchers, a section of machine guns and mortars and a four-man team from the BSF occupied a post on a high sand dune in the area Longewala, which stood smack at the Indo-Pak border. Their meager fire was supplanted with the fire support of two field artillery batteries. The post dominated the area around it which, due to the shifting, loose sand, was virtually intractable by vehicles. The post fell in the path of the Pakistani offensive which planned to capture Longewala, go on to Ramgarh and then capture Jaisalmer. "Breakfast at Longewala, Lunch at Ramgarh and Dinner at Jaisalmer" was how the Pakistanis envisaged the operation.

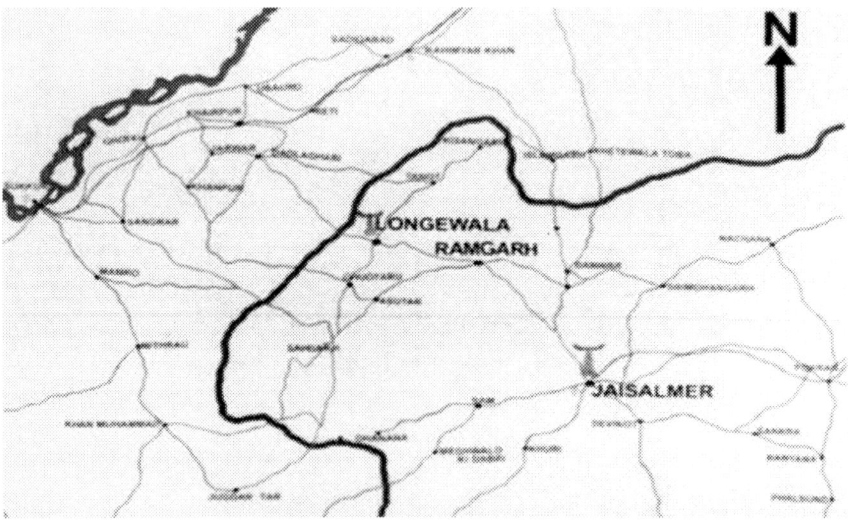

Planned move from Longewala-Ramgarh-Jaisalmer

The Pakistani plan called for one brigade (206 Infantry Brigade) and an armoured regiment (38 CAVALRY based on T-59 tanks) to capture Longewala on the first night and then another force of 51 Infantry Brigade and 22 CAVALRY would move ahead to capture Ramgarh and Jaisalmer. With the overwhelming superiority, it was a workable plan. Where it failed was that it did not have any air support, nor had they conducted reconnaissance of the area. Had they done so, they would have realized that the soft sands could not really sustain the movement of tanks and other vehicles.

War had broken out on 03 December, and the next night, on the night of 4th December, the Pakistani force crossed the border. Fortunately, Maj Chandpuri had sent a patrol under Lt Dharam Vir ahead to get advance information of any enemy movement. Dharam Vir reported a 20-kilometer-long column moving towards Longewala, information which Major Chandpuri reported to his battalion headquarters, located at Sadhwal, 17 kilometers away. He was told that there were no reinforcements that could be sent to him, and he was given the option to stay put and fight or withdraw.

Major Chandpuri decided to stay, and the decision shaped the outcome of the coming battle. His men hastily laid the few anti-tank mines at their disposal, sited their anti-tank and machine guns and braced themselves for the coming assault. The enemy contacted them around midnight and at 12.30 the first assault came in. A massive artillery barrage killed the camels of the BSF detachment, and behind it came tanks followed by infantry in assault formation. The defenders waited till they were around 150-200 meters away and then let loose with all they had. The solitary jeep-mounted RCL and two anti-tank launchers fired, and since they were firing from a height, their rounds were able to hit the thin armour on the tops of the tanks. The tanks were carrying external fuel tanks (to sustain them for the thrust to Jaisalmer) and they caught fire, illuminating the area and providing light for the defenders to engage their targets. As the tanks tried to maneuver to avoid the torrent of fire, many got bogged down in the soft sand, and were hit as they struggled to extricate themselves; 12 tanks were hit and the assault stalled. To make matters worse for them, the leading infantry and tanks ran into a three-strand barbed wire fence around the post, which they presumed marked a minefield. For two hours, the engineers tried to clear the minefield, only to discover that there was no minefield. The defenders had placed the wire around the post to keep away dogs and other animals. That delay would be costly.

The Defenders

The Pakistani Attack

The next attack came around 4 in the morning from another direction. But the tanks and Armoured Personnel Carriers got struck in the soft sands and couldn't make any headway. All night Maj Chandpuri continued to guide fire on the attackers and now at 6, the sun peered over the desert dunes.

The arrival of daylight also saw the arrival of Hawker Hunter fighter bombers. A message had been sent out to the Jaisalmer forward airbase at night itself, but the aircraft did not have night vision devices and could not operate by night. A flight of two Hunters led by Wing Commander Bawa streaked towards their targets, guided on by the airborne Forward Air Controller, Major Atma Singh, who circled overhead in his observation aircraft. Volleys of Matra T-10 rockets and 30-mm cannon raked the targets below. As the tanks struggled desperately to escape, the Hunters had a field day. Flight after flight, two aircraft appeared in relays, attacked, returned to base, refueled and rearmed and then returned to attack again. A total of 40 sorties were launched. The Pakistani Air Force did not appear, nor did the column have effective Air Defence cover. Many Pakistani tank commanders were killed trying to operate the Anti-Aircraft Machine Guns atop the tank turrets, but to no avail. It was, as a pilot described, "a turkey shoot"; 22 tanks were destroyed from the air, an additional 12 from ground fire. Over a hundred vehicles were destroyed as they tried to retreat down the solitary track from Longewala to the border. That same day 20 LANCERS and 17 RAJRIF launched a counterattack on the enemy forcing them to finally abandon their plans and withdraw in disarray.

Hunters taking off for the kill

In terms of casualties, this was one of the most lop-sided operations of the war. Two Indians were killed at the cost of over 200 Pakistani soldiers, 34 tanks and over 100 vehicles. It had another spin-off. Its abject failure put paid to any offensive plans in the West. However, India did not follow the success, and carried the battle into Pakistani territory. Both sides remained static here, till the ceasefire came about on 17 Dec and brought the curtain down on one of the finest feats of arms by the Indian Army.

36

16 December 1971
GALLANTRY ON BOTH SIDES OF THE BASANTAR

Battle of Basantar/Nawapind

Most actions of the 1971 Indo-Pak War were focused on the Eastern Theater (see 'Creating a Nation in 13 Days'). The Western Theater comprising West Pakistan was the scene of notable actions, especially in the Battles of Longewala (see 'Breakfast at Longewala') Chhamb, Hussainiwala and Fazilka, but most significantly in the Shakargarh Bulge. It was here, along the line of the Basantar Nala, that some of the most dramatic events of the war played out.

The Shakargarh Bulge is like a tongue protruding from Pakistan into India and provides it with a perfect launch pad for an offensive into India. To overcome this vulnerability, India launched an offensive into the Shakargarh Bulge with 1 Corps, its prime offensive formation. Facing it was Pakistan's own 1 Corps which had occupied a formidable defence of the area.

The Shakargarh Bulge where the Indian offensive was launched

1 Corps launched its offensive on 05 December 71, with 54 Infantry Division with 16 Independent Armoured Brigade on the left and 36 Infantry Division with 2 Independent Armoured Brigade on the right. Yet the move was unduly cautious and advanced just 8 kilometers in 11 days. On the night of 14/15 December, the two Divisions reached the line of the Basantar Nala, a small tributary of the Ravi River and set about crossing it and establishing a lodgment on the other side.

As is the norm, infantry crosses the minefield and obstacle on foot, and establishes a lodgment on the other side. A lane is then cleared in the minefield, by the Engineers over which tanks cross to join up with the infantry on the other side. On the night of 14/15 December, the Indians had contacted the Basantar Nala and after bitter fighting, the infantry succeeded in getting across the Nala. 47 Infantry Brigade (the leading brigade of 54 Infantry Division) crossed the Basantar and established a bridgehead in an area known as the Lalial Reserve Forest, only to be furiously counterattacked by Pakistani tanks and Infantry. The attack was barely held back by the infantry, but the situation was critical and the brigade commander asked for tanks to be immediately sent in to support them.

Indian troops in defence, and on the offensive

47 Brigade was supported by 17 Poona Horse, one of the most illustrious Cavalry regiments of the Army, commanded by Lieutenant Colonel Hanut Singh (later Lieutenant General), a deeply religious man. The minefield lane had not been made, but seeing the gravity of the situation, he himself led his tanks, moving cautiously in a single file across the minefield. Not a single tank came over a mine as they traversed the minefield, crossed the Basantar Nala and joined up with the infantry on the other side. Folklore has it that the very next day, another Armoured Personnel Carrier tried to cross using the same tank treads only to hit a mine and be disabled.

By early morning of 16 December, Poona Horse had established itself across the Basantar with a Squadron in the Lalial Reserve Forest, B Squadron in the area of Ghazipur, A Squadron in reserve behind the Basantar. The Indian crossing of the Basantar had raised alarm bells amongst the Pakistani defenders, and at 0515 hours, 13 Lancers – an old and illustrious Pakistani Armoured Regiment known as 'The Spearheads' – was tasked to counterattack the Indian bridgehead. The first attack, launched by a squadron of Patton tanks came in around 7.30 am. It was daylight by then and their movements were detected as they formed up and then launched the attack. Indian tanks, artillery and anti-tank weapons opened up and the enemy attack was repulsed with heavy casualties. They withdrew leaving behind eight burning tanks. But an hour or so later, the rest of the regiment reformed and launched another ferocious attack under cover of a smoke screen with two full squadrons. This attack was launched in the direction of Jarpal which was held with just two troops of B squadron of 17 Horse. As the attack came dangerously close, the Squadron Commander radioed for help. His radio transmission was heard by Second Lieutenant Arun Khetrapal, a young officer who had not even done his basic training course after being commissioned. He moved with his troop of three tanks at high speed towards the advancing enemy. On the way, he encountered enemy strong points and anti-tank guns which he engaged and destroyed. One of his tanks was destroyed and another developed a mechanical problem, but he continued, interposing himself in the path of the enemy counterattack, firing rapidly and keeping them at bay. The enemy attack faltered and ten enemy tanks were destroyed, four by Arun Khetrapal himself. But in the firefight, his own tank was hit and caught fire. Ordered to withdraw, he refused, saying that his gun was still firing. He hit one more tank, but then his tank too was hit by an enemy tank barely 200 yards which killed the gallant officer instantly.

2/Lt Khetrapal

A Pakistani Patton emits smoke as it is hit

The enemy counterattack, though perilously close to success, was halted with over 22 tanks destroyed. Another counter attack, this time by another regiment, 31 Cavalry, was launched in the evening, but it did not close in and merely adopted a blocking position ahead of the Indian bridgehead. The next day, on 17 Dec, the last day of the war, Pakistan launched another attack, this time with 35 Frontier Force, a newly raised Infantry Battalion. The attack, led personally by the Commanding Officer Lt Col Akram Raja, was launched in daylight, without adequate artillery or armour support and doomed to failure. The attacking battalion was mowed down by Indian fire, but still managed to advance to almost 50 meters from the Indian positions, before the commanding officer himself was killed and the attack broken virtually as the ceasefire came about at 0830 hours that morning. Over 80 bodies lay on the battlefield in what was a futile last-ditch effort to clear the Indian bridgehead. Lt Col Akram Raja was awarded the *Hilal-i-Jurrat*, and significantly the award was based on the citation written by none other than the Commanding officer of the Indian Battalion opposing him, one of the few such instances when the adversary himself respected the courage of his opponent. Courage was a plenty in this battle. Two Indian officers received the Param Vir Chakra (Lt Khetrapal and Major Hoshiar Singh for his dogged defence of the bridgehead against repeated enemy attacks).

The guns came silent on the Western Front at 0830 hours on 17 December when Mrs Gandhi declared a unilateral ceasefire. (The Pakistani Eastern Command had already surrendered a day earlier on 16 December.) Pakistan, which had hoped for successes in the Western front to compensate for their total loss in the East, suffered grievous losses in this sector as well. At the end of the war, India held on to over six hundred square kilometers of territory in this sector, which had been captured with heavy losses on both sides. A total of 43 Pakistani tanks were destroyed with 10 captured with 15 destroyed or damaged on the Indian side; 222 Pakistani soldiers were killed, 900 wounded and 60 taken prisoner, with the Indians suffering similar losses of 169 killed, over 500 wounded and 17 taken prisoner or reported missing. There was no dearth of gallantry, all right.

There is a tailpiece to the story.

Thirty years later in 2001, Lt Khetrapal's father, Brig M L Khetrapal, now 81-year-old, decided to visit his birthplace in Sargodha, Pakistan. At the airport itself, he was met by a certain Brig Khwaja Mohammed Naser, who took it upon himself to be his host and guide. Brig Naser went out of his way to ensure that Brig Khetrapal had a very satisfying and nostalgic visit to his old home in Sargodha and then insisted that he stay with him as his personal guest at his home.

Brig Khetrapal was overwhelmed by the kindness and courtesy bestowed upon him by the entire family. He was treated with utmost respect and deference and then on the night before his departure, Brig Khwaja came up to him and confided, "Sir, there is something I wanted to tell you for many years, but could not get the opportunity. I am the man who killed your son, Arun."

"On that night of 16 December 71, I was leading the counterattack of 13 LANCERS against the Indian bridgehead at Basantar. Your son was on the opposite side, standing like a rock. In the battle, tank casualties were high. Finally it was just the two of us in our tanks facing each other just 200 meters apart. We both fired simultaneously. Yet it was destined that I was to live and he was to die."

"It was only later, when your son became a national hero, that I realized who was the brave opponent facing me and how young he was. We were both soldiers doing our duty for our nations. I salute your son for what he did. I salute you too, Sir, because seeing you, I know where he received the values that made him such a courageous young man."

Brig Khetrapal was shaken. To be faced with the man who killed his son would have hurt, but he was a soldier himself and realized that what Brig Khwaja had done was a soldier's act in the line of duty. He sat silent for a while, then walked up to his son's opponent, shook hands and embraced him lightly. No words were spoken, none were really needed.

The next day photographs were taken, and Brig Khetrapal was escorted and seen off at Lahore Airport by his gracious host. Two weeks later, the photographs of his visit reached him at his Delhi address, along with a personal note from Brig Khwaja.

> *"With warmest regards to Brig M L Khetrapal, father of Shaheed 2 Lt Arun Khetrapal, PVC who stood like a unsurmountable rock between the victory and failure of the counter attack by the SPEARHEADS–13 LANCERS on 16 Dec 1971."*
>
> **—Brig Khwaja Mohammed Naser, 13 LANCERS**

37

13 April 1984
THE COLDEST WAR

Siachen

In Balti, they call it as Siachen – the abode of wild roses. It is a strange name for an icy glacier, 19,000 feet above sea level, where not a blade of grass grows. It is stranger still that this silent, ice-shrouded land should become the highest battleground of the world, where guns have roared since April 1984. Even today, though the guns are silent, Indian and Pakistani armies remain locked in eyeball-to-eyeball confrontation in these forbidding heights.

The roots of the conflict go back to the 1949 Karachi Agreement signed after the ceasefire of the 1947-48 Indo-Pak War (see "The Race to Srinagar" and "Saving Kashmir"). This demarcated the ceasefire line between India and Pakistan at map coordinate NJ9842 at the foot of the Siachen glacier. Beyond this, the line ran 'thence north to the glaciers'. This ambiguous line was interpreted by Pakistan as running Northeast towards the Karakorum Pass, which gave it control over the glaciers. India claimed that from NJ9842 the line ran along the nearest watershed, the Saltoro Ridge which put Siachen into Indian territory.

Indian and Pakistani claim lines

Through all of the 50s, 60s and 70s, this barren, inhospitable region was ignored by both sides. It was only in the late 70s that Pakistan published maps showing the area as theirs. They also began issuing permits for mountaineering expeditions, often accompanied by a Liaison Officer of the Pak army, *de facto* claiming the area as their own.

India awoke to this gambit thanks to the efforts of Col Narender 'Bull' Kumar, a skilled mountaineer and Commandant of the High Altitude Warfare School. He laid hands on the map which showed the area as Pakistan's and decided to counter the Pak moves by launching mountaineering expeditions of his own. After much persuasion, he received permission to lead his own expedition in 1978. The expedition detected huge quantum of debris with Pak Army markings, which convinced him that Pakistan was subtly laying claim to the glacier. He decided to counter Pak Oropolitics (use of mountaineering expeditions to stake claim) by a series of Indian expeditions, and in 1981 led a 70-man team across the glacier which was tailed by a Pakistani helicopter. Both sides were now awakening to the importance of the glacier.

The Indian expeditions had alarmed the Pakistani planners at GHQ, Rawalpindi, who now decided to occupy the glacier by military force. The aim of the operation was to occupy the heights of Saltoro Ridge, and its main passes of Sia La and Bilafond La and Gyong La. Yet, they made a small but significant error. They ordered large quantities of Arctic weather gear from a supplier in London who also supplied to the Indian Army, and he tipped them off about the large Pakistani order. That set off alarm bells in the Indian Northern Command who now were convinced that Pakistan was planning something in Siachen.

India began procuring its own Arctic equipment to pre-empt the Pakis by occupying Siachen before they did. Intelligence reports stated that they were likely to move in around 17 April and it was decided to move in our own troops by 13 April. Though considered an unlucky day, it was Baisakhi, and the Pakistanis would be least expecting activity on this day. 4 KUMAON and troops from Ladakh Scouts – hardy troops from the mountain regions – were selected for the operation, codenamed OPERATION MEGHDOOT, after Kalidasa's famous poem.

Around end March, troops of 4 KUMAON and Ladakh Scouts marched out in full battle order through the Zojila Pass towards the base of the glacier. Simultaneously, MI-17 and Chetak helicopters carried provisions to be deployed along the route and began stocking up the base camps. Four teams were deployed for the task under Brigadier V N Channa, who was responsible for the operation. One was to occupy Bilafond La, the other Sia La and the third moved towards Gyong La, the three passes leading to the glacier from the Pakistani side. Simultaneously, the positions on the high ground of Saltoro Ridge were to be occupied to deny access to the glacier. Once these positions were occupied, it would be virtually impossible for an enemy to evict them from these heights.

The troops marched up to the base camps in secrecy for the next phase of move to the heights. Yet, the Arctic equipment which was essential for survival at these altitudes, and which was being specially procured from across the world for this operation, was delayed. The first sets reached the base camps only around 5 in the evening on 12 April 84. (In the final briefing before the operation, the troops agreed to move up even if the Arctic gear was not available.) Next morning, on 13 April, Maj R S Sandhu led his platoon on foot to the heights of Saltoro Ridge, being the first Indian officer to be deployed there. Simultaneously, at 0530 hours a Cheetah helicopter, piloted by Squadron Leader S S Bains, took off from the base camp, carrying Capt Sanjay Kulkarni and his radio operator and winged its way towards the Bilafond La pass. The helicopter could only carry two persons and in the wind-swept conditions could not land at the snow-covered heights. The Cheetah hovered a few feet from the ground, Capt Kulkarni and his operator said a small prayer and jumped, their fall cushioned by the soft snow. 17 such sorties took place, and by 10 in the morning, around 30 men, a platoon worth, were on Bilafond La. In a raging blizzard, the Indian tricolor was raised there for the first time.

Yet, the first day was a forerunner of things to come. In just three hours, the radio operator contracted pulmonary edema, and had to be evacuated. By noon, the weather packed up as well, making any operations towards Sia La and the other heights impossible. In heights of over 19,000 feet, another soldier, Lance Naik Ramesh Singh fell to the dreaded high-altitude illness and passed away on 16 April. Although radio transmission was strictly forbidden, Capt Kulkarni made a single transmission to his HQ informing them of his situation. That transmission was picked up by the Pakistani and now they were alerted.

In spite of the terrible weather, they too began moving troops of their elite Special Services Group and Northern Light Infantry on foot towards the glacier.

After three days, the weather cleared and on 17 April, the IAF launched 32 sorties to drop Major Bahuguna and his platoon of Ladakh Scouts in the vicinity of the next objective, Sia La Pass. The platoon walked five kilometers in knee-high snow and secured the pass by mid-day. Indian troops also occupied important heights around Saltoro Ridge and the glacier was securely in Indian hands.

Indian troops assembling for the Siachen Operation

The Pakistanis had been beaten in their plans to occupy the glacier by three days. They now launched their own operation – codenamed OPERATION ABABEEL – to evict the Indians. SSG commandoes reached Bilafond La on 23 April, after a three-day trek on the snow and around 4 in the evening, the first attack came in. A burst of fire killed the Indian sentry at the Observation Post and the silent peaks reverberated with the sounds of gunfire. Yet the Indians were on high ground, and held the advantage. For the Pakistanis, movement in the knee-deep snow was slow and tortuous and their attack was repulsed with 26 Pakistani soldiers were killed in the first assault. Another attack came in the next day, and then again on 27 April which was similarly repulsed. Other attacks followed in May and in June, on each of the newly established Indian posts but to no avail. The Indian positions were being gradually reinforced day by day and at these altitudes recapturing a high ground was virtually impossible. Pakistani attacks, though courageous, were simply beaten back.

Over the next few months, both sides built up their forces. With the passes in Indian control, the Pakistanis tried to seize the adjoining heights. Both sides set about occupying posts to dominate the other – a strategy that continued throughout the war. In July 1984, Pakistani NSG commandoes seized a high feature overlooking the Bilafond La pass in a daring helicopter-borne assault and occupied it. This feature, renamed Quaid Post, dominated Indian positions for over three years, till it was recaptured in July 1987 by Naib Subedar Bana Singh (see 'From Quaid to Bana') and renamed Bana Post.

The Pakistani Army did not give up its attempts to recapture Siachen. Chastened by its failure to defend Siachen, Benazir Bhutto called the Pakistani Army "only fit to fight its own people" and suggested that its generals wear bangles. A series of attacks and counterattacks on each other's positions continued for over a decade, with major Pakistani offensives launched in 1987, 1989, 1992, 1995 which were repulsed with heavy casualties. In 1999, General Musharaff launched the Kargil War, hoping to cut off the supply line to Siachen and force India to vacate their positions. (He himself was a Brigade Commander there and the failures suffered there would have rankled him.) The Kargil operation too failed (see 'The Heights of Victory').

Both sides have around 3000 troops in 150–200 small posts in the crucial heights and the line held by both sides has become the Actual Ground Position Line (ACPL). The Indians hold on to the 76-kilometer-long glacier, and occupy most of the heights and passes around it. Even though the guns have been silent since June 2003 after a ceasefire, appalling weather conditions and the treacherous terrain claim casualties on both sides. In 2012, an avalanche hit the Pakistani Gayari base killing 126 soldiers and 10 Indian soldiers were recently buried alive in a similar landslide in 2016. Over 2000 casualties have taken place on either side. The cost of just maintaining a presence there is around $300 million a year for India and around $200 million for Pakistan. They have the logistical advantage of being located at the Western base of the glacier which can be accessed by roads. Indian posts, even today, largely rely on helicopters for sustenance.

So, is it worth holding on to these inhospitable heights? Yes it is. Vacating the hard-earned positions at Siachen will simply allow the Pakis to move in and then regaining them will be impossible. Siachen also will prevent a Chinese–Pakistani nexus in the area. And it already holds an important position in the psyche of both nations. For a permanent solution to Siachen, clearly marked and delineated boundaries along the AGPL with iron-clad guarantees would be required, something difficult in the environment of distrust. But till the solution is found, the Indian soldier holds vigil in those forbidding heights, suffering hardships that would have broken most armies. And all we can do is raise a prayer and a salute for him.

Quartered in snow, silent to remain. When the bugle calls, they shall rise and march again. "
-The scroll of honour at the Siachen Base Camp

38

23-27 June 1987
FROM 'QUAID' TO 'BANA'

The Capture of Bana Post

In April 1984, Indian troops beat Pakistani soldiers by just four days to occupy positions on the Siachen glacier (see 'The Coldest War'). This set of a series of Pakistani attacks to evict them. When that failed, they too occupied a series of posts on the heights. The occupation of posts on heights to dominate the other was a strategy followed by both nations in this two-decade-long war.

One of the lynchpins of the Pakistani positions was the Quaid Post –

named after Quaid-e-Azam, Mohammed Ali Jinnah, the father of their nation. At 22,153 feet, it was the highest peak in the area, which enabled them to see 80 kilometers away, across the entire Siachen glacier. From here, they could also observe the important Indian positions on Sonam and Amar posts adjoining the Bilafond La pass, and bring down fire on the helipads used to resupply them. Held by elite troops of the Shaheen Company of 3 Special Services Group, it was commanded by Subedar Atauallah Mohammed with a squad of around 15–20 men and considered virtually impregnable.

A Pakistani Sentry stands guard at the Quaid Post

Occupying the remote height was a difficult proposition, but the Pakistani held on to it doggedly, using its heights to advantage. On 18 April 1987, Pakistani troops from Quaid fired at the Indian Sonam Post killing two soldiers. It was then that the Indians decided to capture the post and eliminate the threat once and for all. 8 Jammu and Kashmir Rifles, a unit recently inducted into the area, was selected for the task.

On 29 May, a 13-man patrol under young Second Lieutenant Rajiv Pande was sent to discover the best approach to Quaid post. The 'best approach' was a misnomer. The post was surrounded by ice walls with gradients of 80–85 degrees on three sides, with the fourth side covered by the Pakistanis. The young officer and his men reconnoitered the route marking it with crampons and ropes. They began climbing up the 85-degree ice wall, establishing pitons in the ice that would provide footholds for the subsequent assaults. They also passed a rope through the coupling links which could be used to climb up for a subsequent assault. As they climbed up the 500-meter-high ice wall, they were detected just 30 meters from the top. A Pakistani machine gun opened up, and raked the small team with fire, killing ten soldiers including Lieutenant Rajiv who fell to his death.

Climbing the Ice Wall

The deaths of the young officer and his men put a pall of gloom over 8 JAKLI (Jammu & Kashmir Light Infantry). This mood soon gave way to one of anger and revenge. Another hand-picked assault group was assembled under Major Varinder Singh Minhas (later Brigadier) and his Second-in-Command Captain Anil Sharma, three JCOs (Subedar Harnam Singh, Subedar Sansar Chand and Naib Subedar Bana Singh) and 57 other ranks. This operation was code named Operation Rajiv, in honour of Lieutenant Rajiv Pande.

The assault group assembled in Sonam Post on the night of 23 June, and the next night (24 June), a 10-man team led by Subedar Harnam Singh set out on the same route taken by Lt Rajiv. The route from Sonam post was along a razor-sharp spur, where a single misstep could hurl them hundreds of feet below. The party found the rope buried beneath the snow which led them to the footholds, so painstakingly made by Lt Rajiv's earlier team. They also found the bodies of Lt Rajiv and his men, still preserved in the sub-zero temperatures. As Harnam Singh's men moved forward, they were detected by the Pakistanis who brought down machine gun fire on them. They were unable to return the fire since their own weapons had frozen solid. (It was later discovered that the Pakistanis kept a lit kerosene stove beneath the Machine Gun to ensure it remained warm and could continue firing.) Two men were killed in the fire and the rest withdrew, bringing with them the bodies of their comrades.

The next night (25-26 June), Major Varinder launched another attack. The Indian teams climbed upto Quaid top under intense covering fire brought down on the Pakistani positions from Sonam Post. Subedar Sansar Chand and his party of five reached the top and wanted additional men to rush in towards the Pakistani positions. At this critical juncture, his radio set failed, its batteries freezing in the cold, and he was unable to communicate with Maj Varinder who was just 100 meters behind him. This attack too had to be aborted.

The Indians were now exhausted after three days in the open. The men were reduced to licking icicles to quench their thirst and had burrowed in the snow to avoid detection and enemy fire. Hallucinations and mental breakdowns were common in the heights and Maj Varinder had to ask each man his name and the names of their comrades to ensure that their mental faculties were intact. Each had left behind a 'last letter' to their families, and were painfully aware of how dangerous their mission was. Even though the attack was being monitored at the highest levels and Quaid post was now under fire by virtually every Indian artillery gun in range, for the final assault the small team would be on its own.

The next morning, on 26 June, two teams – one of eight men led by Major Varinder and another of five led by Naib Subedar Bana Singh climbed up the icy wall and reached the vicinity of the post. Fortunately, they were still undetected. The weather was atrocious and a blizzard was raging. Though it was noon, it was almost pitch dark. The Pakistanis obviously did not expect an attack in these conditions.

It was now or never. Varinder Singh decided to launch a daylight attack from two sides. At exactly eleven minutes past noon, the assault went in. Varinder's own team outflanked the post, and Bana Singh with his small team of Rifleman Chunni Lal, Laxman Das, Om Raj and Kashmir Chand assaulted the Pakistani bunker on the post. As they closed in on the bunker, to their horror, their weapons jammed in the intense cold and refused to fire.

Undeterred, they closed in and Bana Singh hurled a grenade inside, closing the door to compound the effect. The occupants were killed, but other Pakistani soldiers closed in. In the hand-to-hand fighting, six Pakistanis were bayoneted to death. A few others jumped off the cliff. Major Varinder himself was severely wounded when an artillery airburst injured his chest and torso, but continued with his men. Ironically, he was saved, because his blood congealed in the intense cold and prevented further blood loss. The Pakistani machine gun which had caused so much havoc was now turned towards the Pakistani positions. The kerosene stove which the Pakistanis used to keep it warm was used to cook rice, the first real meal the men had in three days. Quaid post had changed hands, but it was done without much fanfare. As Bana Singh himself put it, at 22,000 feet no one has the energy to do a *'bhangra'* or even emit a victory whoop.

The audacious capture of a post at 23,000 feet, in sub-zero conditions, after scaling a 1500-foot ice wall, and then through hand-to-hand combat has few parallels. Subsequent Pakistani attempts to recapture it failed and the post remains secure in Indian hands even now. Bana Singh received the Param Vir Chakra, and became a national hero. Subedar Harnam Singh was awarded a Maha Vir Chakra, while Major Varinder and Lieutenant Pande received Vir Chakras. Riflemen Chunni Lal (who would go on to become India's most decorated soldier) and Om Raj were awarded Sena Medals for their courage in the final assault. And just a day after its capture, Quaid Post – the symbolic and strategic centerpiece of Pakistani operations in Siachen – was renamed as Bana Post. And that is how it still remains.

39

14 October 1987 – March 1990
INDIA'S FORAY INTO SRI LANKA

Operation Pawan

On 13 Oct 1987 the Indian Army launched OP PAWAN – a war against the world's deadliest terrorist group, the Liberation Tigers of Tamil Eelam. The operation began with an ill-fated action to take over the LTTE stronghold of Jaffna and then went on for three grueling, inconclusive years.

Let us go to where it all began. The origins were actually in the early 80s when the Tamil militant groups intensified their actions against the Sri Lankan government demanding greater autonomy and freedom for the Tamil-dominated areas of North and East Sri Lanka. The Sri Lankan army launched a vicious crack down and this only led to the resentment. By mid-80s, Sri Lanka was in the grip of a civil war. In June 1987, the Sri Lankan Army had besieged Jaffna, where the LTTE leadership was hiding, and had cut off food and supplies to the town. As the suffering to innocent civilians increased and the humanitarian crisis unfolded, the Indian Prime Minister, Rajiv Gandhi, decided to airdrop essential supplies into the town.

On 4 June 1987, five AN-32 aircraft accompanied by MIRAGE 2000 fighters airdropped essential supplies into Jaffna. The show of force had the desired effect. It brought President Jayawardhane to the negotiating table and resulted in the signing of the Indo-Sri Lankan Accord. (The ceremony of the signing of the accord had an ugly incident. A Sri Lankan sailor in the Guard of Honour for Rajiv Gandhi hit him with the butt of his rifle to protest Indian interference.) As per the accord, India would provide a Peace Keeping Force to keep the Sri Lankan and the LTTE away from each other, disarm the LTTE and ensure the sovereignty and integrity of Sri Lanka. When 54 Infantry Division, the first element of the Indian Peace Keeping Force (IPKF) arrived in Sri Lanka in end June 87, there were no plans for active operations. In fact, they did not even carry most of their heavy equipment. It was to be a Peacekeeping Operation after all, but the operation was to soon go awry.

OPERATION PAWAN

Relations between the LTTE and the IPKF were fine initially. But the LTTE did not hand over their weapons (except a few symbolic ones) as they were meant to do. Then in early October, two LTTE leaders who were in the custody of the Sri Lankan Army committed suicide and the LTTE turned against the IPKF. The IPKF was now tasked to finish the LTTE and capture their stronghold and *de facto* capital of Jaffna. With this, OPERATION PAWAN was launched.

The first battle of OP PAWAN was the heli-borne assault on Jaffna University where the LTTE leadership (including Prabhakaran) were supposedly based. One Para Commando battalion, 10 PARA COMMANDO, and an Infantry Battalion, 13 SIKHLI, were to be heli-dropped inside the Jaffna University grounds hoping to eliminate their leadership and bring an early end to the battle. Two battalions were to move on foot towards Jaffna, enter the town and link up with the commandoes inside. The operation, launched on the night of 12/13 Oct, was a disaster. The troops were sent without maps or adequate intelligence and had no idea of either their locations or what awaited them there. Worse, the LTTE had intercepted IPKF radio transmissions and set up machine guns on the roofs of the university buildings. As the helicopters approached and the force began to disembark, the LTTE opened fire, forcing the helicopters to abort their landing and fly back. Only seven helicopters managed to disembark 30 soldiers of 13 SIKHLI and 17 Commandoes from 10 Para Commando. The troops landed on the open grounds of the Jaffna University football fields were mowed down with fire on all sides. On that cruel night, 29 of the 30 soldiers of 13 SIKHLI were killed – Sepoy Gora Singh was captured alive and survived to tell the tale. Two Para Commandoes were also killed and the rest holed up inside a university building. On the outskirts of Jaffna, 4/5 Gurkhas approaching the town to link up with the heli-dropped force , was ambushed and 35 men were killed, including their Commanding Officer and three other officers.

None imagined that the LTTE would have been so heavily armed or would have prepared the defences of Jaffna so strongly. It required tanks to finally extricate the trapped Commandoes. The leading tank went over an improvised mine – which was a barrel filled with over 200 kg of high explosive – and was hurled 30 feet in the air. The roads had been heavily mined and there was no way to get inside. Finally, one troop of tanks accompanied by infantry managed to get inside using a railway embankment and extricated the trapped Commandoes from within.

In one night, the IPKF had lost 70 men and they realized the Jaffna would be a tough nut to crack. Additional troops were flown in and Jaffna was surrounded from all sides and blockaded from sea by the Indian navy. Marine Commandoes launched two daring raids, destroying LTTE naval craft inside

LTTE Cadres with Prabhakaran

Jaffna Harbour. Slowly the IPKF advanced towards Jaffna, finding mines at virtually every few hundred meters, and facing intensive sniper fire along the way. Finally, a foothold was established and then gradually expanded. Fighting took place at every house and street, and the town was cleared, lane by lane, building by building. What should have been a 72-hour operation, took 20 days, and Indian troops gained control of the town only around end of November.

The Battle for Jaffna was just the start. Most of the LTTE leadership had melted away in to the jungles of Northern and Eastern Sri Lanka. For the next three years, the IPKF waged a slow, difficult battle against the LTTE in the jungles of Batticaloa, Trincomalee and Vavuniya. The LTTE were one of the most dangerous opponents faced by the Indian army. They were excellent guerilla fighters, who were rarely seen, but sniped and fired constantly, and chose to commit suicide by a cyanide pill rather than be captured alive. For three years, the slow war continued, without tangible gains. When the IPKF was finally called back by the then Prime Minister V P Singh, there was little to show for it. They had compressed the LTTE in the areas around the jungles of Vavuniya, but the leadership, including Prabhakaran, were still alive and at large. They still held on to their bases deep in the jungles and the IPKF lost 1157 officers and men with over 3000 injured. To add insult to injury, when they returned to Chennai, the Tamil Nadu Chief Minister Mr MG Ramachandran refused to receive them. Yet, as Lt Gen A S Kalkat, the Commander of the IPKF said, 'They came as proud soldiers. They leave as proud soldiers'.

The inconclusive operation has shaped our reluctance to wage overseas operations thereafter. It had another fall-out. In May 1991, former Prime Minister, Rajiv Gandhi was assassinated by a LTTE suicide bomber for his role in sending the IPKF into Sri Lanka, changing the political equations of the country completely.

40

03 November 1988
INTO OPERATIONS WITH A TOURIST MAP

OPERATION CACTUS in the Maldives

In the late afternoon of 03 November 1988, maroon-bereted troops of India's elite 50 Independent Parachute Brigade filed into the holds of two IL-76 transport aircraft in Agra airfield. At that point of time, few of them knew where they were headed or what exactly they were going to do, but in the next few hours they would help shape India's image as a regional power.

The theatre where the drama was to unfold lay 3000 kilometres away – in the picture postcard islands of Maldives. There, around 200 heavily armed mercenaries of the People's Liberation Organisation of Tamil Eelam (PLOTE) backed by Maldivian businessman Abdullah Latif and his henchmen had stormed the capital of Male, took over the television and radio stations, surrounded the Presidential Palace and forced President Maumoon Abdul Gayoom to seek shelter in the Headquarters of the National Security Service. Besieged there, President Gayoom sent out frantic messages of help to the USA, the Soviet Union, Pakistan and India. And though none of the other powers responded, India acted with a speed that amazed the world.

News of the coup was received in New Delhi around 6 in the morning and conveyed to Prime Minister Rajiv Gandhi. India was then embroiled in the operations of the Indian Peace Keeping Force in Sri Lanka (see 'OP PAWAN – India's Foray into Sri Lanka') and were loath to undertake another operation in a foreign country. But Rajiv Gandhi made the decision rapidly and ordered the despatch of Indian troops to the Maldives to assist President Gayoom. By 7.15 am, the IAF had been instructed to keep aircraft ready and 50 Independent Para Brigade located at Agra was ordered to be ready for immediate move. The Brigade Major, Major Vinod Bhatia (later Lt Gen Vinod Bhatia) rapidly coordinated the move. The brigade was widely dispersed on training and security duties, but 6 PARA and 3 PARA, the only available units in station, were rapidly mobilised for the operation.

IL-76 readies for take off

At that time, nobody, not even the Commander, Brigadier Faroukh Bulsara ('Bull' as he was nicknamed) knew the complete situation. They were given a one-line brief, 'To rescue the President of Maldives and escort him safely back to India.' They had no information of the layout of the 1200 odd islands that make up the Maldives. None of them had ever seen the place and the only maps available were tourist maps and brochures. Brigadier Bulsara, requested

Mr Ashok Banerjee, the High Commissioner to the Maldives who was present for the final briefing, to accompany them so that his local knowledge and expertise could be used. Banerjee readily agreed, picked up his toothbrush, and joined the troops in the leading aircraft to become the first IFS officer to participate in military operations.

As the powerful engines whined to life, the paratroopers raised their battle cries of "*Chattri Mata ki Jai*" (Victory to the Parachute) and the two IL-76 transport aircraft lifted off from Agra and began the 3000-kilometre flight towards the Maldives. OPERATION CACTUS was on its way. The 4.5-hour-long flight was used to brief the troops, study the tourist maps and make their plans. As per the initial plan, Hulhule airfield – the Maldivian airport located on an island which was separated from Male by a kilometre-wide stretch of water – was to be first secured by the paratroopers. They would then cross over the straits, reach Male and head for the NSS Headquarters where President Gayoom was taking refuge. The entire operation hinged on securing Hulhule airfield, but they had no way of even knowing if Hulhule had been taken over by PLOTE mercenaries or was still in the hands of loyal government troops.

Brigadier Bulsara had two options. Drop 60 paratroopers (only 60 pre-packed parachutes were available to the brigade when they took off) onto the airfield, secure it and then land the rest of the force. On the narrow, wind-swept island, there was no dropping zone large enough. The paratroopers could get swept off by the wind and get carried into the waters, which could cause needless casualties. The other option was to take a chance and land directly at the airport, secure it and then rush to save the President.

It had been decided that should Hulhule airfield be held by government troops, the signal 'HADIYA' would be transmitted by the ATC. The runway lights were to be switched on only at the last moment to prevent the terrorists from being alerted of the arrival of the Indians. As they approached Hulhule, Group Captain Bewoor, flying the lead aircraft, received the code word 'HADIYA' and Brigadier Bulsara decided to land. The giant, fully loaded IL-76 descended towards the dark, unlit runway. Just 200 meters away, the runway lights came on, enabling Bewoor to land. As the wheels touched down, the lights switched off again and the aircraft rushed forward in darkness, coming to a halt just short of the runway's edge. In the darkened fuselage, the tightly packed paratroopers gripped their weapons and let out a collective sigh of relief. It was now 9.48 pm on 3 December and the Indian army had landed in the Maldives.

The leading troops of 6 PARA rushed out of the aircraft and secured the airfield, the ATC and the airport buildings. Ten minutes later, the second IL-76 landed, bringing with it a company of 3 PARA along with the Engineers, Medical and Artillery component of the Brigade. As the troops fanned out, PLOTE fighters in the vicinity of the airfield slipped away and they encountered no hostile activity in Hulhule airport. But from the direction of Male, sounds of gunfire could be heard. The terrorists had made the critical mistake of leaving the airport unoccupied. Else, even one single truck place on the runway would have put paid to all plans.

With the airport secured, at around 11 pm, a company of 6 PARA, under Colonel S C Joshi and Major R J S Dhillon, commandeered boats and ferries and sailed across to Male which was on an island around a kilometre away. Another company of 3 PARA moved on boats towards the north-eastern part of the island so that they could approach from two different directions. Guided by loyalist troops, they reached the NSS HQ where President Gayoom was sheltering. The walls of the HQ were pockmarked with bullet holes and mortar bursts – a testimony to the attacks it had been subjected to by the PLOTE fighters. At around 2.10 am, Col Joshi and his men linked up with NSS soldiers and were taken to Gulistaan House where the President was taking refuge. He was shaken, but greeted his Indian rescuers warmly and then was escorted away to safety. As his car moved out, paratroopers formed a tight cordon around it, their eyes alert for snipers that could be hiding in any of the adjoining buildings. President Gayoom was placed in a safe house and around four in the morning made a telephone call to Prime Minister Rajiv Gandhi to thank him for India's help. He however refused to leave the Maldives and insisted on remaining in his capital.

But the drama was not yet done. Even as operations were underway to secure the President, PLOTE terrorists received news of the Indian Army's arrival and decided to flee. Taking 14 hostages, including the Maldivian Minister of Education, they hijacked a freighter M V PROGRESS LIGHT and at around 11 pm of night 03 December – just as Indian troops were making their way to Male – fled the Maldives. Their movement was detected, and the hijacked vessel fired upon by guns of 17 Para Field Regiment, which

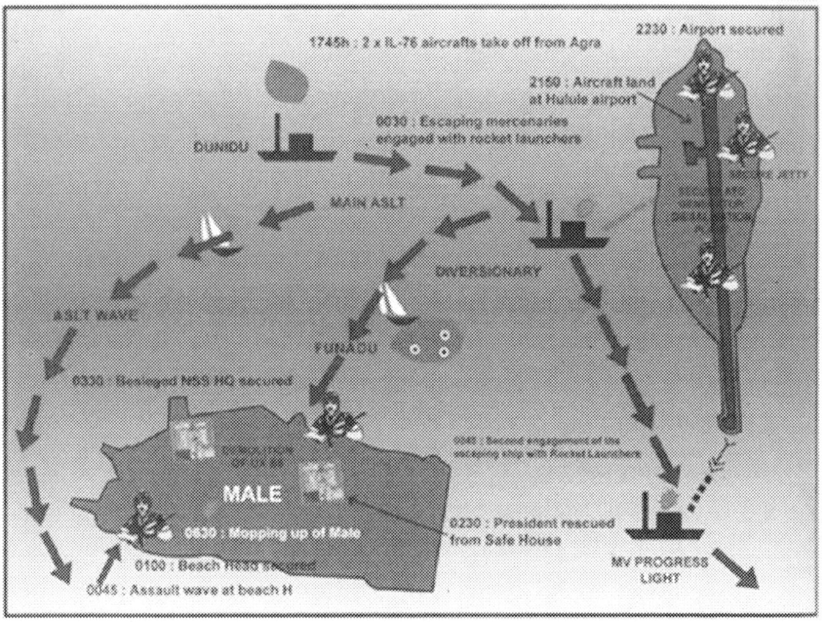

scored hits but could not prevent the ship from slipping out into the open ocean. Tracked by reconnaissance aircraft of the Indian navy, the MV PROGRESS LIGHT was intercepted by the frigates INS GODAVARI and INS BETWA which blocked its path and ordered it to halt. The terrorists refused to surrender and the frigates launched helicopters to drop depth charges around it. With the ship damaged and listing, and the terrorists stunned by heavy firing, Naval Marine Commandoes (MARCOS) clambered aboard, overpowered the terrorists and swiftly took control of the ship.

Indian troops after the Operation

Eleven civilians (including four hostages) and eight Maldivian soldiers were killed in the failed coup. There were no casualties amongst the Indians – just a soldier injured in the foot when his gun went off accidentally. More troops were flown in from India and the situation stabilised. Then with the situation completely under control, Indian troops once again embarked on their aircraft two weeks later, on 17 November, and flew back, with its mission impeccably executed.

M V PROGRESS LIGHT Intercepted by the Navy

The successful overseas operation in Maldives garnered international praise from world leaders ranging from Margaret Thatcher, Ronald Reagan and even China. In its wake, TIME magazine did a cover story, 'Super Power Rising' stating "India asserts its place on the world stage." Though small in scale, the action highlighted Indian capabilities and reach. It showcased its ability to launch a major regional operation in just a few hours, guided by courage, 'Chattri Mata' and a few tourist maps, and perhaps set India on its course to becoming a regional power.

41

05 May – 26 July 1999
THE HEIGHTS OF VICTORY

Kargil

On 05 May 1999, a five-man patrol led by Capt Saurabh Kalia moved across the rugged, mountains of Kaksar, in the Kargil Sector. It was a patrol sent to confirm news of likely Pakistani intrusions in the area and the patrol party was cautious. As they approached the ridgeline adjoining the Line of Control, a movement atop caught their eyes, which was followed by volleys of gunfire. The surprised patrol returned the fire till they ran out of ammunition. Surrounded by Pakistani soldiers – whose presence they, and the rest of the

Indian Army were not aware of – they were captured and brutally tortured to death. The first shots of the Kargil War had been fired and had claimed its first casualties.

The ambushing of Capt Kalia's patrol was the first real indicator of the Pakistani infiltration on the heights adjoining the Indian side of the Line of Control in the Kargil Sector. This 180-kilometer-long sector from Kabal Gali in the West to Chorbatla in the East comprised Dras (Southwest of Kargil), Kargil and Batalik (to its Northwest) sub-sectors. Its forbidding heights overlooked the National Highway 1D, the critical 2-lane road which was the only line of communication from Srinagar to Leh. Pakistani occupation of these heights meant that they could dominate and cut off India's lifeline to Ladakh and Siachen.

OPERATION BADR, as the Pakistani plan to occupy the Kargil heights was called, was the brainchild of General Parvez Musharraf, the then Army Chief and later President of Pakistan. The plan was not new and had been put up by earlier Chiefs to President Zia and Benazir Bhutto, only to be rejected. Musharraf, reactivated the plan when he took over as Chief of Army Staff (COAS), perhaps as a way to get back to the Indians for their capture of

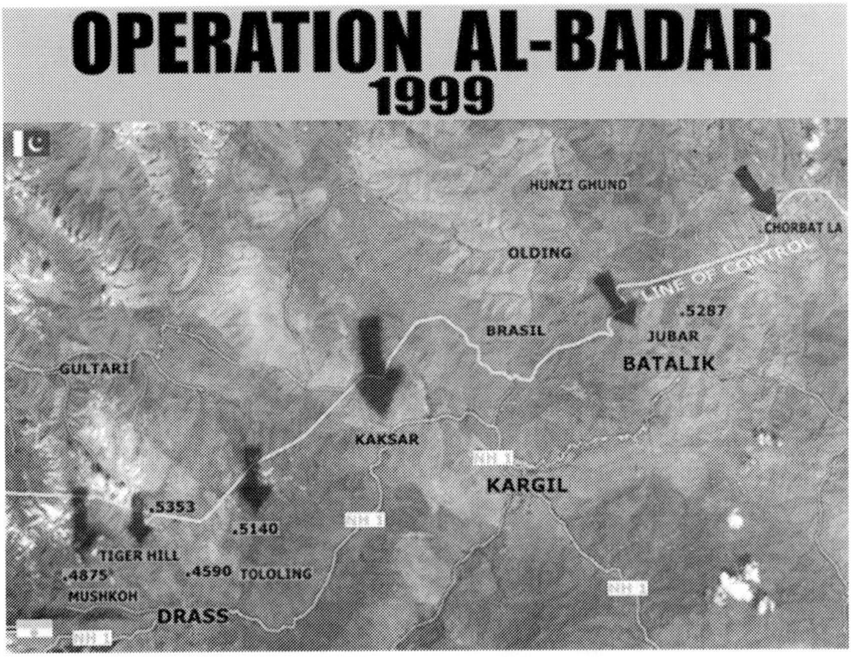

Siachen (see 'The Coldest War' for Siachen Operations), and to get attention to the Kashmir issue. He had been a Brigade Commander in Siachen and the reversals he suffered there must have angered him. Although rehearsals and planning had been going on for over two years, the operation was actually set in motion in November 1998 – ironically at the same time when Prime Ministers Nawaz Sharif and Vajpayee were having their historic meeting at Lahore and talking peace.

The jury is still out as to whether Musharraf consulted his Prime Minister and took him in confidence. As per accounts, he briefed Nawaz Sharif – in vague details – around April 99 when the plan had already been set in motion. From February 1999, troops of the Special Services Group and around seven battalions of the Northern Light Infantry (a paramilitary regiment which was under, but not a part of, the Pakistani Army at that time) began climbing up the heights of the Marpo La Ridgeline in Dras, in Kaksar, near Kargil and Batalik right up to Turtok near Siachen. The Indian posts along the LOC heights were unoccupied in winter and their move was undetected. Strict radio silence was observed, and the move to the heights was done gradually in a phased manner to prevent detection. Pakistani troops were dressed in *salwar kameez*, to give the impression that they were *mujahideens*, so-called freedom-fighters from Kashmir – a stance they maintained till their cover was blown. In fact even within the armed forces, only a handful of people knew of the plan, and even the Air Force and Navy had not been taken into confidence. This secrecy enabled the early success of the operation, but also led to its eventual unraveling.

Detection and Eviction

The 180-kilometer-long Kargil Sector was then occupied by 121 Independent Infantry Brigade with four battalions. The positions had vast gaps between them and in many cases, Indian positions along the heights had been vacated in the winter months. Neither RAW, nor military intelligence had any indication of the gathering storm till a shepherd passed news of armed men in black uniforms at the Kargil heights on 03 May. Reports had started coming in all along the front of activity being detected on the heights, and the disappearance of Saurabh Kalia's patrol on 05 May set alarm bells ringing. On 09 May, shelling from the heights destroyed an ammunition dump at Kargil and Pakistani artillery fire began targeting traffic on the NH 1D. The scale of the threat now became apparent and on 15 May the Indian Army launched OPERATION VIJAY to evict the Pakistani intrusions in Dras, Kargil, Kaksar and Mushkoh sectors.

The initial attacks to clear the Pakistani positions were disjointed and unprepared. For a long time, the troops were told that it was just a minor intrusion 'by a few rats' who had to be thrown out. It was when the first attacks went in, to be met with heavy machine gun, mortar and artillery fire, that it became apparent that this was not a minor intrusion, but a full-scale offensive.

Indian troops moving in

The army may have slipped up in not detecting the intrusions in time, but when it reacted, it moved efficiently. Fortunately, the Zoji La pass (the only pass on the Srinagar–Leh road) which was blocked by snow all of winter, opened a month early that year, on 22 April and was useable by 10 May enabling reinforcements to be pumped into the area. Over 200,000 troops were mobilized, though only two divisions (3 and 8 Divisions) were committed in the Kargil sector and over 250 guns moved in. Yet while military actions began to retake the heights, there was a caveat. The government had laid down that the LOC was not to be crossed, and operations were not to be initiated in other sectors to prevent escalation of the war. The IAF also launched air operations and the navy began aggressive patrolling of the Arabian Sea to choke Pakistan's maritime routes, if required. Slowly, the wheels of the war machinery were set in motion.

121 Independent Brigade, in whose area this sector fell, was tasked to contain the intrusions while additional troops were pumped in to clear them. The major priority was to evict the Pakistani positions at Tiger Hill and the Tololing Heights which overlooked the NH 1D. The clearing of these heights took over a month and saw the bitterest fighting of the war. In those rarified heights, it was not possible to walk ten steps without pausing for breath and assaults were made in the face of withering fire from above. At these nameless heights – known only by Numbers Point 5410, Point 5432, Point 4100 and so on (which depicted their height above sea level) – our officers and men fought and died to recapture them one by one.

The first success of the war came with the securing of Tololing on 13 June. This feature set the stage for the recapture of other positions on the ridgeline. On 4 July, Tiger Hill fell after an 11-hour-long battle. All along the front, from Yaldor, Batalik, Kaksar, Kargil and Dras, Indian attacks intensified as they closed in and regained the occupied positions. The news streamed into Indian homes via television, and names like Captain Vikram Batra, Major Rajesh Adhikari, Lieutenant Manoj Pandey, Grenadier Yogendra Singh Yadav, Major Vivek Gupta, Lieutenant Hanifuddin and so on became household names. Battalions that participated in these assaults – 2 RAJRIF, 18 GRENADIERS, 13 JAKRIF, 1/11 GORKHA Rifles, 17 JAT, 8 SIKH and a host of others – became more than numbers. Images of their men standing victoriously with the national flag atop a captured peak imprinted themselves on the national psyche.

The IAF too came into the fray. It suffered an initial setback on 27 May when a MIG-27 'flamed out' after a rocket attack (apparently gas fumes from the firing of its rockets were sucked into the engine causing it to stall – a freak occurrence). Its pilot Flight Lieutenant Nachiketa bailed out and was taken Prisoner of War. Squadron Leader Ajay Ahuja, flying a MIG-21 fighter on an escort mission overhead, came low to detect where Nachiketa had parachuted and his aircraft was hit by a Stinger missile. Ahuja bailed out, but was killed in cold blood by his captors. His body was returned, riddled with bullet wounds.

The IAF in action

A day later, on 28 May, a MI-8 helicopter flown by Squadron Leader Rajeev Pundir on a rocket attack mission over the Tololing Heights was hit by a Stinger missile killing all four crew members. The IAF maintained high-altitude attacks thereafter, using Mirage 2000s with laser-guided bombs for attacks on Pakistani positions. 'Dumb' bombs were also modified for precision bombing but identifying and engaging targets at those heights was virtually impossible. The IAF too had the strict command that they could not cross the LOC which in a way eliminated encounters with the PAF, which could have escalated the war.

Pakistani Withdrawal

By 4 July, the situation was getting critical for Pakistan. The Indian Army was on the offensive and remorselessly recapturing its lost areas, peak by bloody peak. Its artillery, especially the Bofors guns, was taking a terrible toll. Although the Indians did not cross the LOC (the option to cross the LOC and strike at Pakistani bases was considered, but refused), they had interdicted all supplies to the Pakistani forward troops who were now running out of supplies and ammunition. Casualties were mounting by the day, and the Pakistani Higher Command even refused to take back their dead bodies as it would amount to admitting their involvement. Yet the wounded were pouring into Skardu Base Hospital and the news was slowly leaking out of the debacle taking place at these heights.

On 04 July, Prime Minister Nawaz Sharif flew to Washington for a meeting with the US President Bill Clinton, in a futile bid for intervention, only to be bluntly told "withdraw your troops." By then, the Indian Army had already recaptured most of the positions in Kargil and Dras and were pushing forward in Batalik and Turtuk as well. Faced with lowly defeat, the Pakistani started retreating, harassed by artillery fire along the way, leaving their dead behind. The Indian army continued moving forward and by 26 July 1999 – a day marked as Kargil Vijay Diwas – the last position was cleared. Each of the peaks was back in Indian hands.

Condemned for its failure in what has been called 'Pakistan's greatest blunder' and 'a disaster bigger than East Pakistan', the Pakistani Army came under increasing criticism. Prime Minister Nawaz Sharif laid the onus of the defeat entirely on the Army and relations between him and General Musharraf broke down completely. On 12 Oct, Musharraf staged a coup, ousting Sharif, and another period of military rule began in Pakistan.

But the story did not end here. Just two months later, an Indian MIG-21 shot down a Pakistani Atlantique Reconnaissance aircraft which had intruded into Indian territory in the Rann of Kutch. Two years later, in Dec 2001, the two nations again came to the verge of war after the attack on Indian Parliament by Pakistani-sponsored terrorists. The eternal story of Indo-Pak enmity continued as it will for perhaps decades more.

42

February 2019
KASHMIR

Pulwama, Balakot and Beyond

The vexed issue of Kashmir is the classical game of snakes and ladders. It takes months, if not years, of painstaking effort to move a few steps ahead and then one false step puts it back to Square A. Since the inception of the Kashmir problem (see 'The Race to Srinagar' and 'Saving Kashmir'), each forward step towards normalisation has usually been countered by an action – usually from across the border – that puts the issue back on boil. Three wars and a two-decade-long insurgency have done little to resolve the issue and now in February 2019, it has reached another flashpoint.

2019 could well be the watershed moment for Kashmir. It reached a dangerous point on 14 February 2019, when a Kashmiri youth rammed his explosive-laden SUV into a CRPF convoy killing 46 troopers in the single worst strike on security forces. That indiscriminately high death toll of soldiers across the country resonated all over India.

For way too long Pakistan had been under the perception that they could keep the pot on the boil and continue bleeding India with a thousand cuts under the shadow of nuclear deterrence. Yet under the muscular nationalistic policies that are now being followed, attacks traced back to Pakistan have met with responses that carry the battle into the other side. In September 2016, a Fedayeen attack on an Army camp in Uri killed 19 Indian soldiers, with the smoking gun pointing squarely to Jaish-e-Mohammed, and its handlers in Pakistan. Just 11 days after the strike, teams of Special Forces of 4 and 9 PARA COMMANDO along with the Commando platoons of the two battalions that had suffered casualties during the Uri attacks, infiltrated across the Line of Control shortly after midnight on the night of 29 September. Two teams from 4 PARA crossed the LOC in the Naugam Sector of Kupwara, while teams from 9 PARA crossed over in the Poonch sector. With artillery fire covering their move, the teams converged on to their objectives – terrorist camps 2-3 kilometres inside enemy territory, where militants assembled before infiltrating into India. The movement of the teams was undetected and the teams took up positions around the camps attacking them with grenades, missiles and rocket launchers. The short, intense fire assaults virtually eliminated the militants holed up within and in less than two hours, the teams exfiltrated back across the LOC into India. That daring raid was executed without a single casualty, save one soldier who was injured in a mine blast.

As per a post-strike assessment, 38 militants and 2 Pakistani soldiers were killed in the action. Radio intercepts revealed names of leaders killed in the action. Locals reported the arrivals of ambulances and body bags in military and civilian hospitals and mortuaries. Pakistan, predictably denied the damage, but the message was clear. The LOC was no longer inviolable and retributory action could be expected across it.

The LOC has been some kind of Rubicon. Even during the Kargil War, Indian troops or aircraft were not permitted to cross it. This *'Lakshman Rekha'* was a self-imposed constraint and the surgical strike proved that it no longer held good.

On the night of 26 February 2019, the myth of inviolability of the LOC was broken once and for all. That night, twelve MIRAGE 2000s aircraft, armed with SPICE 2000 and Popeye precision-guided munitions crossed the LOC and headed towards Balakot in the Khyber Pakhtunkhwa Province. The aircraft were part of a strike package supported by 4 Sukhoi 30 MKIs, Netra and Phalcon AWACS, a Heron UAV and two Ilushin IL-78 aerial refuelling aircraft. To act as decoy, four other Sukhoi 30s were launched towards Bahawalpur in South Punjab while the main package raced towards Balakot, unleashed their deadly load and returned – all this in 20 minutes and with no damage to themselves.

The audacious IAF strike at the Jaish-e-Mohammed terrorist training camp at Balakot was the direct outcome of the attack on the CRPF convoy in Pulwama 13 days earlier. But it was the result of months of planning. The increasing actions of Pakistani-based terrorist groups had to be met with pro-active response and retribution had to be punitive and proportionate. It was decided to attack terrorist camps within Pakistan so that a clear message would be sent. A target list of 15 different terrorist camps was prepared and homed on to three main camps: Bahawalpur in Pakistani Punjab, Sawai Nallah near Muzaffarabad (PoK) and the Balakot in the Khyber Pakhtunkhwa Province.

The Camp at Balakot

The main Jaish-e-Mohammed camp at their Headquarters in Bahawalpur was the initial target. It would have the greatest impact, but the camp had expanded over the years and was in a densely populated civilian area which would have caused civilian casualties. Eventually, the Jaish camp at Balakot was selected. It was an ideal choice. The Markaz Syed Ahmad Shaheed Camp was on the crest of a ridge called Jaba Top. It was around 3 kilometres from the nearest village which meant that collateral damage would be minimal. Spread over 8 acres, it held 10 major buildings in which over 200 recruits underwent training. It was known to have received a fresh influx of recruits who were all set to be inducted into India. A strike here would send out a strong message.

Air Chief Marshal Birendra Singh Dhanoa received the go-ahead on 19 February and the plan was set in motion. The Pakistanis would be expecting some kind of a response and maintaining surprise and secrecy was essential. Routine night flying by IAF aircraft was thus increased all along the International Boundary and LOC so that movement of aircraft on the night of the actual strike would not draw attention. The aircraft were drawn from different air bases so that no unusual activity would be noticed. The Mirages took off from their bases in Agra and Bareilly and as they overflew Delhi, a dark corridor of air space was created to mask their move. En route they were refuelled mid-air by IL-76 tankers for their long flight to Pakistan and back. As they approached Pakistani airspace, a flight of 4 Sukhois headed for Bahawalpur (where the main Jaish-e-Mohammed camp was located). These aircraft were deliberately flying high and were detected by Pakistani radars and F-16 fighters were scrambled to intercept them, thus drawing them away from the main force. The main formation of low-flying MIRAGE 2000s roared in across the LOC towards Balakot where they acquired the targets and let loose their specially selected SPICE (Smart, Precise Impact and Cost Effective) munitions on them.

The Israeli-built SPICE are not bombs. They are guidance kits which are fitted on to bombs to convert them to 'smart' weapons. The kit has an on-board GPS and optical cameras which can guide the bomb to targets over 60 kilometers away with an accuracy of three metres. Penetrative bombs were selected for maximum damage. These bombs had a hard nose which could penetrate the concrete of the roof and enter the rooms, with a delayed timer that would make bombs explode within the confines of the room, enhancing the blast and shock effects. Five such bombs struck the target at around 3.45 am, three of them hitting the main residential complex which held around

80–100 recruits, one hitting the main building which held the core leadership team of the camp and the fifth hitting the trainer's complex.

The entire strike took just 8 minutes. By the time PAF fighters moved to intercept them, the Mirages were already in Indian airspace. Damage caused would have been extensive. According to Intelligence agencies, reports of ambulances carrying bodies were received from as far off as Abbottabad. Pakistani sources stoutly maintained that no casualties were caused and the only damage done was "to some trees and some crows."

SPICE Munitions

Yet the story was not over yet. The very next day on 27 February, Pakistani aircraft launched a retaliatory strike on Indian targets. Indian and Pakistani fighters clashed in a dogfight and in a high-speed encounter, a Pakistani F-16 and an Indian MIG-21 were shot down. Wing Commander Abhinandan Varthaman was taken prisoner after he bailed out of his stricken aircraft. This was the most serious clash of arms since the Kargil War and the first time the two sides had engaged in an aerial encounter since August 1999, when an Indian MIG shot down a Pakistani Brequet Atlantique 91 N maritime patrol aircraft that had intruded into the Rann of Kutch in the aftermath of the Kargil War. Wing Commander Abhinandan was released two days later and the two sides slowly pulled back from the brink.

The air strike at Balakot cannot be measured just in terms of casualties and damage caused. It was a significant departure from the reactive strategies of the past. The Indian willingness to cross the LOC and taking the attacks into Pakistani territory implied that the cost of supporting terrorism could be made very high for Pakistan. It was a marked climb up the escalatory ladder and showed that the nuclear bluff which Pakistan banked upon to prevent significant retaliation had been called. But then the danger of climbing up the escalatory ladder is that it is difficult to step back, and each subsequent response takes you higher still. Any one of the steps could lead to a fatal miscalculation.

Uri, Pulwama and Balakot are just another part of the never-ending conflict of Kashmir. This has been the battleground in the wars of 1947-48, 1965, 1971, the Kargil War of 1999 and the 20-year slow burn of insurgency since the late 1980s. Perhaps the abrogation of Article 370 for Kashmir will aid the process of integrating it completely with India and could finally bring peace into the valley. This battle has gone on for too long. In this battleground, the flames never really subside and the embers never get a chance to cool. The battle in the air has added another dimension to it and provided one more chapter to the long conflict. Unfortunately, there may be many more till the troubled story of Kashmir finally finds closure.

43

'OP SINDOOR': India's Retaliation against Terror

"There is no distinction between terror sponsors and Terrorists. India will no longer see terrorist leaders and the governments sheltering them as separate entities."

—**Prime Minister Narendra Modi**

The Tortuous History of Terrorism in India

The scourge of Pakistan-sponsored terrorism in India goes back to 1947. Just two months after Pakistan was created based on the flawed "Two-nation theory," it sent armed tribesmen, led by Army officers and men in civilian clothing, to wrench Kashmir by military force. (Also see "The Race to Srinagar"). That invasion was repelled, and Kashmir was saved, but the legacy of the 'Kabalis' continues to this day, and Pakistan's policy of using state-sponsored terrorism remains undiminished.

Pakistan followed the same playbook when they launched OPERATION GIBRALTAR and sent armed raiders into Kashmir as a prelude to the 1965 war (Also see "Bloody September"). Defeats in the 1965 and 1971 wars did not seem to deter them. In the late 1980s, spurred by the policies of General Zia-ul-Haq, Pakistan began a vicious programme of state-sponsored terrorism in Kashmir, which continued for over two decades.

In 1999, Pakistan launched the disastrous Kargil operation, using regular Army troops and passing them off as *'Mujahideen'* – a lie which was exposed entirely later (See "The Heights of Victory"). But the main scourge of terrorism hit India in the first decade of the millennium, when attacks took place virtually across the country. The Red Fort was attacked by terrorists in December 2000, and the car bombing of the Jammu and Kashmir legislative assembly took place in October 2001. Then on 13 December 2001, the Indian Parliament was attacked by five terrorists of the Jaish-e-Mohammed, who were thankfully eliminated before significant harm could be done. This led to a two-year stand-off, as both sides mobilised troops along the border. But though war was averted, the attacks continued. Akshardham temple in Gujarat was attacked in September 2002, train bombings took place in Varanasi, Mumbai, Ahmedabad, and on the Samjhauta Express. The most heinous act was the 26/11 attacks in 2008, when ten members of the Lashkar-e-Taiba entered Mumbai by sea, and hit the Chhatrapati Shivaji railway terminus, the Oberoi Trident Hotel, the Taj Hotel, Leopold Cafe, and other locations across the city, killing 175 innocent people. One of the attackers, Ajmal Kasab, was captured alive and admitted to his training and indoctrination by the Lashkar-e-Taiba, and also of the active complicity of the Pakistani Army and ISI in the

The Taj Hotel

Ajmal Kasab: The Captured Terrorist

operation. Despite proven Pakistani involvement in the attack, the Indian response remained muted.

The lack of response perhaps emboldened the Pakistani establishment to think that it could continue the policy without fear of retaliation. The turning point came in September 2016, when militants of the Jaish-e-Mohammed attacked an army camp in Uri, killing 19 soldiers in the deadliest attack on security forces in three decades. Just 10 days after the strike, Indian commandos crossed the Line of Control and attacked terrorist launchpads inside Pakistan-Occupied Kashmir. What changed the equation was the Pulwama attack, when 40 CRPF troopers were killed in a suicide attack on 14 February 2019 – a strike claimed by the Jaish-e-Mohammed. This time, the Indian response was even stronger. Indian aircraft struck a terrorist camp at Balakot (See "Kashmir...Pulwama, Balakot and Beyond"). It was a clear signal that retaliation could come even across the border, and, significantly, terrorist actions reduced drastically after that.

But perhaps the deterrence of Balakot was wearing off. With the abrogation of Article 370 and a slew of developmental and security measures, Kashmir was coming back to normalcy and was awash with tourists and prosperity. It was a situation that Pakistan could not accept. On 22 April 2025, Pakistani-sponsored terrorists killed 26 tourists in Pahalgam and the die was set for another response.

The Terrorist Attack at Pahalgam

In the afternoon of 22 April 25, around four or five terrorists, dressed in camouflage fatigues, armed with M4 carbines and AK-47 assault rifles, approached the popular tourist spot of Baisaran—a beautiful valley in Pahalgam, often called "Mini-Switzerland'. They selected a place that was accessible only on foot or by pony, thus ensuring that the security response would be delayed. A group patrolled the upper reaches of the mountains to give early warning; another came up to the tourists thronging the area, separated them after ascertaining their religion, and shot them one by one, before disappearing in the thickly wooded mountains adjoining it.

It was a well-planned action, carried out by well-trained terrorists, specifically targeting tourists based on religion. Kashmir had witnessed a surge in tourism after the near normalcy of the past three years, and over two crore tourists had visited the beautiful state in this year alone. Tourism has grown into a Rs 21,000 Crore industry, raising the per capita income of ordinary Kashmiris by 10.6 percent. The mood in Kashmir had changed with a focus on economic prosperity and development, rather than some half-baked notion of separatism, and even local terrorism had declined considerably. Pakistan had to plan 'something big' to disrupt the return to normalcy in the valley.

It was no coincidence that just a few days before the attack, the Pakistani Army Chief, General Asim Munir, issued a veiled warning, calling Kashmir "Islamabad's jugular vein." The invoking of the Kashmir issue was designed to divert attention from Pakistan's political, economic and social mess. The army, too, had lost much of its sheen, and he probably felt that it needed to revive its actions to make it relevant once again.

Immediately after the attack, a little-known terrorist group – The Resistance Front, an offshoot of the banned Lashkar-e-Taiba, claimed responsibility. The terrorists had come in from across the border and had been aided by locals who provided logistics and shelter. And though the locals were later identified and arrested, the actual terrorists slipped away after the strike.

The strike had to have a response, and in its most decisive action ever, India announced the suspension of the Indus Waters Treaty (IWT). The IWT allows Pakistan to use the waters of the western rivers – the Indus, Jhelum and Chenab; while the Eastern rivers – the Ravi, Beas and Sutlej could be used unrestrictedly by India. The lion's share of the waters – a whopping 80 percent – flows into Pakistan. The suspension of this treaty does not mean that water flowing into Pakistan can be shut off like a tap. It will take a decade of building dams, hydroelectric projects, reservoirs, canals and distributaries to harness the waters adequately. But India can now desilt reservoirs and release water without informing Pakistan. This means that water can be released during wet months, which could contribute to flooding, and withheld during the dry season when it is most needed. It will also enable India to proceed with projects such as the Tulbul Navigational Project, the Wullar project, and the Uri hydroelectric project on the Jhelum, among others, which will provide much-needed hydroelectricity and irrigation to Kashmir. This is a measure that would hurt Pakistan, but as Prime Minister Modi stated, "Blood and water cannot flow together."

'OP SINDOOR': The Strike

Yet, more than the non-kinetic measures, a message had to be sent across that Pakistan could not engage in acts of terrorism on Indian soil without retaliation. And the message had to be delivered on Pakistani soil, clearly and unambiguously. The strike was to be a "Focused, measured and non-escalatory strike" targeting only terrorist camps, and no military or civilian installation was targeted.

On the night of 7 May, a strike package of IAF Rafales, Mirage 2000s, and Sukhoi 30 MKI fighters launched a precision strike on terrorist camps within Pakistan, firing SCALP Storm Shadow long-range cruise missiles and Hammer air-to-ground precision bombs, which were launched from well within Indian airspace. Long-range artillery, utilising precision-guided munitions, was employed against targets within closer range. Other aircraft simulated activity all along the front to divide the enemy's reaction. The entire operation was controlled by an Airborne Early Warning and Control aircraft. At the same time, loitering drones sent back videos of the strike and the damage, before they too finally crashed into their designated targets with their explosive payloads.

The entire strike lasted just 24 minutes – from 1:04 am to 1:30 am. By the time it was over, 24 missiles had hit nine terrorist camps – five in POK and four in Pakistani Punjab. These included the Sawai Nala training camp at Muzzafarabad, the Bilal camp in POK, the Gulpur camp in Kotli, the Barnala camp in Bhimbar, the Kotli Abbas camp and the Sarjal camp in Sialkot – all around 9-30 kms deep. The more significant targets were deeper in Pakistani Punjab. Markaz Taiba camp in Muridke, near Lahore - the HQ of the Lashkar-e-Taiba – from where its chief Hafiz Saeed planned the Mumbai blasts and other terrorist attacks – was levelled with a high precision missile strike. At Bahawalpur, over 100 km deep, the Markaz Subhan camp, HQ of the Jaish-e-Mohammed, was similarly eradicated. Over 90 operatives were reportedly killed in this strike, the losses confirmed by radio intercepts and messages. But it is telling that Pakistani officers and politicians were present for the funerals of dead terrorist– a indictment of the deep nexus that exists between them and the terrorist groups they have raised and sponsored.

The attack also saw the first long-range air battle between Indian and Pakistani fighter aircraft. Around 125 aircraft on both sides engaged each other at ranges up to 100 kilometres using Beyond Visual Range missiles. Indian Rafales, Mirage 2000s, Sukhoi 30s and MiG-29s, engaged Pakistani J-10 and J-17 Chinese-made multi-role fighters equipped with PL-15 air-to-air missiles. The aerial engagement is estimated to have lasted around an hour. Pakistan claimed to have shot down 3–5 Indian aircraft, but without any substantive proof. There would have been some damage to the equipment, but not a single pilot was lost. More importantly, the strike hit the designated targets with precision and impunity, inflicting considerable damage and sending a clear statement of intent.

The Escalation

The Pakistani reaction came the very same day, as it launched its own OP BUNYAD-UN-MARSOOS. At around 2030h, Pakistan targeted 15 military establishments all the way from Bhuj to Srinagar, striking with drones and missiles. The very next day, on 08 May, the conflict escalated even further as Pakistan fired over 500 rockets and drones at military and civilian locations. The missiles were intercepted and shot down – 8 in the Jammu region itself – but several drones did get through, inflicting localised damage. It was the first time since 1971 that both sides had targeted each other's cities – something that was not done even during the Kargil War. That same afternoon, India attacked Pakistani military installations at Rawalpindi, Gujranwala, Mianwali, Bahawalpur, and as far as Karachi, destroying the HQ-9 Air Defence system at Lahore with Harpy Kamikazi drones. The attack was quite ingenious. Drones mimicking the radio and electronic signals of aircraft were flown towards the target, which made them activate their radars. The Harpy drones homed in on the radar emissions and smashed into them, destroying radars and AD systems. Pakistan claimed to have targeted Indian S-400 Air Defence systems similarly, but later accounts proved that not a single AD battery was penetrated by the Pakistanis.

On the night of 8/9 May, Pakistan launched its third round of attacks using around 300 drones – most of them Turkish-built Songars – in a strike directed at 26 installations along the western border. The attacks came in swarms, with sophisticated attack drones mingled with dozens of cheap expendable drones, to swamp the defences. It is to the credit of India's air defence systems that not a single drone or missile managed to hit a defence installation. Most of the drones were shot down by Air Defence guns (thus preserving precious AD missiles for more dangerous targets). A Pakistani Fatah II missile was also shot down near Sirsa – presumably headed for Delhi – as the non-contact war escalated. No naval or ground attacks took place, though the navy had already taken up positions in the Arabian Sea and was poised to hit naval targets, if required. Formations had also mobilised and moved towards the border, but no ground action took place. But along the LOC, the ceasefire broke down completely as artillery and mortar duels and small arms firing raged along its entire frontage.

India's Attack on Pakistan's Air Bases

The night of 9/10 May was perhaps the most significant of the war. On that night, India struck 8 PAF airbases and three radar locations with devastating missiles and drone strikes. The targets were spread across the entire length and breadth of the country and covered the major air bases of all three Air Commands – the PAF Northern, Central and Southern Air Commands.

At 02.09 am on the night of 10 May, Nur Khan airbase at Rawalpindi, which was located close to their nuclear storage plant at Kirana Hills, was hit by a series of Brahmos missiles. The shock of the explosions could be heard as far as Islamabad, and led to fears that their nuclear weapons had been targeted, and forced a radioactive sweep of the area to check for any leakage. At 2.30 am, the Chief of Army Staff, Gen Asim Munir, called up Prime Minister Shahbaz Sharif, informing him of the strike. Speaking after the war, Prime Minister Sharif admitted the devastating effect of the Indian strikes, "We had decided that at 4.40 am, after the Fajr prayers, Pakistan armed forces, ably led by Chief Syed Asim Munir, would launch an attack to teach a lesson to our enemy. But before that, Indians launched missile attacks, Brahmos and others, which hit Pakistan's various provinces, including Rawalpindi and other places."

The effect of the strikes was indeed devastating. A series of missiles hit Rahimyar Khan – most probably Brahmos – which damaged the runways and hangars, rendering them inoperable. The PAF's most crucial strategic asset – the Sargodha base, which is HQ to its Central Air Command and houses Mirage 5, J-7, JF-17 and F-16 squadrons – the mainstay of its air force – was virtually crippled by a pinpoint strike that hit the center of two sections of runway, declaring them inoperable. Bholari – Pakistan's newest and most advanced base, located 270 kilometres deep, which houses JF-17 Thunder and F-16 squadrons, along with the latest SAAB 2000 Airborne Early Warning & Control aircraft. The Indian attack killed Squadron Leader Usman Yusuf and four airmen on the ground, and a SAAB 2000 was damaged when a missile hit the hangar it was sheltering in.

The air bases at Chakwal, Shorkot, Jacobabad and Sukkar were also hit. Only the Rafiqui airbase at Shorkot could activate its Air Defence sufficiently to prevent major damage. All others suffered significant damage, which slowly emerged through satellite photos, admissions by Pakistani sources, and even international tenders that were put up by the PAF seeking contractors to repair the damage caused to these bases by the Indian strikes. The strikes proved that Pakistani Air Defence could be penetrated with ease, and no part of Pakistan was safe from Indian strikes. Radar stations at Sialkot, Pasrur, and Chunian, as well as those located as far off as Malir in Karachi, were also hit, causing huge gaps in their air defence that could have been exploited for subsequent attacks. The Air Force and even the Navy were raring to have another go when the ceasefire was suddenly announced.

The effect of these strikes led Pakistan to ask for a ceasefire. The circumstances behind the ceasefire have different versions. President Donald Trump tweeted that he had asked the two sides for a ceasefire, and claimed credit for it – a claim that later proved unfounded. Both sides claimed that the other had initiated the request. However, in effect, their DGMO had been in touch with his Indian counterpart all morning, and the proposal was finally agreed upon in the afternoon of 10 May. The ceasefire came into effect at 1700 hours on the same day.

But it was for the best that the hostilities ended at that juncture. Beyond that, India could have imposed more damage on Pakistan, but the effects would have been counterproductive. The message had been delivered to Pakistan. Further escalation could have led to all-out war, and then, a climbdown would have been more difficult.

The Lessons for India

India made a clear statement of intent that Pakistani-sponsored terrorism would not be condoned. There is no difference between terrorist sponsors and the terrorists, and the costs imposed on Pakistan for its policy of state-sponsored terrorism could be severe. Uri and Balakot demonstrated that India would not hesitate to cross over into enemy territory in retaliation for a strike. Pakistan had long lived under the illusion that its nuclear capability would deter any Indian attack, irrespective of the provocation. OP SINDOOR has broken the fallacy and proved that India is willing to take punitive action in the event of any misadventure by Pakistan, and the response would come at a time and place of our choosing.

However, the conflict also offers some valuable lessons to take away. It was a short, intense war – just four days – but a war it was. It was, in many ways, a 'non-contact war' since the exchange of fire took place at long ranges and the intense physical battles of the past were avoided. The war saw extensive use of drones and long-range precision munitions striking deep into each other's territory. Perhaps that could be the norm for future engagements as well. This time, we were able to counter enemy drones and missiles, preventing damage to our soil. But our surveillance and Air Defence networks need to be enhanced and integrated even further, because subsequent attacks could be even more sophisticated. And at the same time, our ability to overcome enemy air defences and strike deep needs to be enhanced. Brahmos proved to be one of the major success stories of the war. Brahmos missiles managed to penetrate deep into enemy territory and strike targets with pinpoint precision. It marks a significant success of our ATMANIRBHAR campaign. It should be followed up in the development of indigenous defence equipment, ranging from artillery guns, drones, specialised ammunition, naval ships, aircraft and armoured fighting vehicles. Besides self-sufficiency, it will also provide a considerable boost to defence exports.

Yet, one cause of concern is how India was unable to disseminate its narrative and was slow in the information domain. Pakistan issued its disinformation over social media and global news channels, which often carried their version, providing them with a 'first-mover advantage.' India's information campaign was slow and often reactive. Utilising all branches of the government to craft a strong and consistent narrative, and ensuring its dissemination worldwide, is crucial if we are to win the war of perception, which is often as important as winning the actual battle.

We have also made a statement to Pakistan that the Indian response will be hard and could even pose an existential threat to them. That should serve as a deterrent for a while. But we cannot afford to let our guard down. If anything, our intelligence and internal security need to be heightened. The ball in now in Pakistan's court. It is unlikely to change its ways, but it would be well warned of the dangers of sponsoring terrorism on Indian soil. If that message drives home, OP SINDOOR would well and truly have attained its aims.

Terror Camps that were Hit

- Markaz Taiba, Muridke. The HQ of the Lashkar-e-Taiba and the Jamaat-ud-Dawa. The terrorists who participated in the Mumbai attacks of 2008 were trained and indoctrinated here.
- Markaz Subhanallah, Bahawalpur. The HQ of the Jaish-e-Mohammed is over 100 km from the IB. It was used for the Pathankot and Pulwama attacks.
- Sawai Nala Camp, Muzaffarabad. A major LeT camp where the Pahalgam terrorists trained.
- Syedna Bilal Camp, Muzaffarabad. Camp for LeT and JeM, where training is provided by personnel of Pakistan SSG.
- Barnala Camp, Bhimber. Just 9 km from the LOC, it serves as a launch pad for infiltrators into Kashmir.
- Abbas Camp, Kotli. Indoctrination and training camp for Fidayeen.
- Sarjal Camp, Narowal. Near the IB in Pakistani Punjab. Used for infiltration in the Jammu sector
- Gulpur Camp, Kotli. Base for LeT units active in Poonch and Rajouri districts.
- Mehmona Joya Camp, Sialkot. HeM camp that serves as a launchpad for terrorists entering Punjab and Jammu.

Pak Air Bases Hit by India

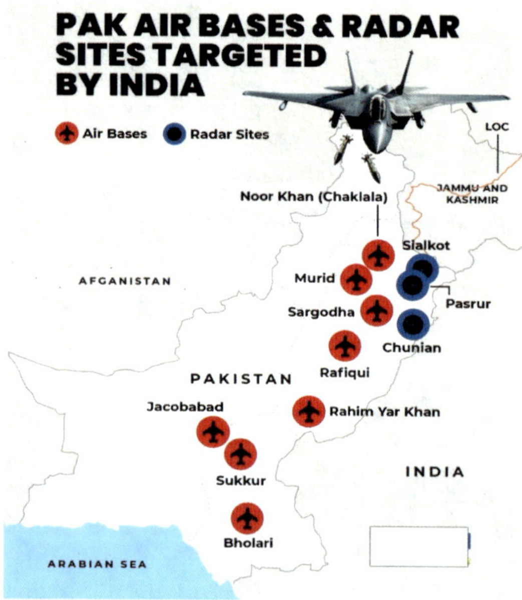

- PAF Base, Nur Khan, Rawalpindi. Close to the Pakistani Army GHQ and their nuclear command.
- PAF Base, Murid, Chakwal. Home base for Pakistan's drone fleet, housing eight hangars of UAVs.
- PAF Base, Mushaf, Sargodha. The most vital strategic base of the PAF, housing the frontline squadrons of the PAF, including F-16s, Mirages, JF-17s and J-7s.
- PAF Base, Shahbaz, Jacobabad. Served as a crucial NATO base for their actions in Afghanistan. F-16 base.
- PAF Base, Rafique, Shorkot. Base for JF-17s and Mirage 5 fighters.
- PAF Base, Sukkur. The HQ of the Southern Air Command is a significant operational base for the PAF.
- PAK Base, Rahimyar Khan. Forward Operational Base of Central Air Command. Indian strikes and base rendered inoperable knocked out its runway.
- PAF Base, Bholari, Jamshoro. PAFs, the newest base, which also houses their AWACs. A Saab 2000 AWAC was hit during the strike here.

Radar Sites Attacked

- Sialkot
- Pasrur
- Chunian
- Lahore
- Malir Cantt, Karachi

Index

26/11 attacks, 238

A

Abdali's Army, 82
Abdullah Latif, 218
Abdullah Uzbeg, 39
Abhimanyu, 5
Actual Ground Position Line (ACPL), 207
Adil Shah Suri, 38
Admiral S M Nanda, 186
Afghan Army, 22, 30
Agni Astras, 6
Ahmad Shah Abdali, 79, 80, 82
Ahmedabad, 238
Air Chief Marshal Birendra Singh Dhanoa, 234
Air Defence Guns, 243
Air Marshal Arjan Singh, 160
Airborne Early Warning and Control Aircraft, 241
Akbar, 38, 41-42, 44, 51-52, 56
Akhnur, 151
Akshauhinis, 3, 4
Albert Museum, 95
Alexander the Great, 7-9, 12
Alexander's Army, 10
Ali, Hyder, 91-92, 95
ANGAR, 189
Anglo-Maratha battles, 97
Anglo-Mysore Wars, 90
Anglo-Sikh Wars, 101, 107, 111
Appa Desai, 97
Arabian Sea, 183
Aravali Hills, 52
Army Chief Gen Sam Manekshaw, 171
Arthur Wellesley, 94
Ashok Banerjee, 220
Atmanirbhar, 245
Attack on Karachi, 186
Aurangzeb, 57-60, 63

B

Bahadur Shah Zafar, 33, 110-12
Bahawalpur, 242
Bahawalpur, Markaz Subhanallah, 247
Bairam Khan, 44
Baisaran, 239
Balaji Vishwanath, 68
Balakot, 236, 239, 245
Banas River, 53
Bangladesh Navy, 183
Bapu Gokhale, 97
Basantar Nala, 196, 198
Battle for
- Goa, 134
- Jaffna, 217
- Kashmir, 118

Battle of
- Basantar/Nawapind, 196
- Bhima Koregaon, 96
- Buxar, 86, 102
- Chausa, 33
- Ghaghra, 30
- Haldi Ghati, 51
- Hydaspes, 7
- Jhelum River, 7
- Khanua, 25
- Kurukshetra, 1
- Longewala, 191
- Nathu La and Cho La, 161
- Palashi, 74, 86
- Palkhed, 68-69
- Plassey, 109
- Rakshasi–Tangadgi, 45
- Rezang La, 144
- Samugarh, 57
- Saragarhi, 114
- Talikota, 45
- Tarain, 13
- Tuglaqabad, 37
- Zojila, 129

BBC, 174
Beas River 12, 106, 240
Bengal Native Infantry, 110
Bengali militia, 172
Beyond Visual Range Missiles, 242

Bhagirathi River, 75
Bhagwat Gita, 4
Bhima River, 96-97
Bhimbar, Barnala camp, 241, 247
Bhishma, 4
Bholari, 244
Bholari Base, 248
Bhuj, 242
Bhutto, Benazir, 207
Bibighar, 111
Bilafond La, 204-05
Blackest Day in Indian History, 79
Bloody September, 238
Bombay Native Infantry, 97
Brahmos missiles, 243-45
Brig Faroukh Bulsara, 219
Brig J C Katoch, 125
Brig Khwaja Mohammed Naser, 200-01
Brig L P Sen, 125-26
Brig M L Khetrapal, 200-01
Brig Mohammed Usman, 128
Brig Rajinder Singh, 120
Brig T N Raina, 145
Brig V N Channa, 205
British, 93-94
  Cavalry Regiment, 105
  Force, 93, 111
Buxar, 87-89

C

Camel's Back, 163-64
Capt Anil Sharma, 211
Capt Dagar, 163-64
Capt G S Gill, 168
Capt Kamaljit Singh, 122
Capt Sanjay Kulkarni, 205
Capt Saurabh Kalia, 224-25
Capt Vikram Batra, 228
Capture of Bana Post, 209
Capture of Sinhgarh Fort, 62
Carnatic Wars, 75
Cavalry Brigade, 105
Chabutra Ridge, 131
Chakravyuh, 5
Chakwal, 244
Chand Bardai, 17
Chattri Mata, 223
Chausa, 24
Chauth, 70, 72
Chawinda, 155
Che Dong, 141
Chenab River, 240
Chetak, 55
Chhamb, 151, 196
Chhamb-Jaurian, 157
Chhatrapati Shivaji railway terminus, 238
Chhatrapati, 70
Cho La, 165
Christian Missionary Hospital, 120
Chunian, 244, 248
Chushul, 144-45, 147
Circar of Guntur, 92
Clive, Robert, 75, 78
Col Burr, 97
Col Narender 'Bull' Kumar, 204
Col S C Joshi, 221
Cusp of Victory, 13
Cyril Radcliff, 118

D

Dacca Race Course, 175
Dara Shukoh, 58, 60-61
Das, Laxman, 212
Daulat Khan, 20
Deccan, 72-73, 85
Deccan Armies, 49
Deccan Sultanates, 47
Defence of Pakistan, 155
DGMO, 244
Dharma, 2
Dhola Ridge, 141-42
Doklam, 165
Dongri Cliff, 64
Dronacharya, 4-5
Duryodhana, 3, 6

E

East India Company, 97, 104, 107, 109
Emperor Shah Jahan, 58
Enfield P–53 rifle, 109

F

F-16 squadrons, 244
Fajr Prayers, 243
Fateh Ali Sahab Tipu, 90
Fazilka, 196
First Anglo-Mysore War, 91
First Battle of Panipat, 19, 37
First War of Independence, 107
First-mover Advantage, 246
Flt Lt Ganapathy, 169
Flt Lt Ghuman, 180
Flt Lt Parvaiz Mehdi Qureshi, 169
Flt Lt Roy Andrew Massey, 169
Flying Bullets, 179
Flying Officer Donald Lazarus, 169
Fort Lockhart and Gulistan, 116
Fort of Kondhana, 62

Fourth Anglo-Mysore War, 94
French Revolution, 93
Fricker, John, 159

G

Gandhi, Mrs Indira, 171-72, 200
Gandhi, Rajiv, 215, 217, 219
Ganges River, 30, 35
Gangtok–Lhasa trade route, 161
Gardi, Ibrahim Khan, 83
Gen A K Niazi, 173
Gen Askari, 30
Gen Aurora, 164
Gen Ayub Khan, 152
Gen Campbell, 112
Gen Hector Munro, 87
Gen Hugh Gough, 104
Gen Manekshaw, 164, 172
Gen Meleager, 10
Gen Mir Mardan, 76
Gen Parvez Musharraf, 207, 225
Gen Sagat Singh, 162-64
Gen Sam Manekshaw, 162
Gen Thimayya, 132
Gen Zia-ul-Haq, 238
Ghaghra River, 24, 30-32
Ghorchurras, 103
Ghorpade, 64
Goa, 134
Godavari River, 71
Governor Gen Manuel de Silva, 138
Grand Trunk Road, 36
Greece, 12
Greek Army, 10
Greek Phalanx, 9-11
Grenadier Yogendra Singh Yadav, 228
Gujarat, Akshardham Temple, 238
Gujranwala, 242
Gyong La, 204-05

H

HADIYA, 220
Haider Mohamed, 39
Haji Khan, Afghan Chief, 39
Haji Pir, 148-51, 153, 155
Haldi Ghati, 52-53, 56
Hammer air-to-ground precision bombs, 241
Harpy Kamikazi drones, 242
Havildar Ishar Singh, 115-16
Hector Munro, 88
Hemchandra/Hemu, 38-44
High Altitude Warfare School, 204
Himalayan Ranges, 148
Hindu Kush Mountains, 8, 21
Holkar, 84
HQ-9 Air Defence system, 242
Humayun, 26, 33-38
Hussainiwala, 196

I

Ibrahim Lodi, 20
Ibrahim Lodi's army, 22-23
Iccha Mrityu, 4
Ichhogil Canal, 154
India, 237-38, 240, 245-46
  Pak Air Bases Hit, 248
India's First War of Independence, 108
India's Gnats and Hunters, 158
Indian Air Force (IAF), 157-59, 177-78
Indian Army, 149, 204
Indian Gnats, 179
Indian Navy, 182
Indian Peace Keeping Force (IPKF), 215, 217, 219
Indo-China border, 141
Indo-Pak War, 1965, 124, 151-53, 157, 162, 166, 170
Indo-Sri Lankan Accord, 215
Indus Waters Treaty (IWT), 240
INS BETWA, 137, 222
INS GODAVARI, 222
INS KATCHALL, 187
INS KHUKRI, 184
INS KILTAN, 187
INS KIRPAN, 184
INS NIPAT, 187, 189
INS NIRGHAT, 187-88
INS POSHAK, 187
INS TALWAR, 190
INS TRISHUL, 190
INS VEER, 187, 189
INS VIKRANT, 136, 182
INS VINASH, 190
Intelligence Bureau, 141
ISI, 238
Islamabad, 243
Islamabad's Jugular Vein, 240
Israeli-built SPICE, 234

J

J 10 and J-17, 242
Jacobabad, 244
Jaish-e-Mohammed, 233, 238-39, 242, 247
Jalep La, 162
Jamaat-ud-Dawa, 247
Jammu and Kashmir, 238
Jamshoro Base, 248
JF-17 Thunder, 244
Jhansi, 112

Jhelum River, 8, 240
Jinnah, Mohammed Ali, 119, 210

K

Kabalis, 237
Kalanaur, 38
Kalyan Darwaza, 62
Kannauj, 35
Karachi Agreement, 1949, 203
Karachi, Malir Cantt, 244, 248
Karan, Khem, 155
Kargil Sector, 224, 226
Kargil War, 207, 236, 242
Karna, 5
Kasab, Ajmal, 238
Kashmir, 152, 231, 237-39
Kashmir Chand, 212
Kashmiri Gate, 111
Kaurava Army, 4
Kaurava, 3-6
Khamnor Village, 53
Khan, Ali Quli, 42
Khan, Bijli, 46, 48
Khan, Jalal, 35
Khan, Khalil Ullah, 60
Khan, Khanwar, 35
Khan, Rustom, 60
Khan, Yar Latuf, 75, 77
Khanua, 24, 26, 37
Khooni Darwaza, 111
Khooni Ghati, 52
Khushwaha Rajputs, 52
Khyber Pass, 80
Killer Squadron, 190
King Porus, 7
Kirana Hills, 243
Kishenganga, 153
Kohinoor Diamond, 107
Koli Dynasty, 63
Kondhana Fort, 63, 66
Koregaon, 98, 100
Kotli, Abbas Camp, 241, 247
Kotli, Gulpur Camp, 241, 247
Krishna, 4-5
Krishna Deva Raya, 46
Krishna River, 48
Krishna's Sudarshan Chakra, 6
Kurukshetra, 1, 2, 4

L

Ladakh, 145
Ladakh Scouts, 204, 206
Lahore, 241, 248
Lance Naik Ramesh Singh, 205
Land and Air Battle at Garibpur, 166
Lashkar-e-Taiba, 238, 240, 242, 247
Lazarus, Donald, 169
Leh, 120
Leopold Cafe, 238
Liberation Tigers of Tamil Eelam (LTTE), 214-16
Line of Control, 239, 243
Lohaganj River, 174
Longewala, 193, 196
Lt Col Akram Raja, 200
Lt Col Dewan Ranjit Rai, 121
Lt Col Hanut Singh, 198
Lt Col Pritam Singh, 127
Lt Col R K Singh, 167
Lt Col Rai, 122-23, 163
Lt Col Sher Jung Thapa, 130
Lt Dharam Vir, 193
Lt Francis Staunton, 97
Lt Gen A S Kalkat, 217
Lt Gen B M Kaul, 142
Lt Gen J S Aurora, 162
Lt Hanifuddin, 228
Lt Manoj Pandey, 228
Lt Rajiv Pande, 211

M

M V Progress Light, 221
Mahabharata, 2, 5-6
Mahar Regiment, 100
Maharaja Duleep Singh, 107
Maharaja Hari Singh, 119, 121, 124
Maharaja Jaswant Singh, 59
Maharaja Ranjit Singh, 101
Maharani Jind Kaur, 105
Maj (later Brig) Kuldip Singh Chandpuri, 191, 193
Maj Atma Singh, 194
Maj Bahuguna, 206
Maj Chandpuri, 194
Maj Gen Akbar Khan, 119
Maj Harbhajan, 163
Maj Harwant Singh, 122
Maj Prithi Chand, 131
Maj R J S Dhillon, 221
Maj R S Sandhu, 205
Maj Rajesh Adhikari, 228
Maj Ranjit Singh Dayal (later Lt Gen R S Dayal), 150
Maj Shaitan Singh, PVC, 146
Maj Somnath Sharma, 123, 125
Maj Varinder Singh Minhas, 211
Maj Vinod Bhatia, 219
Maj Vivek Gupta, 228
Majma-ul-Bahrain, 58

Makar Sankranti, 79
Malik-e-Maidan, 47
Man Singh, 56
Man Singh's Army, 52-53
Mandhovi River, 138
Maratha Army, 69, 73, 81-82, 93, 97
Marathas, 72-3, 80, 92-94, 96
Markaz Subhan camp, 242
Markaz Syed Ahmad Shaheed Camp, 234
Marpo La Ridgeline, 226
Menon, Krishna, Defence Minister, 141
Mianwali, 242
MiG-29s, 242
Mihtar Khan, 54
Mini-Switzerland, 239
Mir Jafar, 75, 77-78
Mir Mardan, 76
Mir Qasim, 86
Mir Sadiq, 94
Mirage 2000s, 241-42
Mirza Raje Jai Singh, 63
Modi, Narendra, Prime Minister, 237, 240
Mohammed Bin Tughlaq, 63
Mohammed Ghori, 13-18
Mohammed Mirza, 22
Mughal Army, 26, 35, 41
Mughal Empire, 37
Mujahideen, 238
Mukand Ridge, 131
Mukti Bahini, 174, 175
Mumbai, 238
Munir, Gen. Asim, 240, 243-44
Murad Bakshi, 59-60
Muridke, Markaz Taiba Camp, 241, 247-48
Murshidabad, 75, 78
Mushaf Base, 248
Muzaffarabad, Syedna Bilal Camp, 247
Muzzafarabad, Sawai Nala, 241, 247
MV Progress Light, 222
MV Sabarmati, 135
MV Venus Challenger, 189

N

Nabha Akal, 168
Naga Astras, 6
Naib Subedar Bana Singh, 207, 211-12
Naib Subedar Gyan Bahadur Limbu, 165
Najib-ud-Daulah, 80
Namka Chu Valley, 142
Narmada River, 73
Nathu La, 161, 163-65
Nawab Siraj-ud-Daulah, 75
Nawab's artillery, 89
Nehru, 136, 141-42, 152
Nizam of Hyderabad, 91-92, 94
Nizam's vast army, 71-72
Nizam-ul-Mulk, 70
Noor Khan, 46, 48
North West Frontier Province, 119

O

Oberoi Trident Hotel, 238
Om Raj, 212-13
OP BUNYAD-UN-MARSOOS, 242
OP SINDOOR, 241-42, 245-46
Operation Ababeel, 206
Operation Badr, 225
Operation Bison, 132
Operation Cactus in the Maldives, 218
Operation Cactus, 220
Operation Gibraltar, 153, 157, 238
Operation Gulmarg, 119
Operation Meghdoot, 204
Operation Pawan, 214-15
Operation Python, 190
Operation Trident, 187, 190
Operation Vijay, 227
Operational Readiness Platform, 179

P

PAF fighters, 235
PAF, 158-59, 179, 244
Pahalgam, Terrorist Attack, 239-40
Pakistan, 149, 155, 200, 237-38, 240, 245
Pakistan Air Force (PAF), 157, 194
Pakistani Army, 171, 207, 238
Pakistani Fatah II missile, 243
Pakistani Gayari base, 207
Pakistani Punjab, 241
Pakistani Tanks Clashing, 155
Pakistani Troops, 174
Pakistan-Occupied Kashmir, 239
Palkhed, 73
Panaji, 138
Pandavas, 3, 4, 6
Pandey, Mangal, 109
Panipat, 82
Pasrur, 244, 248
Pass of Blizzards, 129
People's Liberation Organisation of Tamil Eelam (PLOTE), 218, 220-21
Peshwa, Baji Rao II, 97
Peshwa's Forces, 99
Phillaura, 155
PL-15 air-to-air missiles, 242
PNS DACCA, 190
PNS Ghazi, 182

PNS Khaibar, 187, 190
PNS Muhafiz, 189
PNS Rajshahi, 183
PNS Shah Jahan, 189
PNS Sylhet, 183
POK, Bilal Camp, 241
Pontoon Bridge, 106
Poona Auxiliary Horse, 97
Poona Garrison, 97
Poona Horse, 198
Porus, 8, 11
Porus Scouts, 9
Porus's Army, 8
Princess Sanyogita, 13
Prithviraj Chauhan, 13-15, 18, 40
Pulwama, 236
    Balakot and Beyond, 231
Pune Darwaza, 62
Pune-Ahmadnagar highway, 96
Purana Qila, 40

Q

Quaid Post, 207, 209, 212-13
Qutb-ud-din-Aibak, 17
Qutub Minar, 39

R

Radar Sites Attacked, 248
Radar Stations, 244
Rafales, 241-42
Rafique Base, 248
Rahimyar Khan Base, 244, 248
Rai Durlabh, 75, 77
Raja Uday Singh, 52
Rajput Army, 16-17
Rama Raja Raya, 46-50
Rana Pratap, 52-55
Rana Sanga, 25, 27-28, 30
Rani Lakshmi Bai, 112-13
Ranjodh Singh Majitha, 105
Rao, Baji, 70-71, 73
Rao, Vishwas, 81
Rathod, Uday Bhan, 64-65
Ravi River, 197, 240
Rawalpindi, 242, 244
Rawalpindi, Nur Khan Airbase, 243, 248
Red Fort, 111
Rezang La, 144-47
Rifleman Chunni Lal, 212-13
Righteous Wars, 2
River Gambhir, 26

S

S-400 Air Defence systems, 243
SAAB 2000 Airborne Early Warning & Control Aircraft, 244
Sabre Slayers, 169
Sadashiv Bhau, 81, 85
Saltoro Ridge, 204
Samjhauta Express, 238
Samrat Hemchandra Vikramaditya, 40
Saragarhi, 115
Saragarhi Gurudwaras, 117
Sardar Vallabhai Patel, 126
Sardeshmukhi, 70, 72
Sargodha base, 244, 248
Saurabh Kalia, 226
SCALP Storm Shadow, 241
Scindia, 84
Se La, 143
Sebu La, 163-64
Second Anglo-Sikh Wars, 107
Second Battle of Panipat, 41
Second Lt Arun Khetrapal, 199
Second Lt Rajiv Pande, 210
Seringapatnam, 93
Shadi Khan Kakkar, 42
Shah, Ali Adil, 47-48
Shah, Ibrahim Qutb, 48
Shakargarh Bulge, 197
Sham Singh Attariwala, 105-06
Sharif, Nawaz, 226
Sharif, Shahbaz, 243, 248
Sher Shah Suri, 33-35, 38
Shihabuddin Muizzuddin Mohammed Bin Sam, 13
Shirur–Pune road, 98
Shiv Nala, 72
Shivaji, 62-63, 66
Shivaji's Legacy, 68
Shorkot, Rafiqui airbase, 244, 248
Shuja-ud-Daulah, 86-88
Sia La, 204-05
Siachen, 202, 207-09, 213
Sialkot, 244, 248
    Mehmona Joya Camp, 247
    Sarjal Camp, 241, 247
Sidi Hillal, 65
Signalman Gurmukh Singh, 116
Sikh Army, 101, 103, 105
Sikhs, 106-07
Sikkim-Tibet border, 161
Singh, Dilip, 101
Singh, Lal, 101-02, 105
Singh, V P, the then Prime Minister, 217
Sir Hugh Gough, 103

Siraj-ud-Daulah, 75-76, 80, 86
Siraj-ud-Daulah's Camp, 78
Sirsa, 243
Sisodiya Rajput Warriors, 52
Sonam Post, 211
Southern Tibet, 141
Special Service Group (SSG), 158
Sq Commander Maj D S Narang, 168
Sq Leader M M Alam, 160
Sq Leader S S Bains, 205
Sri Lanka, 219
Srinagar, 120, 126, 242
SS GULF STAR, 190
SS HARMATTAN, 190
Subedar Harnam Singh, 211
Subedar Sansar Chand, 211
Sukhoi 30 MKI fighter, 241-42
Sukkar, 244
Sukkur Base, 248
Sun God, 5
Suri, Hakim Khan, 52
Sutluj River, 106, 240

T

Taj Hotel, 238
Taj Mahal, 61
Tanaji Malusure, 64, 66
Tanaji, 64-65
Tapi River, 70
Tarain, 14-15, 17
Tardi Beg Khan, 38, 42
Tatya Tope, 112-13
Taur Silhadi of Raisen, 26
Tej Singh, 101-02, 105-06
The Heights of Victory, 238
The Race to Srinagar, 237
The Resistance Front, 240
Thermopylae of Mewar, 56
Third Anglo-Mysore War, 93
Third Battle of Panipat, 45, 79
Tibet, 142
Tiger Hill, 228
TIME Magazine, 223
Tipu Sultan, 90-91, 92, 94-95
Tirumalla Deva Raya, 50
Tololing Heights, 228
Tora Nala, 89
Tourism, 240
Treaty of Moongi-Paithan, 72
Treaty of Purandhar, 63
Tribakji Dengle, 97
Tughlaqabad, 41
Tuglaqabad fort, 39
Tulbul Navigational Project, 240
Turkish formation, 22
Turkish-built Songars, 243
Two-nation Theory, 237

U

Uri, 236, 239, 245
    Hydroelectric Project, 240
US Seventh Fleet, 175
USS ENTERPRISE, 175

V

Varanasi, 238
Vasco Da Gama, 134, 138
Vice Admiral R N Krishna, 184
Victoria, 95
Vijayanagara Army, 48-50
Vijayanagara Empire, 46-48

W

War, 179
West, 64, 125, 141, 157, 172, 177-79
West Pakistan, 171, 196
Wing Commander Bawa, 194
Wodeyar Dynasty, 95
Wullar project, 240

Y

Yamuna River, 82
Yudhisthira, 4, 6

Z

Zahir-ud-Din Mohammed or Babur, 19, 21-26, 30, 32-33, 37
Zamburaks, 84
Zojila Pass, 129, 131-33, 205, 227